This book provides a selection of annotated translations from Ernst Kurth's three best-known publications: *Grundlagen des linearen Kontrapunkts* (1917), *Romantische Harmonik und ihre Krise in Wagners "Tristan"* (1920), and *Bruckner* (1925).

Kurth's contemporaries considered these books to be pioneering studies in the music of J. S. Bach, Wagner, and Bruckner. The translated passages were chosen because they articulate Kurth's pre-analytical attitudes and illustrate many of his analytical strategies. The book includes Kurth's commentary on over 100 music examples.

An extensive introductory essay discusses the intellectual and sociocultural environment in which Kurth was writing, referring to aspects of the early twentieth-century cultural renewal movements and to intellectual developments of the day in phenomenology, aesthetics and psychology. In this essay and in the commentaries on the translated passages there are numerous references to hitherto unpublished correspondence between Kurth and his close friend the composer-theorist August Halm (1869–1929).

CAMBRIDGE STUDIES IN MUSIC THEORY
AND ANALYSIS

GENERAL EDITOR: IAN BENT

ERNST KURTH: SELECTED WRITINGS

Titles in this series

1 *Haydn's "Farewell" Symphony and the idea of Classical style*: James Webster
2 *Ernst Kurth: Selected writings*: Lee A. Rothfarb

ERNST KURTH: SELECTED WRITINGS

Edited and translated by
Lee A. Rothfarb
Associate Professor, Music Department, Harvard University

CAMBRIDGE UNIVERSITY PRESS
Cambridge
New York   Port Chester
Melbourne   Sydney

Published by the Press Syndicate of the University of Cambridge
The Pitt Building, Trumpington Street, Cambridge CB2 1RP
40 West 20th Street, New York, NY 10011, USA
10 Stamford Road, Oakleigh, Melbourne 3166, Australia

© Cambridge University Press 1991

First published 1991

Printed in Great Britain at the University Press, Cambridge

British Library cataloguing in publication data

Kurth, Ernst, *1886–1946*
Ernst Kurth: selected writings. – (Cambridge studies in
music theory and analysis)
1. Music. Theories
I. Title II. Rothfarb, Lee A.
781

Library of Congress cataloguing in publication data

Kurth, Ernst.
Ernst Kurth: selected writings / edited and translated by Lee A.
Rothfarb.
p. cm. – (Cambridge studies in music theory and analysis)
Includes bibliographical references.
ISBN 0-521-35522-2
1. Music – Theory. I. Rothfarb, Lee Allen. II. Title.
III. Series.
MT6.K995E715 1990
781 – dc20 90–1591 CIP

ISBN 0 521 35522 2 hardback

ME

Contents

Foreword by Ian Bent	page xi
Preface	xiii
Notes on the translation	xvi
Introduction	1

Part I *Grundlagen des linearen Kontrapunkts*   35
(Foundations of linear counterpoint)

1 Polyphonic structure	37
Approach to compositional technique	37
The effect of harmonic cohesion	41
The interplay of contrasting elements	43
Conclusion: fundamental approach to the theory of counterpoint	45
Staggering of apexes and intensifications	49
The influence of dynamics on harmonic relationships	55
2 Thematic and motivic processes	58
Consolidation and dissolution of thematic motion	58
The process of thematic dissolution in the melodic content of transitional passages	65
The generalization of dynamic progressions	70
3 Polyphonic melody	75
The polyphony of a single line	75
Implications of polyphony in the single line	78
Richness of apparent polyphony in Bach's melodic lines	80
The monophonic episodes from the C-major Fugue for Violin	83
The evolution and dissipation of apparent voices	90
The interaction of apparent voices and the actual voice	92

Contents

Part II	*Romantische Harmonik und ihre Krise in Wagners "Tristan"* (Romantic harmony and its crisis in Wagner's "Tristan")	97

4 Details of Romantic harmony 99
   Effects of color contrasts 100
   Harmonic shading 103
   The intensive alteration style 110
   On the technique of neighbor-note insertion and its connection with chordal alteration 111
   Distortion of harmonies and harmonic progressions 116
   The interior dissolution of color in Romantic harmony: the effect of the absolute progression 119
   The destruction process and its countereffect in tonality 121
   The absolute harmonic effect 125
5 Broader dimensions of Romantic harmony 130
   Chromatic connections of harmonies 130
   Paths of melodic disruption: the sequential technique of the Romantics 135
   Paths of tonal development: paths of harmonic expansion 143

Part III *Bruckner*

6 Bruckner's form as undulatory phases 151
   The symphonic wave: introductory example and general characteristics 151
   Additional characteristics in individual illustrations: parts and whole 162
   The illimitability of the interior processes: the symphonic melos 177
7 Details of Bruckner's symphonic waves 188
   Wave and linear dynamics: an exploration of additional features 188
   The relationship between developmental dynamics and thematic content 195
   The perspective on larger contexts: the art of motivic unity 198

Appendix: Complete tables of contents for Kurth's 208
*Grundlagen des linearen Kontrapunkts, Romantische Harmonik
und ihre Krise in Wagners "Tristan" and Bruckner*

Select bibliography 219
Index of musical examples 228
General index 230

Foreword by Ian Bent

Theory and analysis are in one sense reciprocals: if analysis opens up a musical structure or style to inspection, inventorying its components, identifying its connective forces, providing a description adequate to some live experience, then theory generalizes from such data, predicting what the analyst will find in other cases within a given structural or stylistic orbit, devising systems by which other works – as yet unwritten – might be generated. Conversely, if theory intuits how musical systems operate, then analysis furnishes feedback to such imaginative intuitions, rendering them more insightful. In this sense, they are like two hemispheres that fit together to form a globe (or cerebrum!), functioning deductively as investigation and abstraction, inductively as hypothesis and verification, and in practice forming a chain of alternating activities.

Professionally, on the other hand, "theory" now denotes a whole subdiscipline of the general field of musicology. Analysis often appears to be a subordinate category within the larger activity of theory. After all, there is theory that does not require analysis. Theorists may engage in building systems or formulating strategies for use by composers; and these almost by definition have no use for analysis. Others may conduct experimental research into the sound-materials of music or the cognitive processes of the human mind, to which analysis may be wholly inappropriate. And on the other hand, historians habitually use analysis as a tool for understanding the classes of compositions – repertories, "outputs," "periods," works, versions, sketches, and so forth – that they study. Professionally, then, our ideal image of twin hemispheres is replaced by an intersection: an area that exists in common between two subdisciplines. Seen from this viewpoint, analysis reciprocates in two directions: with certain kinds of theoretical inquiry, and with certain kinds of historical inquiry. In the former case, analysis has tended to be used in rather orthodox modes, in the latter in a more eclectic fashion; but that does not mean that analysis in the service of theory is necessarily more exact, more "scientific," than analysis in the service of history.

The above epistemological excursion is by no means irrelevant to the present series. Cambridge Studies in Music Theory and Analysis is intended to present the work of theorists and of analysts. It has been designed to include "pure" theory – that is, theoretical formulation with a minimum of analytical exemplification; "pure" analysis – that is, practical analysis with a minimum of theoretical underpinning; and writings that fall at points along the spectrum between the two extremes. In these capacities, it aims to illuminate music, as work and as process.

However, theory and analysis are not the exclusive preserves of the present day. As subjects in their own right, they are diachronic. The former is coeval with the very study of music itself, and extends far beyond the confines of Western culture; the latter, defined broadly, has several centuries of past practice. Moreover, they have been dynamic, not static fields throughout their histories. Consequently, studying earlier music through the eyes of its own contemporary theory helps us to escape (when we need to, not that we should make a dogma out if it) from the preconceptions of our own age. Studying earlier analyses does this too, and in a particularly sharply focused way; at the same time it gives us the opportunity to re-evaluate past analytical methods for present purposes, such as is happening currently, for example, with the long-despised methods of hermeneutic analysis of the late nineteenth century. The series thus includes editions and translations of major works of past theory, and also studies in the history of theory.

Legendary in their linguistic difficulty, overawing in their complexity of thought, elusive in their subtlety of expression, the writings of Ernst Kurth have a certain monumental unapproachability. Lee Rothfarb's translations put us vividly in touch with those writings and with Kurth's intricate thought processes. By bringing together passages from three books, and by cross-relating them with footnotes on theoretical issues, the editor conveys the essential continuity and homogeneity of thought embodied in Kurth's 2,000 and more pages. The selected passages given here offer countless insights, and Kurth's footnotes, as well as his main text, can be startling in their richness. If they leave the reader hungry for more – for the analyses of the symphonies and other works that make up the second volume of *Bruckner*, for example, or the chapter on musical Impressionism in *Romantische Harmonik* – then this volume will have served a second purpose, that of emboldening the reader to tackle Kurth in the original, aided by Rothfarb's definitions of terminology and explanations of Kurth's highly individual ideas.

Preface

This reader introduces the work of Ernst Kurth (1886–1946) to those modern-day scholars, composers, and performers who, because of the formidable German language barrier, have had very limited, or no, direct access to the ideas of one of the most original and influential theorists of the early twentieth century. The book offers the first extended translations from Kurth's work, with commentary, allowing English-speaking audiences to meet and learn from Kurth directly, rather than through secondary literature. The translations include passages in which Kurth lays out the conceptual groundwork for analysis, but focus primarily on the analyses themselves, both for their historical significance as well as for their value as suggestive points of departure for today's theorists. The present volume might be considered a companion to my monograph, *Ernst Kurth as Theorist and Analyst* (University of Pennsylvania Press, 1988). There, I provide an overview of Kurth's work and place it in historical perspective by presenting and interpreting key theoretical viewpoints and analytical strategies along with those of his predecessors and contemporaries.

For various reasons, Kurth's writings faded from interest during the 1940s, having peaked in popularity during the 1920s and 30s. In the changed intellectual climate of the post-World-War-II period, Kurth's unfashionable idealistic outlook and metaphor-laden prose style put him at first on the periphery and then outside of the mainstream of music-theoretical research. Additionally, critical assessments made by Schenkerian disciples such as Oswald Jonas and, more recently, Hellmut Federhofer have hindered a fair reading of Kurth's work. In the 1960s and 70s, when music theory was emerging as an independent discipline, Schenkerian theory held center stage in studies of tonal music, leaving no room for someone like Kurth, who in his heyday was in fact more widely read than Schenker. However, in light of the increasing diversity in contemporary music theory, as evidenced by the recently published "State of Research in Music Theory," I believe today's professionals will be more receptive to Kurth's modes of thought and analysis than just ten years ago, when the aforementioned journal was launched.[1] In particular, the interest in phenomenological, literary-critical, and semiotic approaches to the analysis of tonal music indicates that Kurth will find sympathetic readers. If contemporary theorists heed Leo Treitler's call for "analytical methodologies that are less normative and more phenomenological and historical. . .that concern themselves not with structures alone, but with the relations of structure and meaning," and if they strive for a synthesis of "music theory and criticism, reception and transmission, performance practice, aesthetics and semiotics," then Kurth's writings are sure to be of interest in the next phase of music theory's development.[2]

I begin the selected readings with an introductory essay, which provides the necessary cultural and ideological background for reading Kurth. The essay opens with a sketch of the *fin-de-siècle* socio-cultural renewal movement that gave rise to Kurth's work, and continues with a discussion of the intellectual context, specifically the relationship of Kurth's ideas to phenomenology, psychological aesthetics, and Gestalt psychology. Finally, the essay gives an overview of the leading ideas of the three works represented in this volume, *Grundlagen des linearen Kontrapunkts* (1917), *Romantische Harmonik und ihre Krise in Wagners "Tristan"* (1920), and *Bruckner* (1925), and takes up the issue of the reception of Kurth's work. Throughout the essay, as well as in the commentary on the translations, I refer to unpublished correspondence between Kurth and his close friend, the composer, aesthetician, and theorist August Halm (1869-1929). The letters illuminate the relationship between the two men as well as Kurth's view of musicology in his day. Preceding the translations, I discuss briefly the problems of rendering Kurth in English in the "Notes on the Translation." Six chapters topically organize sections of Kurth's books: Polyphonic structure; Thematic and motivic processes; Polyphonic melody; Details of Romantic harmony; Broader dimensions of Romantic harmony; Bruckner's form as undulatory phases; and Details of Bruckner's symphonic waves. Each chapter begins with a few short, introductory paragraphs that explain the context of the material to follow, so that the reader will understand how the translated sections fit into the books from which they are taken. An appendix provides translations of the complete tables of contents for *Grundlagen* and *Romantische Harmonik*, and for the first volume of *Bruckner*.

Several people have assisted variously in the preparation of this book, and I am delighted to acknowledge them here. I am greatly indebted to Clare Parsons, of

---

[1] *Music Theory Spectrum* 11.1 (1989). This volume of *Spectrum* is devoted to "The State of Research in Music Theory: Papers of the Plenary Session, Rochester, 1987." The first issue of *Spectrum* appeared in spring, 1979.

[2] Leo Treitler, "Structural and Critical Analysis," *Musicology in the 1980s*, ed. D. Kern Holoman and Claude V. Palisca (New York: Da Capo, 1982), 77. In some ways, Kurth's work exemplifies what Joseph Kerman, another commentator on music theory of the past decade, calls "criticism" (*Contemplating Music* [Cambridge, Mass.: Harvard University Press, 1985], 16-19, 66-69).

the Comparative Literature Department at Harvard, for the many hours she spent editing my drafts of the translations. On countless occasions she came up with just the right word or phrase that captured in English the sense and style of the German. I am grateful to Daniel Beller-McKenna, of the Music Department, who read the manuscript and made many valuable suggestions for including commentary; and to Carl Leafstedt, also of the Music Department, who facilitated my initial work on the project by doing a large amount of bibliographic research. Dan and Carl also deserve thanks for assembling the musical examples, and for alerting me to errors and textual variants in the examples printed in Kurth's books. I am especially grateful to Kathryn Welter for her diligent and thorough work in preparing the index. I would also like to acknowledge the Deutsches Literaturarchiv/Schiller-Nationalmuseum (Marbach am Neckar), the Archiv der deutschen Jugendbewegung (Burg Ludwigstein, Witzenhausen), and Hans Kurth, Ernst Kurth's son, for providing me with the correspondence between Kurth and Halm. I am grateful to the American Council of Learned Societies for their financial support, which allowed me the leisure in the summer of 1987 to do the initial research for the project. Finally, I would like to thank Professor Ian Bent for offering me the opportunity to do this reader, and for his unfailing support and encouragement as it took shape.

Notes on the translation

Those who have tried to read Kurth may disagree with his ideas, or with one another over their interpretation. But they all agree on one thing, that his German ranges between difficult and impossible to understand. Novice readers may respond by demanding that Kurth *should* be translated into English, more experienced readers that he *could* be translated, and seasoned readers, or bilinguals, that he in fact *cannot* be translated into English – technically perhaps yes, spiritually no. Kurth can of course be rendered in English, though not easily, nor without losing some of the characteristic "spiritual" quality that imbues his work with much of its mystique and allure. As with any translation, the intrinsic qualities of the source language hinder an idiomatic mapping of both structure and style into the goal language. Those two elements will necessarily be weighted, often partially, or wholly, sacrificing some of one to preserve more of the other. Consequently the translation will be more or less "faithful" to the structure or to the style of the source.

The present translation variously weights and modifies structure and expression in order to preserve the third and most important element of the source texts, the sense. That task was not always easy because I often had to walk a fine line between translation and paraphrase. With Kurth the balancing act is a constant one. His prose is scattered with metaphors that vex the most diligent translator; the English – and with it, Kurth – can easily sound trite and silly. For example, in *Bruckner*, vol. I (311, 312, 314) Kurth speaks of *Klangwehungen* and *Wellenatem*, which literally mean roughly "sonic winds" and "wave breath," respectively. Contextual circumstances and linguistic sensitivity disallowed translating such words literally, or even the same way each time. In this volume, *Klangwehungen* are "sonic wisps" and *Wellenatem* variously symphonic "ripple," "undulatory motion," or simply "wave." Such tamed metaphors may still strike the reader as silly. However, routinely neutralizing Kurth for modern ears can make him sound too slick and falsifies the original tone. Translating him too literally, on the other hand, can make him sound melodramatic. Once again, the line is often a fine one.

Another problem is terminology. Academic convention demands that at least terms, and even other recurrent expressions, be translated uniformly. Apart from a few standard harmonic and melodic terms (e.g., dominant, motive, phrase, etc.), which I have translated consistently, Kurth uses very few words that we can call terms as such. He commonly speaks of kinetic and potential energy, and these, too, are translated uniformly. In other cases, however, Kurth is inconsistent. In *Bruckner*, for example, he speaks variously of *Anspannungen* and *Steigerungen*, *Entspannungen* and *Absteigerungen*, *Nachwellungen* and *Nachbebungen*, etc., without distinguishing among them or using them strictly as terms. I have translated flexibly in such cases, depending on context and the momentary linguistic needs.

Synthetic compound words are another stumbling block. German routinely combines two or more simple, graphic words to express an abstract idea. The language possesses enough common synthetic compounds as it is to keep translators thumbing their dictionaries and thesauruses late into the night. But Kurth manages to invent yet more synthetic compounds, often involving metaphors. Such creative eloquence was part of his appeal and quickly became a trademark. For the translator, his resourcefulness compounds (excuse the pun) the difficulty of translating metaphors and necessitates multi-word locutions that bloat an already prolix text. Synthetic compounds challenge a translator to find an equivalent English expression, or to invent one. In general, I have tried to hold the translation within acceptable linguistic bounds, though in searching for English equivalents I have surely overlooked that elusive ideal word or expression. In trying to preserve Kurth's style to some extent I may have indulged him on some occasions when I might have neutralized the text a bit more. For such indulgences, I take responsibility and ask, in turn, for the reader's indulgence.

The reader is organized in three sections: chapters 1–3 contain passages from *Grundlagen* (3rd edn.), 4–5, from *Romantische Harmonik* (3rd edn.), and 6–7 from *Bruckner*, vol. I. Each chapter begins with a short introduction that identifies the excerpts to follow, and explains how they fit into their respective books as a whole. Numbers in square brackets within the text indicate Kurth's page numbers. The "K" numbers in square brackets at the head of each musical example, e.g. [K67], signal Kurth's example numbers as they appear in the editions cited above. My annotations and Kurth's footnotes are distinguished from one another by initials in square brackets, e.g. [LR], [EK].

Introduction

In an unusually brief publishing career of roughly fifteen years – about half that of Heinrich Schenker and one-third that of Hugo Riemann – the Berne professor Ernst Kurth (1886–1946) wrote four lengthy, strikingly original and probing music-theoretical studies. Blending harmonic and melodic analysis with psychological interpretation, he explored contrapuntal techniques in Bach's keyboard and solo string works, harmonic practices in Wagner's operas (chiefly *Tristan und Isolde*), and formal processes in Bruckner's symphonies. In a final, summary work Kurth studied the cognitive-psychological implications of the musical techniques examined in his earlier books.

Kurth published five books, *Die Voraussetzungen der theoretischen Harmonik und der tonalen Darstellungssysteme* (Berne: Drechsel, 1913), *Grundlagen des linearen Kontrapunkts* (Berne: Drechsel, 1917), *Romantische Harmonik und ihre Krise in Wagners "Tristan"* (Berne: Haupt, 1920), *Bruckner* (2 vols., Berlin: Hesse, 1925), and *Musikpsychologie* (Berlin: Hesse, 1931).[1] Additionally, he wrote two large essays, "Die Jugendopern Glucks bis zum 'Orfeo'" (1913), a revision of his doctoral dissertation (1908); and "Zur Motivbildung Bachs: ein Beitrag zur Stilpsychologie" (1917), which expands certain ideas presented in *Grundlagen*.[2] The magnitude of the

---

[1] *Grundlagen* is subtitled *Bachs melodische Polyphonie*. It had second and third editions (Berlin: Hesse, 1922, 1927), and several reprintings of the third edition (Berne: Krompholz, 1946, 1956; Hildesheim: Olms, 1977), as well as a translation into Russian by Boris V. Asaf'yef (Moscow, 1931). The translations in the present volume are from the Krompholz reprint (1946) of the third edition. *Romantische Harmonik* had second and third editions (Berlin: Hesse, 1922, 1923) and two reprintings (Olms, 1968, 1975), and was translated into Russian (Moscow, 1975). Our translations are from the Olms reprint (1975) of the third edition. *Bruckner* appeared in only one edition and was reprinted once (Olms, 1971). *Musikpsychologie*, which also had a single edition, has been reprinted twice (Berne: Krompholz, 1947; Olms, 1969).

[2] Ernst Kurth, "Die Jugendopern Glucks bis zum 'Orfeo'," *Studien zur Musikwissenschaft* 1 (1913), 193–227; orig. "Der Stil der opera seria von Gluck bis zum 'Orfeo'," (Ph.D. diss., University of Vienna, 1908); "Zur Motivbildung Bachs: ein Beitrag zur Stilpsychologie," *Bach-Jahrbuch* (1917), 80–136. Arnold Schering, then editor of the *Bach-Jahrbuch*, solicited the article on Bach's motivic procedures. He repeatedly coaxed a reluctant Kurth to submit the essay by promising a review of *Grundlagen* in the same issue. The review, written by Hermann Wetzel, turned out to be highly critical, which greatly irritated Kurth (letter to Halm dated March 6, 1920, Protocol no. 69.833/1, Deutsches Literaturarchiv/Schiller-Nationalmuseum, Marbach am Neckar).

books is staggering: nearly 3,000 pages! In the grand tradition of late nineteenth-century humanistic and scientific researchers such as Wilhelm Dilthey and Wilhelm Wundt, Kurth was, alas, not concise.

The present volume offers translations from three of the five books, from *Grundlagen*, *Romantische Harmonik*, and from the first volume of *Bruckner*. Of the five, these three best serve the goal of this reader: to offer extensive translated passages that articulate Kurth's pre-analytical attitudes and illustrate his analytical strategies. Such passages will be of greatest interest and practical value for readers hoping to learn about and benefit from Kurth's mode of thinking. His *Habilitationsschrift*, *Voraussetzungen*, although noteworthy for its trenchant critique of contemporary theory and for embryonic ideas that surface in Kurth's later writings, is a minor work compared with the other volumes.[3] *Musikpsychologie*, a major work, is rich in insight and historically important for establishing the field of music psychology as a discipline separate from "tone psychology." However, it contains no musical references or examples. It relates to analysis only by implication and thus has less immediate value for the analyst.[4]

Unlike Schenker and Riemann, whose voluminous publications evolve comprehensive theoretical and analytical systems, Kurth left no system. Instead, he evolved various specialized analytical and listening strategies that highlight contextually unique events and reveal certain large-scale formal and harmonic procedures. Because Kurth left no systematic methodology to build on, despite his popularity and impact on music theory in the 1920s and 30s, his ideas have largely passed from

---

Minor articles include "Zur 'ars cantus mensurabilis' des Franko von Köln," *Kirchenmusikalisches Jahrbuch* 21 (1908), 39–47; "Julius Bittners grosse Messe mit *Te deum in D*," *Die Musik* 18.12 (1925–26), 878–83; and "Die Schulmusik und ihre Reform," *Schweizerische Musikzeitung* 70.9 (1930), 341–51, orig. *Schulpraxis* 19 (1930). Kurth also published several previews just before the appearance of his books: "Zum Wesen der Harmonik," *Musik-Blätter des Anbruchs* 2.16–17 (1920), 539–43, 568–71; "Bruckner," *Die Musik* 16.12 (1924), 861–69; "Bruckners Fernstand," *Musik-Blätter des Anbruchs* 6 (1924), 351–57; "Der musikalische Formbegriff," *Melos* 4 (1924–25), 364–70; and "Symbolische und dynamische Primitivformen," *Die Musik* 23.2 (1930), 81–86. Kurt von Fischer, Kurth's most distinguished student, provides a comprehensive bibliography of Kurth's writings, along with a list of literature on Kurth, in "Ernst Kurth – Bibliographie," *Schweizer Jahrbuch für Musikwissenschaft* 6–7 (1986/87), 20–21. The bibliography accompanies a biographical sketch of Kurth ("Ernst Kurth [1886–1946]: Persönlichkeit, Lehrer und Musikdenker," 11–19).

[3] Those interested in *Voraussetzungen* may refer to my translation of the book, entitled "Ernst Kurth's *The Requirements for a Theory of Harmony*: An Annotated Translation with an Introductory Essay," Master's Thesis, West Hartford, Connecticut, Hartt School of Music, University of Hartford, 1971; and to my forthcoming article, "Ernst Kurth's *Die Voraussetzungen der theoretischen Harmonik* and the Beginnings of Music Psychology," *Theoria* 4. Robert Wason refers to *Voraussetzungen* in his book *Viennese Harmonic Theory from Albrechtsberger to Schenker and Schoenberg* (Ann Arbor: UMI Research Press, 1985), 33–34, 155 n. 22.

[4] Albert Wellek evaluates *Musikpsychologie* in a review in *Acta Musicologica* 5.2 (1933–34), 72–80. In an article entitled "The Present State of Music Psychology and its Significance for Historical Musicology," Wellek points out that Kurth's pioneering book initiated the systematic study of music psychology (*Report of the Eighth Congress of the International Musicological Society*, vol. I [Kassel: Bärenreiter, 1961], 121). As an abstract synthesis of Kurth's thought, *Musikpsychologie* deserves a separate study by a modern author sufficiently versed in cognitive psychology and its history, as well as in music theory, to deal properly with the book.

German music-theoretical literature. They never made much headway with English-speaking audiences due in part to a complex, often opaque metaphorical prose style. The present volume of English translations introduces Kurth to the now large English-speaking community of theorists and musicologists who may have begun to read him but have given up because of the language barrier. With increased historical perspective and a broader range of music-theoretical knowledge, today's scholars can read Kurth more objectively, and perhaps more sympathetically, than did some of his contemporaries.

Like many innovators, Kurth had outspoken critics, among them Schenker and Riemann.[5] Other readers, however, enthusiastically acclaimed his contributions. In a review of *Grundlagen*, Paul Bekker, for instance, hailed the book as "one of the most significant achievements in the field of musicological research. . .we have gained here a new, original and fruitful view of the nature of an old style." Bekker specifically recommended Kurth's discussion of polyphonic melody for its "wealth of insight and newness of approach," for which Bekker knew "no equivalent in the Bach literature."[6] After the third edition of *Romantische Harmonik* appeared (1923), Ernst Bücken, then director of the *Musikwissenschaftliches Institut* at the University of Cologne, recognized the historical significance of Kurth's research.

Up until recently, music theory resembled a house that tries to give the appearance of a new building by means of numerous additions. However, despite the most industrious work, ultimately everything remained as it was because the quite necessary renovation was not initiated *from the foundations*, which for music theory is the *rationalistic basis*. . .The overcoming of rationalistic music theory, encouraged and attempted by Riemann [in his essays on *"Tonvorstellungen"*], has only now become a reality in the works of the Berne professor Ernst Kurth.[7]

---

[5] See, for example, Schenker's *Das Meisterwerk in der Musik* (3 vols., Munich: Drei Masken Verlag, 1925, 1926, 1930; reprint Hildesheim: Olms, 1974), vol. I, 93–98; and Riemann's essay "Die Phrasierung im Lichte einer Lehre von den Tonvorstellungen," *Zeitschrift für Musikwissenschaft* 1.1 (1918), 26–39.

[6] Paul Bekker, "Kontrapunkt und Neuzeit," *Frankfurter Zeitung*, vol. 62, March 27, 1918, p. 1. The present volume includes a large section from Kurth's chapter on polyphonic melody (our chapter 3). I should point out that Bekker, in complete contradiction to Kurth's intent, saw in the notion of "linear counterpoint" a stimulus for modern composers (Kurth's new outlook will "not only remain scholarly knowledge but seems certain to be transformed into contemporary creative practice" ["in zeiteigene schöpferische Werte umzusetzen"], ibid.). Kurth expressed himself clearly on the misunderstanding and misapplication of linear counterpoint in *Grundlagen* (Berne: Krompholz, 1948), xiii, and in a letter, dated June 13, 1926, to a close friend, the composer-theorist August Halm (Protocol no. 69.833/13, Deutsches Literaturarchiv/Schiller-Nationalmuseum, Marbach am Neckar).

[7] Ernst Bücken, "Ernst Kurth als Musiktheoretiker," *Melos* 4 (1924–25), 358. Translations from German texts are my own unless otherwise indicated.

Bücken refers to Riemann's two essays, "Ideen zu einer 'Lehre von den Tonvorstellungen'," *Jahrbuch der Musikbibliothek Peters* 21–22 (1914–15), 1–26; and "Neue Beiträge zu einer Lehre von den Tonvorstellungen," *Jahrbuch der Musikbibliothek Peters* 23 (1916), 1–22. Robert Wason and Elizabeth West Marvin will soon be publishing an annotated translation of Riemann's essays, complete with an introduction, in the *Journal of Music Theory*.

Bücken's remarks are telling because they highlight the connection, to be discussed later, between Kurth's style of theory and the anti-Intellectualist sentiment of the time. Kurth's work appealed to musicians who rejected formalist, quasi-scientific, or the diluted varieties of contemporary academic theory, and so readily embraced his non-axiomatic, humanistic variety. After World War II, however, a renewed wave of Positivism and rapid advances in scientific and humanistic fields put Kurth's work into a different, dimmer light. What had once been ideological and methodological assets became liabilities.[8]

Considering Kurth's importance for the history of analysis as well as for the wealth and originality of his ideas, a large-scale translation of his works is long overdue. Kurth has received scant attention compared with Schenker and Riemann, for example, whose major writings are readily available in English. Additionally, modern interpretive secondary literature has been no more generous, in quantity or assessment. Aside from my monograph, *Ernst Kurth As Theorist and Analyst*, until the 1980s there has been comparatively little material available on Kurth in English or in German.[9] There are several reasons for this neglect, which I will discuss later in this introduction. As I have already hinted in connection with

---

[8] In a review of a reprint of *Romantische Harmonik* (Hildesheim: Olms, 1968), Carl Dahlhaus wonders whether Kurth's reputation "rests less on the books themselves than on the rumor of the books" (Dahlhaus, "Ernst Kurth: *Romantische Harmonik und ihre Krise in Wagners 'Tristan'*," *Die Musikforschung* 25 [1972], 225). Nevertheless, Dahlhaus counts Kurth among the significant theorists of the early twentieth century, along with Riemann and Schenker (ibid.).

[9] My book, *Ernst Kurth As Theorist and Analyst* (Philadelphia: University of Pennsylvania Press, 1988), henceforth abbreviated as *EKATA*, is the first monographic study of Kurth. I will refer to it often, in this introduction and throughout, since it covers much of the historical background for Kurth's work, and comments interpretively on many of the musical examples included in this reader. Other discussions of Kurth in English include Dolores M. Hsu, "Ernst Kurth and His Concept of Music as Motion," *Journal of Music Theory* 10 (1966), 2–17; Ira Lieberman, "Some Representative Works from Beethoven's Early Period Analyzed in Light of the Theories of Ernst Kurth and Kurt von Fischer," (Ph.D. diss., Columbia University, 1968); and Patrick McCreless, "Ernst Kurth and the Analysis of the Chromatic Music of the Late Nineteenth Century," *Music Theory Spectrum* 5 (1983), 56–75. I mention Hsu's, Lieberman's, and McCreless's work in *EKATA*, 229. Kurt von Fischer was the first to summarize Kurth's work in the essay "In Memoriam Ernst Kurth," *Der Musik-Almanach*, ed. Viktor Schwarz (Munich: K. Desch, 1948), 228–52. Hellmut Federhofer criticizes Kurth along Schenkerian lines in *Akkord und Stimmführung in den musiktheoretischen Systemen von Hugo Riemann, Ernst Kurth und Heinrich Schenker*, Veröffentlichungen der Kommission für Musikforschung, vol. XXI (Vienna: Verlag der österreichischen Akademie der Wissenschaften, 1981), 33–54. Other modern research in English includes Madelon Bose's article, "The Sound and the Theory: A Novel Look at Work and Music," *International Review of Aesthetics and Sociology of Music* 10.1 (1979), 52–72; and, more recently, Stephen Parkany's article, "Kurth's *Bruckner* and the Adagio of the Seventh Symphony," *19th Century Music* 11.3 (1988), 262–81. As I completed the present introductory essay, the latest issue of the *Schweizer Jahrbuch für Musikwissenschaft* 6–7 (1986–87) appeared, commemorating the 100th anniversary of Kurth's birth. In addition to Kurt von Fischer's biographical sketch and bibliography cited above, the yearbook contains essays on the relationship between Kurth's and Guido Adler's views of the history of style (Manfred Angerer); on Kurth's notion of "absolute melody" (Carl Dahlhaus); on "energy" in Kurth's and Boris Asaf'yef's writings (Hermann Danuser); on Kurth's approach to music psychology (Helga de la Motte-Haber); and on Kurth's idea of "synthetic fusion" (Hans-Peter Rösler).

Bücken's comments, they are related primarily to the socio-cultural and intellectual context in which Kurth's work arose and was read in the early part of our century. It is to those contexts which we now turn.

SOCIO-CULTURAL CONTEXT

I call particular attention to the socio-cultural background of Kurth's approach to music theory, as distinct from the intellectual currents that affected him.[10] I have in mind various aspects of the social reform movement in the decades straddling 1900, characterized by anti-modern and anti-intellectual tendencies, as well as by a crystallizing nationalistic "volkish" ideology. Within the socio-cultural domain I also include the emerging reform pedagogy movement, which altered the material and, crucially, the method of education throughout Europe. Several modern historians have discussed these developments, their origins and effects, in great detail.[11] By intellectual currents I mean, in general, the late nineteenth- and early twentieth-century neo-Idealist approach to "humanistic studies" (*Geisteswissenschaften*), as well as specific developments in the history of ideas: the development of phenomenology (Edmund Husserl), Gestalt psychology (Max Wertheimer), and a psychological branch of aesthetics (Theodor Lipps, Konrad Lange, among others).

A few modern scholars have investigated the intellectual origins of certain music theorists' ideas. However, none has explored the social context very far, and little has been written on these matters with reference to early twentieth-century theorists other than Riemann and Schenker.[12] Knowing something about

[10] I take up some of the intellectual origins of Kurth's work in *EKATA*, chapter 1.
[11] The sources I will be referring to are Henry Stuart Hughes, *Consciousness and Society: The Reorientation of European Social Thought, 1890–1930* (New York: Octagon Books, 1976); Fritz Ringer, *The Decline of the German Mandarins: The German Academic Community, 1890–1933* (Cambridge, Mass.: Harvard University Press, 1969); Fritz Stern, *The Politics of Cultural Despair: A Study in the Rise of the Germanic Ideology* (Berkeley–Los Angeles: University of California Press, 1961); George L. Mosse, *The Crisis of German Ideology: Intellectual Origins of the Third Reich* (New York: Schocken Books, 1981); and Janos Frecot, "Die Lebensreformbewegung," *Das wilhelminische Bildungsbürgertum: Zur Sozialgeschichte seiner Ideen*, ed. Klaus Vondung (Göttingen: Vandenhoeck & Ruprecht, 1976), 138–52. Mosse characterizes "volkish" ideology in *German Ideology*, 13–17, and amplifies on its origins and manifestation on 17–30.
[12] August Halm, Alfred Lorenz, and the co-authors Rudolf Louis and Ludwig Thuille, for example, still await modern critical expositions of their work. Siegfried Schmalzriedt published a collection of Halm's essays, prefaced by a sizable introduction to Halm's thinking on various aesthetic and music-theoretical issues (*Von Form und Sinn der Musik*, ed. Siegfried Schmaltzriedt [Wiesbaden: Breitkopf und Härtel, 1978]). However, he does not go into detail concerning theoretical or analytical matters. There is currently no monographic study on either Lorenz or the Louis–Thuille team. Secondary literature does mention Lorenz occasionally, though often with a decidedly negative tone (e.g., in Patrick McCreless's article "Ernst Kurth and the Analysis of the Chromatic Music of the Late Nineteenth Century," 68; but see Ian Bent, *Analysis* [New York: Norton, 1987], 47–49). Wason discusses Halm and the Louis–Thuille team in *Viennese Harmonic Theory*, 115–32. William A. Pastille studies the philosophical background of Schenker's writings in "*Ursatz*: The Musical Philosophy of Heinrich Schenker," (Ph.D. diss., Cornell University, 1985). Peter Rummenhöller analyzes the philosophical underpinnings of nineteenth-century theory in his ambitious and informative

the socio-cultural context of Kurth's generation is particularly important because of the profound changes in outlook and attitudes that crystallized at the time, and because Kurth's work so strikingly reflects those changes.

Kurth matured during the generation that witnessed the outcome of the German and Austrian industrial booms of the 1870s and 80s, which brought rapid economic and urban growth, as well as the outcome of advances in science and technology.[13] Progress in natural science, for example, allowed a fuller understanding of phenomena that had previously been explained only fragmentarily. In physiological science, lines of inquiry reaching from Johannes Müller through Ernst H. Weber, Gustav T. Fechner up to Hermann von Helmholtz inspired confidence in the ability of science to explain complex biological processes. Mental science, too, advanced with the pioneering research of Wilhelm Wundt, who in founding the first laboratory for experimental psychology in 1879 removed the science of the mind from philosophical speculation and physiological research. With German science leading the way, Positivist doctrine in the last half of the nineteenth century supplanted Idealist doctrine of the first half.[14]

By the late 1880s the consequences of the preceding generation's achievements became clear to both its contributors and skeptical observers. In exchange for modern society, industrialization had brought a loss of community, individuality, and spiritual fulfillment. Externally, there was political unity. Internally, however, there was no sense of cultural unity.[15] Although science could boast impressive accomplishments, even Wundt's experimental psychology was far from explaining the workings of the creative, artistic mind. Educational institutions, in their zeal to transmit facts, had failed to transmit both the cultural legacy that animates those facts, as well as the cultural awareness that appreciates them. Mass education had

---

book *Musiktheoretisches Denken im 19. Jahrhundert: Versuch einer Interpretation erkenntnistheoretischer Zeugnisse in der Musiktheorie*, Studien zur Musikgeschichte des 19. Jahrhunderts, vol. XII (Regensburg: Bosse Verlag, 1967). Rummenhöller summarizes the main ideas of his book in "Die philosophischen Grundlagen in der Musiktheorie des 19. Jahrhunderts," *Beiträge zur Theorie der Künste im 19. Jahrhundert* (Regensburg: Bosse, 1971), 44–57. William C. Mickelsen's translation of part 3 of Riemann's history of music theory opens with a chapter on "Riemann's Predecessors" (Zarlino to Oettingen) but does not discuss the cultural background of Riemann's work (*Hugo Riemann's Theory of Harmony and History of Music Theory, Book III by Hugo Riemann* [Lincoln–London: University of Nebraska Press, 1977], 3–24).

[13] Chapter 1 of *EKATA* contains a biography of Kurth.
[14] Peter Rummenhöller shows how the changes in music-theoretical outlook from the first to the second half of the nineteenth century reflect the changing intellectual outlook, in "Die philosophischen Grundlagen," cited above.
[15] Mosse, *German Ideology*, 2–4; Stern, *Cultural Despair*, xxviii–xxx; Ringer, *German Mandarins*, 1–3, 10–11, 14–15, 42–43; Frecot, "Lebensreformbewegung," 139. Hughes cites the historian Egon Friedell for a characterization of late nineteenth-century cultural decadence: "Men of the seventies and eighties. . .were filled with a devouring hunger for reality, but they had the misfortune to confuse this with matter – which is but the hollow and deceptive wrapping of it" (Hughes, *Consciousness and Society*, 40, quoting Friedell, *A Cultural History of the Modern Age*, trans. Charles F. Atkinson [3 vols., New York: Knopf, 1930-32], vol. III, 299).

cheapened the goals of wisdom (*Wissen*) and learning for its own sake to the level of either knowledge (*Kenntnis*), necessary for a nation's bureaucracy and academies, or of specialized technical skills (*Können*), required for industry. Civilization flourished while culture foundered.[16]

Beginning around 1890, attitudes began to change. The educated middle class and the intellectual elite rebelled against the reigning materialistic, mechanistic, and rationalistic tendencies in an effort to recover the cultural heritage and unity that had earlier been the source of national pride and identity.[17] The emphasis shifted from industrial and commercial goals to the goals of cultural self-definition and -realization. Attaining those goals would, in turn, lead to the desired cultural reawakening and, ultimately, to a genuine, spiritually more satisfying national identity. This new identity would be founded, not on a political order or on economic strength, but on spiritual strength.

During the 1890s, then, ardent anti-modern and anti-Positivist sentiments arose, expressing, on the one hand, a nostalgic remembrance of a past age of higher cultural awareness, and on the other a fascination with the unquantifiable and irrational spirit that produces culture. In the educational realm that desire meant retreating from utilitarian instruction and training in technical skills (*Ausbildung*), and returning to self-cultivation, to the personal cultivation of mind and spirit (*Bildung*) in the tradition of Heinrich Pestalozzi and Wilhelm von Humboldt.[18] In the social realm it meant abandoning the quest for material products in favor of acquiring an understanding and appreciation of cultural products.

Social reform and cultural rebirth, in order to succeed, had to start with individual spiritual well-being and growth.[19] As a means of coping with modernity, adverse external forces were offset by cultivating internal, psychic forces. Those hoping to stimulate a cultural renewal emphasized subjective, intuitive understand-

---

[16] Mosse, *German Ideology*, 6–7; Stern, *Cultural Despair*, 196–97; Ringer, *German Mandarins*, 86–90, 255–56, 265–66, 268. Oswald Spengler contrasted civilization and culture in *The Decline of the West* (Munich: C. H. Beck, 1918), trans. Charles F. Atkinson (2 vols. New York: Alfred A. Knopf, 1926–28), vol. I (*Form and Actuality*), 31–32, 106–8, 353–54.

[17] Hughes, *Consciousness and Society*, 33–66 ("The Decade of the 1890's: The Revolt against Positivism"), gives an excellent summary of the attitudinal changes of the 1890s. Fritz Ringer discusses cultural decadence in *German Mandarins*, 253–69. Hughes quotes Friedrich Meinecke's words concerning a change in outlook just before the turn of the century: "In all Germany one can detect something new around 1890 not only politically but also spiritually and intellectually. . .Politically things were going down; intellectually they were going up again." There was "a new sense for the fragmentary and problematic character of modern life, a sense which sought to penetrate from life's civilized surface to its now terrifying, now tempting depths. . . the period after 1890 can at least boast of better taste than what on the average had prevailed in the two decades after 1870" (Friedrich Meinecke, *Erlebtes 1862–1901* [Leipzig: Koehler und Amelang, 1941], 167–68). Most of the translation given here is from Hughes, 43. The last part, from "a sense which sought. . .," is from Stern, *Cultural Despair*, 165n, who also quotes Meinecke.

[18] Ringer, *German Mandarins*, 258–59; Stern, *Cultural Despair*, 71–81.

[19] Frecot, "Lebensreformbewegung," 146, 148, 152.

ing of the world as an alternative to the objective, calculative methods of physical science. For if, as Dilthey had argued, the methods of science were inadequate for studying artistic products of the mind – what Georg Simmel called "objective spirit" (*objektiver Geist*) – then those products had to be studied with reference to "subjective spirit," the creative mind itself.[20]

In 1921, the philosopher-aesthetician Arthur Wolfgang Cohn wrote of the need for a revival of the emotional side of life to counteract excessive rationalistic thinking.

The external lustre of our powerful state, the material good-life of the so-called "ruling classes," the bloom of capitalism dispensed precisely with internal values. . .In religion, the sophistry of "atheism" got the upper hand, in art the crudity and banality of "verismo," in science the restrictedness of "Positivism." Fluent life was forced into the constraints of spiritual mechanization. . .all emotional life [*Gemütsleben*] was intellectualized. . .The "Intellectualism" that has penetrated art must be eliminated and "emotional" life must be reawakened. This demand articulates the goal of the artistic renewal.[21]

Similarly, nearly fifteen years earlier the musician Karl Grunsky had questioned formalist aesthetics and had advocated what Leonard Meyer would call an "absolute expressionist" viewpoint.

That music is an expression of mental life [*seelisches Leben*] is today admitted, defended, demanded from nearly all sides, since we barely pay attention to Hanslick any longer.

Expressing something musically means resolving the mental (or worldly [*irdisch*]) image into pure motion. Understanding something musically means having a mental, worldly image for the pure motion.

The essence of music [is] the conflict and struggle of various forces in cosmic mobility, detached from materiality.[22]

Of the authors who wrote about fin-de-siècle cultural decadence, and of cultural renewal through a return to subjective knowledge, none was as fiery and fashionable – nor any as erratic – as Julius Langbehn (1851–1907). An eccentric of checkered education, Langbehn anonymously published *Rembrandt als Erzieher. Von einem*

---

[20] In *Consciousness and Society*, 105–60 ("The Recovery of the Unconscious"), Hughes discusses the ideas of Henri Bergson, Sigmund Freud, and Carl Gustav Jung, and their nineteenth-century background. An important element of Eugen Diederichs's neo-Romantic reform program was the cultivation of the spirit and intuition (Mosse, *German Ideology*, 54): "According to Diederichs, the adoption of an irrational, emotional, and mystical world view by each individual German would automatically produce the desired results [social revitalization]" (ibid., 55).

[21] Arthur Wolfgang Cohn, "Das musikalische Verständnis: Neue Ziele," *Zeitschrift für Musikwissenschaft* 4.3 (1921), 129–30.

[22] Karl Grunsky, *Musikästhetik* (Berlin-Leipzig: Göschen'sche Verlagsbuchhandlung, 1907, 1919), 22, 29, 75–76. Meyer distinguishes between formalists and expressionists, and further between absolute and referential expressionists, in *Emotion and Meaning in Music* (Chicago: University of Chicago Press, 1956), 1–3.

Deutschen (1890), a "rhapsody of irrationality," which denounced "the whole intellectualistic and scientific bent of German culture, the extinction of art and individuality."²³ The book was an instant and overwhelming success. In two years it went through forty printings. Writing at a time when the educated middle class began to sense the emptiness of modern industrial society, "Langbehn caught the mood of a groping, discontented, and aspiring people, and they in turn welcomed [Langbehn's] book as an articulation of their own inchoate feelings of discontent."²⁴

Langbehn sets the sharp culture-critical tone at the very opening of *Rembrandt*:

It has gradually become an open secret that the contemporary spiritual life of the German people is in a state of slow decay; according to some, even of rapid decay. . .Moreover, the entire culture of the present is. . .turned backward; it is less concerned with the creation of new values than with the cataloguing of old ones. . .The more scientific it [culture] becomes, the less creative it will be.²⁵

Langbehn rebelled violently against his university studies in natural science and chemistry, as well as against all mechanistic thinking. If there are any themes that unify Langbehn's disjointed harangue against modernism, they are the maladies of Intellectualism and scientism. Throughout the book he rails against science, its tendency toward fragmentary specialization, and against the false objectivity of Positivism.

Science is spiritless [*geistlos*]. For spirit is precisely the relationship of all parts to the whole, and of the whole to all its parts. Modern science luxuriates in details.

*Current science is proud of its objectivity. But it easily forgets that sterility [Farblosigkeit] and tedium [Monotonie] are not truth.*²⁶

Art was for Langbehn the antipode of science and scholarship, and thus became his antidote for all the ills both had caused. By studying and learning to appreciate art, one could develop synthetic thinking and revive the emotional and sub-

---

²³ Stern, *Cultural Despair*, xii. Stern's book contains the most extensive critical exposition in English of Langbehn's background and career. In four detailed chapters Stern covers Langbehn's biography (97–115), the themes of *Rembrandt* (116–136), the political and social effects of the book (137–52, 153–82). Mosse (*German Ideology*, 39–46) and Hughes (*Consciousness and Society*, 43–45) also touch on Langbehn. All are agreed that, despite the pretentious and capricious qualities of *Rembrandt*, the book had a tremendous impact in the two decades preceding World War I.

²⁴ Stern, *Cultural Despair*, 153–54.

²⁵ Langbehn, *Rembrandt als Erzieher*, ed. Dr. Gerhard Krüger, according to the 1st edn., with supplements from the 17th edn. (Berlin: Theodor Fritsch Verlag, 1944), 51–52. The translation given is from Stern, *Cultural Despair*, 121–22.

²⁶ Langbehn, *Rembrandt*, 127, 140. Langbehn specifically addresses "False Objectivity" in a section on pages 142–44. Wilhelm Flitner, sounding much like Langbehn, wrote thirty years later "The primarily scientific education, which sustained itself under lack of true human education, has left us spiritually empty and deceives us out of our last sense of existence" (Flitner, *Laienbildung* [1921], 45, cited in Wolfgang Scheibe, *Die Reformpädagogische Bewegung, 1900–32: Eine einführende Darstellung* (Berlin-Basle: Julius Beltz, 1969), 359.

jective elements of life that science and scholarship had nearly extinguished. Hence the title of Langbehn's book: Rembrandt personified artistic individuality and so symbolized a cultural ideal.[27] Intuition and subjectivity had to replace intellection and materiality in the thinking of the folk before it could achieve cultural distinction.

Langbehn's book elicited mixed, confused reactions, running from unreserved acclaim to vehement denunciation and charges of sophistry. However, the most damning criticism could not dampen the enthusiasm for *Rembrandt*, which became a catalyst for diverse reform movements of the time. For instance the book directly affected the then emerging art education movement, a crusade to reform and expand art instruction in schools and so to raise the cultural level of society. What could have been more beneficial for such a campaign than a book that glorified art as the key to social and cultural renewal? Like Langbehn, Alfred Lichtwark (1852–1914), a leader in the art education movement, believed that art was central for social reform in general.

> The demand for an artistic education does not appear in isolation; from its first hour it was inextricably connected with the contemporaneous, more clearly formulated call of the mid-eighties for a moral renovation of our life. The two fields are inseparable. It is high time now for the moral-religious and artistic forces to reach their full development.[28]

As director of the Hamburg art museum, Lichtwark's main connection with the art education movement was through pictorial art. The conductor and professor Hermann Kretzschmar (1848–1924) was the chief spokesman around 1900 for reform in music education. In a booklet entitled *Current Musical Issues (Musikalische Zeitfragen)*, Kretzschmar laments the decline in popular cultivation of music and the correspondingly low level of appreciation for music in the folk.

> Music must above all be secure in the folk, in receptiveness and understanding. Music must evolve its power and benefits based on a well-supervised involvement with music. Only then can one argue over composers and trends in compositional practice.[29]

---

[27] Stern, *Cultural Despair*, 119.

[28] Quoted in Stern, *Cultural Despair*, 174, from Lichtwark's concluding address to the first of three Art Education Conferences (*Kunsterziehungstage*) in 1901. Wolfgang Scheibe discusses the art education movement in *Die Reformpädagogische Bewegung*, 139–70.

[29] Hermann Kretzschmar, *Musikalische Zeitfragen* (Leipzig: Peters, 1903), 4. Further, "The evolution of composition is influenced ultimately, and perhaps most crucially, by the general musical capability of the folk and country" (ibid., 7). Kretzschmar, like Fritz Jöde, recommended a thorough reform of singing instruction in public schools as a way of raising the music-cultural consciousness of the folk: "Today, singing instruction in schools is the most important source. . .of musical strength for the folk. . .Without reinforcement from the folk, no art can exist, none can remain sound when it loses contact with the domain of simpler cultivation. . . Singing instruction. . .is accordingly not merely a current musical issue but rather a general cultural issue" (ibid., 23).

In order to instill greater musical literacy and appreciation in the folk, besides reforming vocal training Kretzschmar proposed elementary training in aesthetics, based on "hermeneutic" analysis, a latter-day doctrine of affections. In his concert-hall guides and again in two essays explaining the ideology and method of hermeneutic analysis, Kretzschmar hoped to provide a form of musical understanding that would be accessible to the educated lay person.[30] Hermeneutic analysis was intended to reveal the spiritual content (*geistiger Inhalt*) of music by

> distilling the affects from the tones and laying out the structure of their development. Whoever penetrates past the tones and sonic forms to the affects elevates the sensuous phenomena, the formal work, to a spiritual activity.[31]

Purely formalistic analysis was insufficient. For Kretzschmar it was "only an intermediate stage. Forms are means of expression. That which is expressed is something spiritual."[32]

Kretzschmar's emphasis on spiritual as opposed to formal elements in music, the intuitive nature of his hermeneutic analysis, and above all his overriding concern for the folk illustrate clearly his connection with the socio-cultural renewal movement of the early 1900s. Like many of his contemporaries, he believed that elevating the level of understanding and appreciation for art in the folk was essential for renewal.

The reform and growth of art education parallels a larger, general reform of education in the decades around 1900. The adult education movement (*Volksbildungsbewegung*), for instance, under way since the 1870s, escalated during the socio-cultural renewal of the 1890s. The goal of the movement was to set "shared cultural treasures and the solid cultural achievements of [the] folk against material and socialistic tendencies."[33] Primary and secondary education also underwent reform. Kaiser Wilhelm's 1890 address criticizing education in Germany encouraged initiatives to modernize the curriculum and methodology in public schools. Similar

---

[30] Hermann Kretzschmar, *Führer durch den Konzertsaal*, 2nd edn. (Leipzig: A. G. Libeskind, 1891; orig. 1886); "Anregungen zur Förderung musikalischer Hermeneutik," *Jahrbuch der Musikbibliothek Peters* 2 (1902), 45–66; and "Neue Anregungen zur Förderung musikalischer Hermeneutik: Satzästhetik," *Jahrbuch der Musikbibliothek Peters* 12 (1905), 75–86. The two essays are reprinted in Kretzschmar's *Gesammelte Aufsätze* (2 vols., Leipzig: Breitkopf und Härtel, 1910-11), vol. II, 168–92, 280–93. Bojan Bujić gives a translation of the first seven pages of Kretzschmar's first hermeneutics article *Music in European Thought, 1851–1912* (Cambridge: Cambridge University Press, 1988), 114–20. Werner Braun discusses the background of Kretzschmar's hermeneutics, and comments on the two essays in "Kretzschmars Hermeneutik," *Beiträge zur musikalischen Hermeneutik*, ed. Carl Dahlhaus, Studien zur Musikgeschichte des 19. Jahrhunderts, vol. XLIII (Regensburg: Bosse, 1975), 33–39.

[31] Kretzschmar, "Anregungen," 51.

[32] Ibid., 53.

[33] Scheibe, *Die Reformpädagogische Bewegung*, 354. Scheibe discusses the adult education movement on pages 353–86.

reform movements sprang up elsewhere in Europe.[34] One of the essential aims of reform pedagogy, also known as the "New Education," was to eliminate the mindless drilling of abstract facts. Kaiser Wilhelm, arguing against long years of studying classical languages and cultures, declared "We should raise young Germans, not young Greeks and Romans."[35]

Teachers who had become dissatisfied with the authoritarian style of education in Bismarck's Imperial Germany eagerly embraced reform. There was little progress during the 1890s, however, due to ideological and political inertia. Rather than move slowly within the public-school system, some reformers forged ahead by starting private "experimental schools" (*Versuchsschulen*), located in picturesque country settings, away from the afflictions of urban society and culture. There, they could implement their ideas more quickly and completely.[36]

Kurth taught in such an experimental school, the Free School Community (*Freie Schulgemeinde*) in Wickersdorf. After spending several unhappy years as a rehearsal pianist in various German cities, just before taking a post at the University of Berne, Kurth worked at the Free School for a year (1911–12) as head music instructor. It was a turning point in his career. At Wickersdorf, Kurth came into contact with the personality and ideas of August Halm, the school's first music director, and with its co-founder, the contentious educational theorist, Gustav Wyneken (1868–1965).

Wickersdorf, one of the most radical of the experimental schools, institutionalized Wyneken's controversial, neo-Idealist views. After leaving another private

---

[34] I have written on the relationship between reform pedagogy and music theory in an article entitled "The 'New Education' and Music Theory, 1900–1925" (forthcoming). General sources on educational reform in Europe include Frederick Roman's *The New Education in Europe* (London: Routledge, 1924); and William Boyd's and Wyatt Rawson's *The Story of the New Education* (London: Heinemann, 1965). There are several good studies of the reform pedagogy movement in Germany, including Wolfgang Scheibe's *Die Reformpädagogische Bewegung* (see note 26 above); and Thomas Alexander's and Beryl Parker's *The New Education in the German Republic* (New York: John Day Co., 1929), based on the authors' travels through Germany in 1908–13. Earlier accounts include Herman Nohl's *Die Pädagogische Bewegung in Deutschland und ihre Theorie*, 2nd edn. (Frankfurt: G. Schulte-Bulmke, 1935); and Franz Hilker's book, *Deutsche Schulversuche* (Berlin: C. A. Schwetschke & Sohn, 1924). Those interested in German education before 1900 can refer to Friedrich Paulsen's *German Education Past and Present*, trans. T. Lorenz (London: T. Fisher Unwin, 1908); John T. Prince's *Methods of Instruction and Organization of the Schools of Germany* (Boston: Lee and Shepard, 1892); and William H. Winch's *Notes on German Schools, With Special Relation to Curriculum and Methods of Teaching* (London: Longman's Green and Co., 1904).

[35] James Albisetti discusses Kaiser Wilhelm's address on education in *Secondary School Reform in Imperial Germany* (Princeton: Princeton University Press, 1983), 140. See also Dennis Shirley's essay "Paul Geheeb's Leadership of the Odenwaldschule, 1910–1930," (Qualifying Paper, Harvard Graduate School of Education, 1987), 8. Langbehn, complaining about the abstract knowledge peddled in German schools, remarked "German education, which in the meantime has risen to abstraction and brilliance, must henceforth come back down to straightforward and concrete matters, otherwise, like a too highly pitched voice, it could crack" (*Rembrandt*, 255).

[36] Franz Hilker compiled a collection of essays that describe the work of several schools, in *Deutsche Schulversuche*, cited in note 34 above. Martin Luserke discusses the Wickersdorf Free School on pages 77–90.

school – one of Hermann Lietz's "Country Boarding Schools" (*Landerziehungsheime*) – Wyneken co-founded the Wickersdorf school in September, 1906, with Paul Geheeb. Wyneken agressively styled the Free School according to his version of reform pedagogy, hoping to make it a model institution and, ultimately, the birthplace of a new culture.[37] Just as the *Wandervögel* were a realization of the contemporary back-to-nature movement, and Lietz's schools an institutionalization of nationalistic and "volkish" ideologies, so the Wickersdorf Free School was an institutionalization of humanistic aspirations of the socio-cultural renewal.

In general, Wyneken's ideas followed the principles of reform pedagogy: treat and teach the child as child (*vom Kinde aus*), not as miniature adults; stimulate natural curiosity to promote meaningful learning; allow distinctive personality traits and abilities of pupils to unfold naturally; and teach through *direct experiences*, not through academic exercises – in short, tenets of modern-day "developmental" education.[38] Although Wickersdorf was similar in approach to other experimental schools, there were some notable differences. Chief among these, and crucial for our discussion, was Wyneken's emphasis on humanistic studies, on manifestations of "objective spirit" in philosophy, literature, and particularly in *music*. For Wyneken, music was the purest expression of the objective spirit. Accordingly, it was the centerpiece of daily life at the school and became the symbol of its social and cultural mission.

Each day at Wickersdorf began and ended with a short musical performance, usually a Bach keyboard piece, and each week climaxed with a *Konzertrede*, an evening musical lecture-demonstration, given at first by Halm and later by Kurth. The lectures dealt with stylistic and structural aspects of music, illustrated by performances on the piano.[39] Halm's main analytical objective was to highlight

---

[37] Wyneken recounts the founding of the Free School Community in *Wickersdorf* (Lauenburg/Elbe: Adolf Saal, 1922), 1–7. He summarizes his philosophy of education in the pamphlet "Der Gedankenkreis der Freien Schulgemeinde" (Leipzig: Erich Matthes, 1913). Heinrich Kupffer discusses Wyneken's ideas, career, and influence in "Gustav Wyneken: Leben und Werk," *Jahrbuch des Archivs der deutschen Jugendbewegung* 2 (1970), 23–32.

Hermann Lietz, called the "German Pestalozzi," founded his first Country Boarding School in Ilsenburg (April, 1898). He modeled it after Cecil Reddie's pioneering school "Abbotsholme," founded 1889 in Derbyshire, England, where Lietz spent a year in residence (1896–97). Lietz went on to establish two more schools, one at Haubinda (1901), the other at Biberstein (1901), in order to accommodate Ilsenburg students as they grew older. Alexander and Parker discuss Lietz in *The New Education*, 179–83. Lietz wrote of his work in "Zur Einführung in die Bestrebungen der deutschen Land-Erziehungsheime," *Leben und Arbeit* 1 (1913), 1–13.

[38] Dennis Shirley outlines the reform pedagogical agenda in "Geheeb's Leadership," 10–12. He discusses the roots of reform pedagogy and its early development on pages 13–15, 19–20 (Lietz), 21–22 (Wyneken). Evelyn Weber gives the background of modern developmental education in *Ideas Influencing Early Childhood Education: A Theoretical Analysis* (New York: Teachers College Press, 1984).

[39] Wyneken outlines the daily routine in *Wickersdorf*, 11. It resembles the routine at Lietz's schools, which in turn reflects the one Lietz experienced at Reddie's Abbotsholme school. Although Lietz followed Reddie's example, his schools closely resemble the outlook and plan of the nationalistic school model suggested

the dynamic properties of music in order to reveal the formal logic of a work. In doing this, he hoped to heighten the students' *experience* of music as a dynamic process. Halm's stress on experience in learning about and understanding music agrees with reform-pedagogical methods of the time, which stress direct experience as a learning tool in general. Because of the age and training of the audience, Halm had to rely extensively on analogy and metaphor. Technical analysis went only as far as students' preparation. This is not to say that his analyses were superficial or insubstantial. On the contrary, from the published versions of some of Halm's talks it is clear that they were quite penetrating.[40]

The age and training of Halm's and Kurth's young audiences at Wickersdorf forced them to teach musical comprehension within defined limitations. However, neither viewed the limitations as disadvantages. On the contrary, as Kurth wrote in *Bruckner*, amateurs sometimes detect certain musical processes more readily than professional musicians, who with all of their specialized analytical apparatus tend to get mired in detail.[41]

Throughout their careers both men were committed to educating the general public. Teaching at Wickersdorf was but one manifestation of that commitment. During World War I, Halm taught at a pedagogical institute in Esslingen, near Stuttgart, and was a frequent speaker or panelist at teachers' workshops throughout Germany. In his lectures and books Halm endeavored to foster an informed listening public. Professional literature, such as the writings of Schenker, were in Halm's opinion too technical to be useful for a broad audience. Halm criticized Schenker's Beethoven editions, for instance, for taking such a "strongly esoteric approach [which] addresses only musicians, the knowledgeable and able, so that. . .the image of a musical folk, or even of a public [*Gefolge*], has no place." Halm's audience,

---

by Hugo Goering in *Die neue Deutsche Schule: ein Weg zur Verwirklichung vaterländischer Erziehung*, 2nd edn. (Leipzig: R. Voigtländer, 1890). See also Alexander and Parker, *The New Education*, 184–85, 198, 200; Wilhelm Flitner and Gerhard Kudritzke, *Die deutsche Reformpädagogik* (2 vols., Düsseldorf–Munich: Helmut Küpper, 1961–62), vol. I, 74, 323; and Cecil Reddie, *Abbotsholme* (London: George Allen, 1890), 74. Reddie's *Abbotsholme* is bound together with Lietz's account of his year there, *Emlohstobba*. See pages 277, 297, 316.

[40] I discuss Kurth's experience at Wickersdorf in *EKATA*, 5–6, 222–23, and in my essay, "The 'New Education' and Music Theory"). Wyneken describes the evening lectures in *Wickersdorf*, 106–07. He points out that some of Halm's talks from the early years at Wickersdorf appeared in Halm's book *Von Zwei Kulturen der Musik* (Munich: G. Müller, 1913; 3rd edn., Stuttgart: Klett, 1947). Hilmar Höckner gives the most complete discussion of music at Wickersdorf, and of Halm's activities there, in *Die Musik in der deutschen Jugendbewegung* (Wolfenbüttel: Kallmeyer, 1927), 63–89, specifically 85–87 on the lectures.

[41] Kurth, *Bruckner*, vol. I, 283, in the present volume, 156: "Precisely here [in tracing dynamic formal processes in Bruckner] we can observe that amateurs often have one of the many advantages of impartiality over professional musicians." Wallace Berry expresses a similar opinion: "I believe a great deal of understanding of musical process, in its essential terms, to be accessible to the involved layman or amateur. Indeed, many of the most persuasive factors in musical effect and function are delineative of shapes and processes that can be demonstrated, given necessary theoretical and analytical calculations, relatively simply" (*Structural Functions of Music*, [Englewood Cliffs: Prentice Hall, 1976], 3).

in contrast to Schenker's, was to a large extent aspiring musical amateurs, "dilettantes" in the true sense of the word.[42] Wickersdorf was one source of the kind of cultural reform necessary to restore the reputation of the dilettante.

[One] cultural source of new things is the Wickersdorf Free School Community and other educational institutions that emulate and develop the Wickersdorf model. It is surely no coincidence that Dr. Ernst Kurth's aforementioned work [*Grundlagen*] arose in the Wickersdorf Free School Community, where the author worked (even if it was not written there). My book *Von Zwei Kulturen der Musik* also derives from the same source. Both books are part of the work of emancipating the friends of music – and with them, music – from the sovereignty of the musicians caste.[43]

Kurth was profoundly affected by his experience at the Free School, by the unique atmosphere there, and by its strong sense of cultural "mission." Years after he left for Berne, in a letter to Halm Kurth referred to the "spirit of Wickersdorf," which remained an ideal and inspiration throughout his academic career.[44] In response to a query about his experience at the school, Kurth wrote

For me it was a stimulating and momentous time. My activity at the University of Berne remains strongly influenced by the culture and outlook of the whole intellectual life [*Geistesleben*] at the Free School Community, despite the fact that the scholarly activity brought with it other objectives. It is precisely in this regard, though, that I hope not to have obscured the intellectual and cultural outlook that pervades the incomparably lively intellectual climate [*Geistigkeit*] of the Free School Community.[45]

In addition to teaching musicology and theory seminars at Berne, Kurth rou-

---

[42] Halm, *Von zwei Kulturen der Musik*, 3rd edn., xiv. I discuss Halm's views on the dilettante and the need for more *Bildung* and less *Ausbildung* in "The 'New Education'". Schenker maligned the dilettante in *Kontrapunkt* (2 vols., Vienna: Universal, 1910, 1922), vol. I, x–xi; *Counterpoint*, trans. John Rothgeb and Jürgen Thym (2 vols., New York: Schirmer Books, 1987), vol. I, xviii–xix. Schoenberg, by contrast, was more forgiving, even supportive of the layman (*Harmonielehre* [Vienna: Universal, 1911], 463; *Theory of Harmony*, trans. Roy E. Carter [Berkeley–Los Angeles: University of California Press, 1978], 414). Fritz Jöde (1887–1970), another important music-educational reformer of the time, said of Halm's work, "Some may have the impression that, in Halm's work, it is only a matter of discussing musicological issues, which are irrelevant for the cultivated [*gebildete*] non-musician. No evaluation could be more incorrect. Halm does not primarily address professional musicians at all. Rather, he aims at serving today's ever increasing need, precisely outside of this [professional] circle, for insight into the essence of music" (Jöde, in a review entitled "*Von zwei Kulturen der Musik,*" *Der Wanderer* 7 [1916], reprinted in *Die deutsche Jugendmusikbewegung in Dokumenten ihrer Zeit*, comp. Wilhelm Scholz and Waltraut Jonas-Corrier et al. [Wolfenbüttel-Zurich: Möseler, 1980], 70). Halm's comment on Schenker's Beethoven editions is in "Heinrich Schenker," *Die Freie Schulgemeinde* 8 [1917], 15.

[43] Halm, "Gegenwart und Zukunft der Musik," *Das hohe Ufer* 2 (1920), reprinted in *Von Form und Sinn der Musik*, 253–54.

[44] Letters to Halm dated December 11, 1926 and February 17, 1927 (Deutsches Literaturarchiv/Schiller-Nationalmuseum, Marbach am Neckar, protocol nos. 69.833/15 and /20). Kurth and Halm corresponded up until Halm died, in 1929.

[45] Höckner, *Musik in der deutschen Jugendbewegung*, 93–94.

tinely held public lectures for the university community. He also initiated a weekly collegium musicum, attended by music students and amateurs, in which he conducted Renaissance and Baroque choral masterworks but also explained them historically and, as far as possible, technically. While writing *Bruckner*, Kurth regularly lectured on the symphonies and choral works at informal gatherings of lay people and amateur musicians, as well as in public lectures at the university. It is thus fitting that Kurth wrote the book so that it would be "understandable even for the lay person."[46]

Kurth's abiding commitment to music education for the non-professional motivated him to offer a course on the "Fundamentals of Music Instruction: Pedagogy and the Youth Movement" (winter term, 1927–28), and to publish an essay proposing reforms for music education in primary and secondary schools. Kurth's suggestions in the essay are based on the Wickersdorf model. "Introductions to music," he declared, "are. . .necessary for schools and surely welcome for the whole culture." Such introductions were to be "thoroughly graphic," and musical explanations to rely primarily on "intellectual concepts," and "as little as possible on technical concepts."[47]

Spontaneity becomes the focus. Supported by the discussion that accompanies, spontaneity serves the [musical] *experience* [emphasis mine]. . .Understanding of music can be built up gradually on the pure training of instinct.[48]

Kurth's attitudes and activities show that, as an academician, he concerned himself with more than educating professionals, with more than esoteric technical analysis for a small, scholarly audience. Unlike Schenker, Kurth's work was not aimed at the professional musical community alone. He clearly felt responsible for developing a cultural consciousness in the folk. In approaching his work from a humanistic, at times populist point of view, rather than from a formalistic, elitist one, Kurth followed the thinking of Halm and other socio-cultural reformers. As with Halm, Kurth's music-analytical work is not so populist that it becomes insubstantial. His analyses are often quite detailed, but even then they are couched in generally accessible language. Specialized terminology is limited, as in Wickers-

---

[46] Kurth, *Bruckner*, vol. I, vii. "I sought to make specialized music-technical concepts understandable through explanations and the mode of illustration itself. Only the discussions on harmony are an exception, and these can be skipped by readers lacking the requisite training with no loss to the overall intelligibility" (ibid.). During lectures Kurth illustrated his ideas by playing four-handed arrangements of Bruckner's symphonies with his assistant, Elsbeth Merz. They often played for invited groups in towns around Berne. The talks probably resembled the ones he delivered to the students at Wickersdorf. Further, Kurth gave adult education courses on music in the early 1920s. Rudolf Schäfke mentions Kurth's and Halm's commitment to the musical amateur as a distinctive trait of their work, in *Geschichte der Musikästhetik in Umrissen* (Berlin: Hesse, 1934), 418–19.

[47] Kurth, "Die Schulmusik und ihre Reform," *Schweizerische Musikzeitung* 70.9 (1930), 347, 343.

[48] Ibid., 346, 349.

dorf and public lectures. Like Halm, Kurth felt that the direct *experience* of the music, of its dynamic qualities and processive formal logic, was paramount and should not be obscured by analytical schematicism – what Kurth called "reconstructions."[49] Halm's and Kurth's emphasis on aural experience, relatively unencumbered by schematic analysis and theoretical abstraction, aligns their work with the then emerging phenomenological school of thought, which will be discussed shortly.

In the first section of this essay, I have touched on those characteristics of the early twentieth-century socio-cultural revival that shaped Kurth's theoretical, analytical, and pedagogical attitudes. Those characteristics include a distrust of rationalism and "systems" in favor of intuitive, open-ended modes of inquiry; rejection of factual drill and functional education in favor of experiential spontaneity and cultural education; intolerance of academic elitism and instead the fostering of populism; and, in general, a devaluation of exteriority and accentuation of interiority.

The next section of this essay will briefly address three early-century intellectual developments that influenced Kurth's thinking and methodology: phenomenology, psychological aesthetics, and Gestalt psychology. Each of these developments are reactions to then common modes of thought: phenomenology to psychologism, Gestalt psychology to elementism, and psychological aesthetics to formalism. Given the complexity and breadth of these topics, it will of course be impossible to discuss each in detail. We will thus limit ourselves to key ideas, and cite relevant primary and secondary literature for reference.

INTELLECTUAL CONTEXT

Phenomenology is relevant for Kurth's writings because, in accord with its general tenets, his analyses describe and try to elucidate the organic function of manifest aural events. Moreover, his contemporaries counted his work among the newly emerging phenomenological approaches to analysis and aesthetics. The aesthetician Arthur W. Cohn and the musicologists Hans Mersmann, Herbert Eimert, and Rudolf Schäfke, for example, all cite Kurth's research as being phenomenological.[50]

---

[49] Kurth refers to "theoretical reconstructions" several times in *Romantische Harmonik*, for example on pages 281–82, in a discussion of the well-known sequential passage, "So stürben wir. . ." in Act 2, Scene 2 of *Tristan und Isolde* (Schirmer piano-vocal score, p. 178). See also *Romantische Harmonik*, 247, 265, 267n, 301.

[50] Arthur Wolfgang Cohn, "Das musikalische Verständnis," 135 (see note 21 above for full citation); and "Das Erwachen der Ästhetik," *Zeitschrift für Musikwissenschaft* 1 (1918–19), 674; Hans Mersmann, "Versuch einer Phänomenologie der Musik," *Zeitschrift für Musikwissenschaft* 5 (1922–23), 227n.2; and "Zur Phänomenologie der Musik," *Zeitschrift für Ästhetik und allgemeine Kunstwissenschaft* 19 (1925), 375; Herbert Eimert, "Zur Phänomenologie der Musik," *Melos* 5.7 (1926), 242; Rudolf Schäfke, *Geschichte der Musikästhetik in Umrissen*, 410–11. Cohn and Mersmann mention Halm's writings as seminal in developing a phenomenological school of analysis.

Kurth's effort to "bracket" certain common music-theoretical presuppositions and to return "*zu den Sachen*" by analyzing and theorizing about music as direct, aural experience associate him with phenomenological modes of inquiry. Like other early phenomenological researchers, Kurth tried "to get away from the primacy of theories, of concepts and symbols, to immediate contact with the intuited data of experience." Just as Kurth's and Halm's work arose as part of the socio-cultural and intellectual revival, Husserl's search for "apodictic" certainty also arose from a desire to achieve an unshakable foundation for a spiritual and intellectual renewal, amid a threatened civilization.[51]

The development of phenomenology has taken many paths. Its founder, Edmund Husserl (1848–1936) went in a wholly different direction, for example, than did some of his better-known students, who expanded on the early stages of his teachings rather than following his Idealistic path toward "transcendental" phenomenology.[52] Kurth's ideas reflect Husserl's early thinking, up to about 1913 (*Ideen zu einer reinen Phänomenologie*, part 1), as adapted for musical purposes by Cohn and Mersmann. However, Kurth diverges from phenomenological principles in some crucial respects. For instance when Kurth interprets musical events as sonic manifestations of psychic tensions or, in Wagner's music, as psychological or dramatic signs, he contradicts Cohn's phenomenological "musical understanding," which avoids evaluating musical events as "symbols of any sort of psychic motions of its creator."[53] Furthermore, Kurth enters psychologistic territory, which is foreign to the phenomenological realm, when he demands that theoretical reflection arise from "an empathy [*Einfühlen*] and internal resonance with the animated *creative* forces," and says that "the most essential goal in identifying and observing artistic logic [in Bach's counterpoint] is the awakening and stimulating of that art of instinctive empathy." We might take "empathy" here to mean something analogous to

---

[51] Herbert Spiegelberg, "Ways into Phenomenology: Phenomenology and Metaphenomenology," *Doing Phenomenology: Essays on and in Phenomenology* (The Hague: Martinus Nijhoff, 1975), 15; and *The Phenomenological Movement: A Historical Introduction*, 2nd edn. (2 vols., The Hague: Martinus Nijhoff, 1965), vol. I, 85. In the latter volume, Spiegelberg provides a clear presentation of "The Essentials of the Phenomenological Method," 653–701.

[52] In addition to Spiegelberg's books cited above, good introductions to Husserl's phenomenology are Maurice Natanson's *Edmund Husserl: Philosopher of Infinite Tasks* (Evanston: Northwestern University Press, 1973), and Quentin Lauer's *The Triumph of Subjectivity: An Introduction of Transcendental Phenomenology* (New York: Fordham University Press, 1978). Don Ihde gives a clear, practical introduction to phenomenological method in *Experimental Phenomenology* (New York: Capricorn Books, 1977). One of Husserl's brightest students at Göttingen, Adolph Reinach, gives a particularly clear exposition of early phenomenology in "What is Phenomenology?" trans. Derek Kelly, *The Philosophical Forum* 1.2 (1968), 231–56. On Reinach's view of phenomenology, see Spiegelberg, *The Phenomenological Movement*, vol. I, 197–202.

[53] Cohn, "Das musikalische Verständnis," 132. Likewise Alfred Pike: "When music is considered as a system of symbols passing on to extramusical experience it ceases to become music" ("The Phenomenological Approach to Musical Perception," *Philosophy and Phenomenological Research* 27 [1966–67], 251).

Introduction   19

phenomenological intuition.⁵⁴ There is the dual possibility of "phenomenal objectivity" and "phenomenal subjectivity," but the empathy theory tends to equate the objective with the subjective.⁵⁵ However, Mersmann explicitly rejects empathy as a basis for aesthetic discourse: all relations to the self (*Ich-Beziehungen*) must be dissolved. Still, he characterizes Kurth's analyses as phenomenological because they do what is for Mersmann the chief work of analysis: to reveal the organic "evolution of elemental forces" in order to understand the dynamic tectonic structure.⁵⁶

Are Kurth's analyses, then, phenomenological? In the strict sense of the word, no. But if we understand "phenomenological" loosely as "experiential," and if we consider Kurth's conscientious effort to focus on and explain the logic of manifest aural facts, then his work certainly exemplifies a "phenomenological attitude."⁵⁷ Perceptive readers can, and should, see through the quasi-phenomenological interpretations to their syntactical underpinnings, but they will find that Kurth highlights the aural impact of musical events and their hierarchic function in a dynamic continuum, rather than technical abstractions.

The empathy theory, which leads Kurth to "psychologize" musical events, is one of the chief obstacles to considering his analyses genuinely phenomenological. It is of course always possible to disregard Kurth's psychologistic bent and to focus on the intramusical criteria that underlie his analyses. But it is impossible to ignore the consistent references to psychic motivations for those criteria, and the implicit empathetic assumptions for analysis in general. Halm's analyses, by comparison, are more clearly phenomenological, despite some hermeneutic "slips," especially in his earlier writings, due to the typical metaphorical language in non-formalistic, interpretive analyses. As, shown above, Kurth explicitly challenges the listener to empathize with musical events in order to sense the power of their generative psychic forces. Halm cautions against such psychologizing: "In music, one ought

---

⁵⁴ Kurth, *Romantische Harmonik*, 2; *Grundlagen*, 350. Consider, however, Kurth's views that "The process *outside of us* when a melody is played is nothing but the temporal succession of tones. By contrast, what we designate as melody in the musical sense is a tension process *in us*" (*Grundlagen*, 2), and that "Music is. . .not a reflection of nature but rather the experience of nature's mysterious energies *in us*" (*Romantische Harmonik*, 4). One of Husserl's main battles was against psychologism, exemplified in Theodor Lipps's theory of empathy. Spiegelberg discusses "The Critique of Psychologism" in *The Phenomenological Movement*, vol. I, 93–95, 171–72 (Lipps).

⁵⁵ Pike, "The Phenomenological Approach," 253: "*Phenomenal Objectivity* describes the kinetic qualities of various musical patterns. . .*Phenomenal Subjectivity* describes the listener's response and attitudes as evoked by his perception of phenomenally objective sound patterns." Paul Moos discusses Lipps's tendency to equate objective qualities with subjective perceptions in *Die deutsche Ästhetik der Gegenwart* (Berlin–Leipzig: Schuster & Loeffler, 1914), vol. I: *Die psychologische Ästhetik*, 179, 212–13, 231–32, 238–40.

⁵⁶ Mersmann, "Versuch einer Phänomenologie," 374, 376–78.

⁵⁷ Thomas Clifton, *Music as Heard: A Study in Applied Phenomenology* (New Haven: Yale University Press, 1983), ix, 37.

not to take the psychological for the logical." Kurth and Halm part ways over this and other issues.[58]

In adopting an empathetic-psychological slant in analysis, Kurth aligns himself with early twentieth-century psychological rather than phenomenological aesthetics. Psychological aesthetics is a late nineteenth-century outgrowth of the Romantic view of music formulated, for example, by Herder, Hegel, and A. W. Schlegel. For them, music is an abstract, i.e., non-conceptual (*begriffslose*) exteriorization of mental life. Psychological aesthetics takes this Idealistic notion and, as a way of guiding our experience of music's interior content, modifies it with the idea of self-projection (Lipps), "inner imitation" (*innere Nachahmung*, Karl Groos), or "illusion," and "conscious self-deception" (*bewusste Selbsttäuschung*, Konrad Lange), or some variation of these views.[59] Lange, for instance, considers music the strongest case for the illusion theory. The related illusions of motion and force are particularly strong in the perception of music.[60] Kurth tacitly employs this illusion theory when he speaks of individual melodic tones containing energy derived from a pervasive dynamic current (*Bewegungszug*). The current creates a whole that absorbs the parts into a transcendent unity.

This dynamically determined, holistic view of melody links Kurth's ideas to those of Gestalt psychology. Bear in mind that the beginnings and initial development of Gestalt psychology in the early writings of Max Wertheimer, Kurt Koffka, and Wolfgang Köhler are contemporary with *Grundlagen* (1917) and *Romantische Harmonik* (1920). Of course in 1920 the major works in Gestalt psychology still lay ahead, and Kurth may have learned of the research only later. Nevertheless, there are

---

[58] Halm, "Humor und Musik," *Von Grenzen und Ländern der Musik. Gesammelte Aufsätze* (Munich: G. Müller, 1916), 111, cited in *Von Form und Sinn der Musik*, 32. Halm muses "the psychiatrist is declared the rightful judge of music" if its quality depends on the composer's mental makeup ("Unsere Zeit und Beethoven," *Die Rheinlande* 11 [1911], 60; cited in *Von Form und Sinn der Musik*, 153). *EKATA*, 8–9, explains a few of the differences between Kurth and Halm. In a letter (February 3, 1927), Halm alerts Kurth to their disagreement on the genetic status of melody (Deutsches Literaturarchiv/Schiller-Nationalmuseum, Marbach am Neckar, protocol no. 69.562/1).

[59] The relevant early nineteenth-century sources are Georg Wilhelm Friedrich Hegel's *Aesthetics: Lectures on Fine Art* (1820–29), trans. T. M. Knox (2 vols., Oxford: Clarendon Press, 1988), vol. I (part III: 3), 855, 902, 906, 938, and *passim*; Johann Gottfried Herder, *Kalligone* (1800), ed. Heinz Begenau (Weimar: Hermann Böhlhaus Nachfolger, 1955), 146; August Wilhelm von Schlegel, *Vorlesungen über schöne Literatur und Kunst* (1801), in *Die Kunstlehre*, ed. Edgar Kohner (Stuttgart, 1963), 220; in Peter le Huray and James Day, eds., *Music and Aesthetics in the Eighteenth and Early Nineteenth Centuries* (Cambridge: Cambridge University Press, 1981), 266. Relevant passages from Herder's *Kalligone* and Hegel's *Aesthetics* are in le Huray and Day, *Music and Aesthetics*, 255, 257 (Herder); 344, 346 (Hegel). Lipps's treatise is *Ästhetik* (2 vols., Hamburg: Voss, 1903, 1906). He introduces the word *Einfühlung* in vol. I, 120, where he calls it the "inside of imitation." Karl Gross wrote *Einleitung in die Ästhetik* (1892), and Konrad Lange *Das Wesen der Kunst* (Berlin: G. Grote, 1901). Lange speaks of self-deception as the basis of aesthetic enjoyment on page 27, and explains "illusion" on pages 77–79. Paul Moos discusses and critiques psychological aesthetics in *Die deutsche Ästhetik*.

[60] Lange, *Das Wesen der Kunst*, 116, 134, 145. Keep in mind that, for Lange, motion in music is primarily for simulating emotions (*Scheingefühle*), i.e. part of the conscious self-deception theory.

so many similarities between Gestalt principles and Kurth's music-theoretical and cognitive ideas that we could say Kurth intuitively explored in the aural-temporal domain what Gestaltists later scientifically explored and experimentally verified in the visual-spatial domain.[61]

The chief link between Kurth and Gestaltist premises is the idea of dynamically organized, super-summative wholes. Perceptually, a super-summative whole, a "*Gestalt*," depends on organizational forces among its components. According to Koffka, these forces in the behavioral environment are analogous to those in the physical environment. He argues that such forces are genetically primary properties of objects and images, which we associate perceptually according to well-defined criteria because of "actual forces between the members of the group."[62] Kurth puts it this way:

the tones do not exist first and their connection afterwards; rather, the dynamic current [*Bewegungszug*] is the primary element.

The actual sustaining content of the [melodic] line is the dynamic currents that manifest themselves perceptibly in the individual tones. Thus the content is not to be interpreted as a (secondary) connection traced out subsequently from tone to tone but rather as the totality of the dynamic phase [*Bewegungsphase*].[63]

For Koffka, melody "cannot be described by successive states." Just as a "moving body never *is* at one place" but rather "always *passes through places*. . .Just so, a melody. . .never *is* at one note but passes through it." Kurth anticipated Koffka's ideas on melody in *Grundlagen*:

Melody is not a collection [Zusammenfassung] of tones but rather a primal continuity [Zusammenhang] from which the tones are released.

The melodic element resides in the motion through the tones, not in the individual tones through which the motion flows.[64]

---

[61] The main primary sources of Gestalt psychological research are Wolfgang Köhler's *Gestalt Psychology* (New York: Liveright, 1929) and Kurt Koffka's *Principles of Gestalt Psychology* (London: Routledge and Kegan Paul, 1935). Harry Helson traces the early development of Gestalt psychology in "The Psychology of *Gestalt*," *American Journal of Psychology* 36 (1925), 342–70, 494–526; 37 (1926), 25–62, 189–223. David J. Murray gives a succinct, modern account and cites key primary and secondary sources in *A History of Western Psychology*, 2nd edn. (Englewood Cliffs: Prentice Hall, 1988), 281–97. I briefly discuss Kurth's relation to Gestaltist ideas in *EKATA*, 100–01.

[62] Koffka, *Principles of Gestalt Psychology*, 43–44, 46–48, 72, 165.

[63] Kurth, *Grundlagen*, 17; and "Motivbildung," 85.

[64] Koffka, *Principles of Gestalt Psychology*, 434–35. Kurth, *Grundlagen*, 18, 15. See also *Romantische Harmonik*, 7: "the force flows over the empty spaces between the notes and over the notes themselves." Viktor Zuckerkandl, referring to Max Wertheimer's experiments in perceived motion, presents this same line of thought in *Sound and Symbol: Music and the External World*, trans. W. R. Trask, Bollingen Series, vol. XLIV (Princeton: Princeton University Press, 1956), 126–38.

Kurth's account of the perceptual continuity of a melody differs from that of Gestalt psychology. Koffka advances the notion of a mental "trace," produced by the residual force of a tone reaching forward. In hearing a melody, a "trace field" accumulates, perceptually linking each tone with the next to create perceptual continuity.[65] Kurth approaches the issue empathetically. He speaks of individual melodic tones embodying "kinetic energy," which they derive from the overarching dynamic current. Each tone is thus energetically charged and so strives forward. We perceive this striving, empathetically, as the connections between tones. Kurth's so-called "overriding lines" are a more elaborate case. They consist of nonadjacent apex tones, as in compound melody, which are even more strongly energized by virtue of the jagged melodic approach to and departure from them. Such tones strive forward particularly urgently.[66] Kurth's empathetic bias notwithstanding, his linking of nonadjacent tones based on an implicit principle of (frequency) proximity, rather than on a pitch-syntactic model associates his approach to overriding melodic continuities more closely with Gestalt psychology than with the methods of Heinrich Schenker.[67]

THE BOOKS: CONTENT AND RECEPTION

Grundlagen, which established Kurth's reputation as a theorist, departs significantly from the style and content of counterpoint manuals of the day. It is not a didactic primer in composition; it outlines no rules of voice leading and prescribes no exercises. *Grundlagen* is an extended analytical study of Bach's counterpoint, based on certain psychological ideas. Kurth begins the book by presenting his psychological theories of melody and harmony. He then reviews the concept of counterpoint from its early history up through Fux's species and Kirnberger's tonally conditioned counterpoint. Only after a further theoretical section that contrasts Baroque and Classical melodic styles does Kurth finally take up details of Bach's counterpoint. The first important musical example does not appear until page 208!

As explained above Kurth viewed his psychological agenda not just as an alternative to, but rather as a mandatory reform of, music theory. For him theory necessarily had to consider psychological issues lest it founder in abstraction and

---

Wertheimer, very much in sympathy with Kurth on the genetic wholeness of melody, remarks in the posthumously published *Productive Thinking*, "A composer does not usually put notes together in order to get some melody; he envisages the character of a melody *in statu nascendi* and proceeds from above as he tries to concretize it in all its parts" (*Productive Thinking* [1945], enl., ed. Michael Wertheimer [New York: Harper, 1959], 242).

[65] Koffka, *Principles of Gestalt Psychology*, 450–51. Köhler's comments on "dynamical self-distribution" are interesting in this regard (*Gestalt Psychology*, 139–40, 182, 193).

[66] *Grundlagen*, 11. In *Musikpsychologie*, 256–59, Kurth speaks of pro-audition and retro-audition (*Voraushören*, *Zurückhören*) as mechanisms for perceiving overriding lines.

[67] *EKATA*, 100–02, 220–21, discusses the relationship between Kurth and Schenker.

Introduction   23

schematicism. According to Kurth, "real" music resides in psychic motion, beginning with the composer's creative psychic stirrings. Sonic music is the final stage, the last reverberation, of that generative psychic process.

> the whole aural phenomenal form in music, with which the laws of physical sound and physiological perception of tones begins, is already the conclusion of a primal process of interior *psychic* growth. . .The forces activated in us are projected from within onto the surface, where they take shape. The sonic impressions are nothing but the intermediary form in which psychological processes manifest themselves. . .Musical activity merely expresses itself in tones, but it does not reside in them.[68]

Kurth translates this psychological genesis of music into a psychological mode of analysis. His emphasis in theory on the manifest dynamic qualities of music and, in analysis, on the aural immediacy of those qualities reflects the contemporary interest in cognitive issues and, furthermore, the cardinal reform-pedagogical tenet of learning through direct experience. Recall Halm's statement, cited earlier, about *Grundlagen* arising ideologically from the cultural spirit of the Wickersdorf Free School, Wyneken's showcase of reform pedagogy and cradle of socio-cultural renewal.[69] Halm meant that *Grundlagen* reflected Wickersdorf's effort to introduce youth to "objective culture" (here, Bach's contrapuntal art) at an appropriately modified level, in order to spawn an informed, discriminating public (in this case, a generation of knowledgeable musical amateurs). This is not to say that *Grundlagen* is aimed solely at amateurs; the historical and parts of the analytical discussions probably exceeded the understanding of all but extensively trained amateurs. Still, Kurth's descriptive analyses would have been largely accessible to educated non-professionals, although only professionals would have grasped their full technical implications.[70]

Once in the fray of analysis, Kurth does not deal with technical subjects commonly found in counterpoint manuals (e.g. invertible counterpoint, stretto), nor with familiar contrapuntal genres and their formal characteristics (e.g. canon, fugue). For Kurth such analysis was, at worst, too schematic and homogenizing, at best, merely preliminary to revealing the substance and spirit of Bach's music. Rather than starting with technical apparatus, Kurth starts with the element in

---

[68] Kurth, *Grundlagen*, 3, 4, 7. See also *EKATA*, 12.
[69] See note 43 above. *Grundlagen* was probably not written at Wickersdorf. Kurth's letters to the Berne Director of Education during 1912 indicate that, in March, he was still working on *Voraussetzungen*, which he later submitted to the University of Berne in order to qualify as a candidate for a vacancy there in music history and theory (letter dated March 28, 1912, Berne State Archive). Kurth did not finish *Voraussetzungen* until May or June. He submitted the manuscript on June 28, 1912 (letters dated June 20 and 28, 1912, Berne State Archive).
[70] Riemann's and Schenker's criticisms, for example, arise from disagreements over such analytical implications. See *EKATA*, 36–37, 101–2, 220–22, for instance, on differences between Kurth and Schenker. By non-professionals I mean those musical amateurs who, like amateur musicians today, would have had instrumental instruction along with some training in the fundamentals of theory.

Bach's counterpoint that is experientially primary: the flowing melodic line, which through various means of elaboration, expansion, and connection with other lines attains its logical, dynamically determined consummation in form.

The notions of melodic "line" and "linear counterpoint" lie at the heart of the mystique of *Grundlagen*. Those who decide to read it will want to know what Kurth meant by those expressions. Ian Bent has explained "linear" as deriving from three levels of the creative process: Will, which gives music its dynamic thrust (kinetic energy); the manifestation of Will in the creative psyche, which fashions a play of forces (*Kräftespiel*) from the primordial energy; and the sonic realization of the play of forces in melody and, more complexly, in polyphony.[71] In short, for Kurth a melodic "line" is a sonic externalization of a psychic energy vector, powered by the creative Will. Melody in Kurth's sense is "kinetic energy," the quintessential embodiment of psychic energy.[72] Linear counterpoint results when two or more such kinetic melodic strands are combined in a complementary manner. Harmony is a "result" of multiply directed lines, not a pre-existent grid. In genuine counterpoint, harmony consists, not in inert tone stacks, but rather in variously charged configurations of "potential energy," generated when lines "get caught" in chords. In listening to counterpoint, we hear an equilibrium among streaming linear forces (kinetic energy) and congealing harmonic forces (potential energy).[73]

Grundlagen, with its intuitively satisfying ideology, brought Kurth international notoriety. Some scholars, and especially composers, found the book insightful and suggestive. One reviewer of the second edition, for example, agreed with Paul Bekker's evaluation of the book as a strikingly original and fruitful view of Bach's

---

[71] Bent, *Analysis*, 46. See also *EKATA*, 13–14.

[72] Recalling the views of *Voraussetzungen* and *Grundlagen*, in *Bruckner* (vol. I, 274 n. 1) Kurth says, "In earlier works I called the animated force of the monophonic line the *energy* of melody, not in the physical but in the psychodynamic sense of the music."

[73] *Grundlagen*, 61–62, 442, 445. *EKATA*, 109–11. Kurth did not intend the terms kinetic and potential energy to be understood in the precise scientific sense but rather "in analogy to the corresponding physical-mechanical concepts" (*Grundlagen*, 12), and "in free imitation of the mode of designation in physics" (*Romantische Harmonik*, 10). He first used them as music-theoretical terms in *Voraussetzungen*, 71. There, he speaks of "absolute melody" as the pre-sonic prototype of sonic melody (ibid., 60, 61, 70). Carl Dahlhaus discusses absolute melody in the last section of his essay "Absolute Melodik, Ernst Kurths *Voraussetzungen der theoretischen Harmonik und der tonalen Darstellungssysteme*," *Schweizer Jahrbuch für Musikwissenschaft* 6–7 (1986–87), 67–70.

Ian Bent believes Kurth's idea of potential energy is "closely related" to Hindemith's idea of harmonic fluctuation (*Analysis*, 53). Allen Forte, too, in a review of Bent's original "Analysis" article in the *New Grove Dictionary*, says that "Hindemith's notion of harmonic fluctuation is clearly derived from Kurth" ("Theory," *The Musical Quarterly* 68.2 [1982], 165). I believe the two concepts are only superficially similar. Hindemith's harmonic fluctuation derives from the variously tense intervals that *constitute* the vertical structure of a chord. Kurth's potential energy, by contrast, derives from the variously directed melodic strands that *pass through* a chord.

counterpoint.⁷⁴ Other reviewers were less complimentary. Herman Wetzel charged that the book failed totally in its objectives due to the author's insufficient "intuitive-artistic experiential capacity."⁷⁵ Hugo Riemann attacked *Grundlagen* for neglecting norms of phrasing and periodic structure.⁷⁶ Kurth reacted defensively to such criticisms, calling them unobjective and no less biased than his own views. He complained repeatedly in letters to Halm about the disapproving German "authorities" (*die Maßgebenden*), who either neglected his work or distorted its meaning by dwelling superficially on catchwords.⁷⁷

Grundlagen thus brought Kurth considerable frustration professionally, but also financially. Although the book went through three editions and a few reprintings, he earned little from it because he contracted for a single, lump-sum payment at publication. In addition to the aforementioned criticisms, professionally *Grundlagen* caused Kurth much anxiety due to misinterpretations. Readers took "linear counterpoint" for a harmony-free style, which motivated some composers to adopt the expression as a theoretical validation and watchword of their work. Ironically, as a result some readers then interpreted linear counterpoint as a retrospective applica-

---

⁷⁴ Anonymous, "Ernst Kurth: *Grundlagen des linearen Kontrapunkts*," *Neue Zeitschrift für Musik* 86.9–10 (1919), 60. The review is signed with the initial "L." Paul Bekker's review was mentioned at the beginning of this Introduction. I discuss Paul Hindemith's and Ernst Toch's, and Ernst Krenek's reception of Kurth in *EKATA*, 225–26.

⁷⁵ Hermann Wetzel, "Ernst Kurth: *Grundlagen des linearen Kontrapunkts*," *Bach-Jahrbuch* (1917), 173. Wetzel's review appeared simultaneously with Kurth's essay "Zur Motivbildung Bachs" (80–136), which Arnold Schering, then editor of the *Jahrbuch*, convinced Kurth to write on the promise of a review of *Grundlagen* (see above, note 2). Needless to say, Kurth felt betrayed when the review appeared. Because of that and other experiences, he distrusted all journal publishing. Kurth explains the history of "Motivbildung" in a letter to Halm dated March 6, 1920 (69.833/1).

⁷⁶ Hugo Riemann, "Die Phrasierung im Lichte einer Lehre von den Tonvorstellungen," *Zeitschrift für Musikwissenschaft* 1.1 (1918), 26–39. Kurth responded in "Zur Stilistik und Theorie des Kontrapunkts," *Zeitschrift für Musikwissenschaft* 1.1 (1918), 176–82. Hermann Keller criticized Kurth, too, for ignoring points of melodic articulation (Keller, *Die musikalische Artikulation, insbesondere bei Johann Sebastian Bach* [Augsburg: Bärenreiter, 1925], 10–12). Karl Hasse felt Kurth treated Bach's music too much as "absolute music," thereby robbing it of its expressive qualities – a curious evaluation indeed, considering the animated, dynamic picture Kurth gives of Bach's counterpoint (Hasse, *Johann Sebastian Bach* [Bielefeld and Leipzig: Velhagen und Klasing, 1925], 12, 70). Jacques Handschin criticizes *Grundlagen* on various counts, including oversimplified contrasts between the Baroque and Classical styles ("De différentes conceptions de Bach," *Schweizerisches Jahrbuch für Musikwissenschaft* 4 [1929], 18–22). Handschin unsuccessfully applied for the Berne post offered to Kurth. The Philosophical Faculty judged Handschin's submitted writings inferior to Kurth's (memo dated July 27, 1912, protocol no. 1128, in Kurth's file at the Berne State Archive).

⁷⁷ Among others, letters of interest in this regard are those dated March 6, 1920 (69.833/1, Deutsches Literaturarchiv/Schiller-Nationalmuseum, Marbach am Neckar), October 31, 1920 (69.833/2), April 11, 1921 (69.833/3), and February 17, 1927 (69.833/20). Sounding paranoid, Kurth claimed that "official" German musicologists neglected his work rather than lower themselves to deal with an immigrant Austrian. Kurth particularly disliked Arnold Schering for reasons explained in note 75.

tion of modern compositional technique to Bach's music![78] Disgusted, Kurth appealed to Halm for help in correcting such distortions. The outcome was a long passage in Halm's *Beethoven*, which attempts to clarify and defend Kurth's position.[79]

The controversy over *Grundlagen*, and the main focus of criticism, was Kurth's melodic-genetic view of Bach's counterpoint, and his nearly exclusive linear approach to analysis. Critics were quick to point out that Bach's counterpoint was manifestly harmonic, and that to deny, or even to minimize, the harmonic control theoretically or analytically was to distort the structural basis of the music. Kurth contended that he had not meant to deny the role of harmony, only to illuminate the contrapuntal structure from the melodic angle in order to counterbalance the prevailing excessively harmonic view. He maintained that his approach was

> expressly intended as a concept of counterpoint that develops the structure [*Satzgefüge*] from the other side. But it resists the harmonic feeling in order to penetrate it. . .not to evade it. . .Hence not a weakening of harmonic effects is intended but rather a supplementary infiltration of them with the polyphonic-melodic element. . .The contrapuntal suffusion is thus always intended only as one component, not as the entirety of Bach's structure. Not an isolation of two elements is meant with the extreme formulation but rather a better understanding of their relationship.[80]

Although he did argue that "tone for tone. . .the lines must also be harmonically and tonally explainable," he insisted nevertheless that, genetically, "a primal, autonomous process underlies the melodic element, and not any mere dependence on chords." He became impatient with readers' "superficial interpretation that [in *Grundlagen*] the harmonic effects had been ignored or suppressed," and wondered aloud whether his awareness of harmony as a regulative element "should have been hammered home anew page after page."[81]

---

[78] Letter to Halm, dated June 13, 1926 (69.833/13), which outlines three stages of distortion to which *Grundlagen* was subjected. Kurth reiterates the distortions in *Grundlagen*, xiii, and announces that "linearity and atonality have in essence nothing at all to do with one another."

[79] Halm, *Beethoven* (Berlin: Hesse, 1927), 206–12. Kurth, too, tried to clarify certain misunderstandings in the preface to the third edition of *Grundlagen*, xiii–xx. In *Beethoven*, 125–27, Halm also defended Kurth's view of form as articulated in *Bruckner*. Halm even sent Kurth galley proofs of the relevant passages for Kurth's approval. Kurth reworded several passages (Kurth's letter to Halm, January 31, 1927 [69.833/19]), but in the end Halm changed very little (Halm's reply to Kurth, February 3, 1927 [69.562/1]). In corresponding with Kurth about a defense of *Grundlagen*, Halm discovered that he differed fundamentally from Kurth on the role of harmony in counterpoint. Kurth felt it was "secondary," i.e. not generative but regulative, while Halm felt it was primary and organizational. Surprisingly, in the reply to Kurth, Halm called the differences "insignificant" [*unwesentlich*] and stressed their similarities in the *Beethoven* commentary (ibid.).

[80] Kurth, *Grundlagen*, xiv. See *EKATA*, 80, on Kurth's view of harmonic effects in Bach's monophonic works. In the letter to Halm suggesting rewordings for the "defense" in *Beethoven* (see note 79 above), Kurth tried to explain what he meant by a reciprocal permeation of melodic and harmonic forces.

[81] Kurth, *Grundlagen*, xvi, xiv. "The harmonic developments and their. . .constitutive significance are substantiated throughout the present volume." "An essential requirement of any contrapuntal piece is that the coincidence of voices achieves the most compact, autonomous harmonic effects" (ibid., xvi, 439–40).

Kurth's self-defense is well taken. But in light of the book as a whole his rationale is at least partially disingenuous. The melodic-genetic view in *Grundlagen* is more than just a counterbalancing of predominantly harmonic views. It is an explicit ideological commitment. As he would write only a few years later, "The melodic line is the first projection of the will onto 'matter'," the "*boundary* where the creative will and its reflection in sonorous *expression make contact*. . ."[82] More importantly, the view reflects Kurth's psychoauditive approach to analysis. Kurth remarked to Halm that the melodic line had primal significance "on the basis of psychodynamic processes," which for him did not imply that, syntactically, "linearity can claim exclusively primal significance in Bach's music."[83]

Kurth's melodic–genetic ideology naturally affects his analyses of Bach's counterpoint, which do not always agree with modern views. Occasionally, he interprets events melodically when modern analysts might interpret them harmonically, or vice versa, thereby respecting the variable relationship between melody and harmony. In such cases, we must recall Kurth's experiential, psychoauditive method of analysis, which may yield results that disagree with those of a purely syntactic method. Events that are psychoauditively primary may turn out to be syntactically secondary.[84]

Kurth scored a second success in 1920 with *Romantische Harmonik*. Studies of Romantic harmony were not uncommon for theorists of the time. There were books that dealt partially with the subject, as well as detailed, topical articles devoted wholly to it. The entire second part of Rudolf Louis's and Ludwig Thuille's *Harmonielehre*, for instance, discusses chromatic and enharmonic procedures, and a large section of the appendix (pp. 345–69) offers numerous annotated analyses of passages illustrating chromatic-harmonic techniques. Schoenberg's *Harmonielehre* must also be mentioned in this regard.[85] However, up until *Romantische Harmonik* no one had published so sustained an analytical study that documented late nineteenth-century harmony and its roots in early nineteenth-century practices, all copiously documented with excerpts from the literature. Moreover, before Kurth no one had dealt so extensively with the touchstone of chromatic harmony, *Tristan*, whose notorious first chord pair he astutely posited as a microcosm of the whole

---

[82] Kurth, *Romantische Harmonik*, 5.

[83] See note 80 above.

[84] I point out a few examples of such disagreements in *EKATA*, 123–24, 139–40, 143–44, and try to explain Kurth's notion of linear primacy experientially rather than syntactically (ibid., 102, 118–19, 220–21). Carl Dahlhaus comments on the problems of Kurth's melodic-genetic viewpoint in "Bach und der 'lineare Kontrapunkt'," *Bach-Jahrbuch* 49 (1962), 55–79.

[85] Rudolf Louis and Ludwig Thuille, *Harmonielehre* (Stuttgart: Carl Grüninger, 1907). Arnold Schoenberg, *Harmonielehre*. Robert Wason discusses the work of several authors who attempted to modernize Simon Sechter's essentially eighteenth-century teachings to accommodate nineteenth-century harmony (*Viennese Harmonic Theory*, 90–111).

late Romantic style. Further, Kurth ventured into new territory by discussing Impressionistic harmony. Finally, in an extraordinary tour de force, he devoted four chapters to "endless melody." Like *Grundlagen*, *Romantische Harmonik* begins with psychological foundations. In forty-three pages, Kurth outlines a psychological theory of harmony in general, and specifically addresses the psychological bases of Romantic harmony. In outlook, *Romantische Harmonik* picks up where *Grundlagen* left off. Harmonies are *"reflexes from the unconsciousness."* Every chord is "only an *acoustically conceived image of certain energetic impulses*," and music is a "symphony of energetic currents."[86] Not surprisingly, Kurth's Schopenhauerian Idealism, already evident in *Grundlagen*, grew stronger in a study built around *Tristan*: "Sound is dead; what lives within it is the *Will* to sound."

> The usual theory of harmony (especially since Riemann) designates the chord simply as *harmony* [*Klang*]. However, it is primarily *urge* [*Drang*].[87]

The analyses in *Romantische Harmonik*, beginning with "The first chord," must be understood in light of these psychoauditive viewpoints.[88]

No sooner had the first edition of *Romantische Harmonik* appeared than Kurth recognized its shortcomings. He was already planning a second edition, which seemed inevitable owing to heavy sales, again especially in France and Italy.[89] The second edition was delayed because, Kurth speculated, of the negative opinions from the "official" German musicological establishment.[90] *Romantische Harmonik*, like *Grundlagen*, received mixed reviews. Alfred Lorenz reviewed the second edition favorably in *Die Musik*, and deferred to its detailed harmonic analyses in his monumental book on *Tristan*. Hermann Wetzel, an anti-Wagnerian who had earlier condemned *Grundlagen*, was equally critical of *Romantische Harmonik*.[91] Despite negative commentaries, the book became a popular text in advanced harmony

[86] Kurth, *Romantische Harmonik*, 1, 11, 2.

[87] Ibid., 3, 11. In *Grundlagen*, 6, Kurth says that music and its sonic manifestation "relate to one another as Will and its expression." *EKATA*, 12, discusses Schopenhauer's influence on Kurth.

[88] Part 2 of the book includes four chapters, on "The tension of alteration," which analyzes the *Tristan* chord, its relatives and their resolutions; on "The transformations of the internal harmonic dynamics," which discusses enharmonic forms of "the chord"; on "Resolutions of tension" in general; and on "Harmony as a symbol," which takes up the subject of harmonies as motives and symbols in Wagner's music.

[89] Letter to Halm, dated October 31, 1920 (69.833/2). The second and third editions are greatly expanded over the first edition. Both contain many more examples and additional commentary, as well as altered commentary. The analysis of Example 11 in the first edition (p. 58), for instance, differs substantially from the equivalent example in the third edition (Ex. 12, p. 60).

[90] Letter to Halm, dated April 11, 1921 (69.833/3).

[91] Alfred Lorenz, "Ernst Kurth: *Romantische Harmonik und ihre Krise in Wagners 'Tristan'*," *Die Musik* 16.4 (1924), 255–62; and *Das Geheimnis der Form bei Richard Wagner* (4 vols., Berlin: Hesse, 1924–32; 2nd edn. Tutzing: Schneider, 1966), vol. II (*Der musikalische Aufbau von Richard Wagners "Tristan und Isolde"*), 10–11. Hermann Wetzel, "Zur Stilforschung in der Musik: Bemerkungen und Betrachtungen zu Ernst Kurths *Romantische Harmonik*," *Die Musik* 16.4 (1924), 262–69. Note that Wetzel's review was printed back to back with Lorenz's, which Kurth surely interpreted as another jab from the German musicological establishment.

and went through three editions and several reprintings. In addition to being a unique classroom tool, Kurth's *Romantische Harmonik* expressed contemporary anti-rationalistic sentiments in the music-theoretical domain, just as Langbehn's *Rembrandt* had in its day expressed similar sentiments in the socio-cultural domain.[92]

Bruckner, Kurth's most ambitious analytical effort, arose from years of teaching about the symphonies and choral works to a variety of audiences. As mentioned above, he taught the music in public lectures, attended by non-matriculants, and took it upon himself to introduce the symphonies to the wider Berne community in Wickersdorf-style lecture-demonstrations.[93] As early as 1917 he offered a public lecture series on the symphonies, all nine of which were played in four-hand piano arrangements, and in 1918 gave a course entitled "Bruckner as Symphonist." In the winter term of 1922–23 he taught a seminar on Bruckner's harmony.[94] The tone and analytical style of *Bruckner* reflect its formal as well as informal pedagogical origins.

The basis for Kurth's extensive analyses of the symphonies is a portrayal of Bruckner as a visionary, as a quintessential mystic and embodiment of the expiring Romantic period. Like Halm, Kurth considered Bruckner's music the zenith of late nineteenth-century harmonic technique and formal design, a consummate blend of Beethoven's thematic and formal procedures with Schubert's and Wagner's harmonic practices. Musicians and scholars had overlooked Bruckner's genius, Kurth claimed, because they had heard only the superficial traits of the music: the hierarchical binary periodicity, with Bruckner's habitual doubling and halving of rhythmic values and phrase lengths; his predictable three-theme sonata and otherwise transparent ternary movements; or, worse, alleged formal inconsequentiality and gargantuan amorphousness (Eduard Hanslick and his cohorts Gustav Dömpke and Max Kalbeck).[95] For Kurth such qualities were insignificant compared to the convulsive, explosive inner forces that invigorated such externalities. In focusing on static formalities, critics had neglected the dynamic shaping process that imbued the music, not only with grandeur and power, but with the very formal logic and sustained creative strength that Hanslick and others had denied Bruckner's music. As Kurth put it, critics "did not comprehend the large dimension and became lost in details."[96]

The key to understanding Bruckner's music is, therefore, an awareness of its underlying dynamism, its *"control of force through space and time."*[97] Just as counter-

---

[92] Recall Ernst Bücken's comment on Kurth's work, cited in note 7 above.
[93] See note 46 above, and *EKATA*, 17–19.
[94] Letter to Halm, October 31, 1920 (69.833/2).
[95] See chapter 6, note 33.
[96] Kurth, *Bruckner*, vol. I, 290, in this volume, 161.
[97] Ibid., 239. This phrase is Kurth's characterization of the essence of form. Kurth presents his concept of form on pages 233–56. *EKATA*, 190–92 summarizes Kurth's basic ideas on form.

point represents a balance of streaming and congealing forces, similarly form is a balance – a "transition" – between musical dynamicism and formal staticism.

> Form is neither the pure streaming of the formation process nor the pure fulfillment of borders, but rather the transition, the active transformation of the former into the latter. . . In music. . .form is neither movement nor its synoptically grasped rigidity, neither flux nor outline, but rather the lively struggle to grasp something flowing by holding on to something firm.[98]

Not the shape (*Form*) but the shaping (*Erformung*) is crucial. Form is not inert. Rather, it pulsates with tensions and countertensions, which represent the motion of a composer's creative psyche.[99] Kurth calls such pulsations "waves," which range in magnitude from local "component waves" (*Teilwellen*) to cumulative, global "symphonic waves" (*symphonische Wellen*). Formal action consists in variously paced, steadily mounting intensifications, which peak in "apex waves" (*Gipfelwellen*). These are followed by one or more "reverberatory waves" (*Nachwellen*) and a "discharge" (*Entladung*). With his wave theory, Kurth verifies analytically that Bruckner's symphonies are indeed logically shaped "sonic forms in motion."[100]

In order to do this, Kurth probes the interior substance of the music, the *internal* form. He examines escalatory and de-escalatory processes, involving, among other things, increasing and decreasing rhythmic activity; thickening and thinning texture; expanding and contracting register; brightening and darkening timbre; tonally near and distant harmonies (i.e., luminescent "sharp-side" chords and dusky "flat-side" chords); or combinations of these techniques. The waves do not undulate in regularized crests and troughs but rather overlap variously, with no clear boundaries. Larger waves supersede smaller ones irregularly, but with clear processive logic. Kurth refers to "lengthwise" and "crosswise" profiles (*Längsschnitt, Querschnitt*) in order to depict these multidimensional undulations. Exterior form (themes, transitions, etc.) is borne by interior form. Accordingly, we must penetrate to the latter before we can grasp and fully experience the formal logic and vitality of Bruckner's symphonies.

Kurth was of course not the first to delve into Bruckner's music. A number of life-and-works-style books on Bruckner did of course exist, for example Max Auer's *Bruckner* and Oskar Lang's *Anton Bruckner*. But discussions of the symphonies in

---

[98] Kurth, *Bruckner*, vol. I, 239.

[99] Kurth's idea of form as shaping, in particular the shaping of tensions and releases originating the composer's psyche, is prepared in the works of Leo Funtek (*Bruckneriana* [Leipzig: Verlag für Literatur, Kunst und Musik], 1910], 2, 15, 24, 56); Arnold Schering (*Musikalische Bildung und Erziehung zum musikalischen Hören* [Leipzig: Quelle & Meyer, 1911], 63); and Karl Grunsky (*Musikästhetik*, 111; and *Anton Bruckner* [Stuttgart: J. Engelhorns Nachfolger, 1922], 26). Oskar Lang's views closely resemble Kurth's, although they are not worked out analytically in any detail (*Anton Bruckner: Wesen und Bedeutung* [Munich: Beck, 1924], 61, 92).

[100] Eduard Hanslick, *Vom Musikalisch-Schönen: Ein Beitrag zur Revision der Aesthetik der Tonkunst* (Leipzig: J. A. Barth, 1854; 6th edn. rev., enl., 1881), 66: "*tönend bewegte Formen*."

such works were primarily biographical and only topographically or hermeneutically analytical.[101] August Halm's *Die Symphonie Anton Bruckners* is a notable exception in this regard. It is one of the earliest substantive analytical studies of the symphonies. Unlike Kurth's book, it does not offer a complete analysis of each symphony. However, it does probe deeply into the formative processes in each of the movement types (Scherzo, Adagio, etc.) as illustrations of Bruckner's formal dynamism. As such, it was an important forerunner of Kurth's monograph, as was Leo Funtek's booklet *Bruckneriana*.[102]

Like *Grundlagen* and *Romantische Harmonik*, *Bruckner* turned out to be controversial, only more so, partly because of the split opinion on the music itself – remnants of the Bruckner–Brahms feud – and partly because of Kurth's innovative methodology. His psychologically oriented, intuitive methods ran headlong into the traditional German formalistic, scientific methods. Frank Wohlfahrt, author of a book on Bruckner's symphonies, praised Kurth's work for its synthetic quality, its clarity and compellingly objective explanations, and commended Kurth for outstanding scholarly intuition.[103] Georg Göhler asserted precisely the opposite. He accused Kurth of vagueness, unscholarly method, "colossal prolixity," "unnatural expressions," and of general floweriness. "Heaven protect German musicology," Göhler appealed, "from books like Kurth's becoming a school of thought."[104] Halm, in

---

[101] Max Auer, *Anton Bruckner* (Zurich–Leipzig–Vienna: Amalthea Verlag, 1923), 341–73 (on "The Symphonies"). Oskar Lang, *Anton Bruckner*, 60–106 (on "Form and Content"). Another, similar example is Ernst Decsey's, *Bruckner: Versuch eines Lebens* (Berlin–Leipzig: Schuster and Loeffler, 1919, 1922), 175–225 (on "The Symphonies"). Kurth comments on the available literature in *Bruckner*, vol. II, 1316–320.

[102] August Halm, *Die Symphonie Anton Bruckners* (Munich: Georg Müller, 1914). Notes 99 above and 104 below refer to Funtek's work. Like Kurth, Halm intended his Bruckner book for professionals *and* amateurs: "I do not want to overlook addressing myself particularly to those who, for whatever reason, cannot find access to these music-theoretical, primarily technical compositional discussions, or do not themselves want to try to find access. For I would like to have written this my book also for such individuals. . ." (xiv). Kurth was also fond of Karl Grunsky's *Anton Bruckner* (full citation in note 99 above), which gives cursory, hermeneutic analyses of all nine symphonies, movement by movement (53–99). More important than the analyses for Kurth's *Bruckner*, though, is Grunsky's notion of dynamic form (40–41) as an externalization of mental life (26, 40, 45).

[103] Frank Wohlfarht, "Ernst Kurth: *Bruckner*," *Die Musik* 18.3 (1925), 202–3, 204, 206, 208. Wohlfahrt's book on the symphonies is *Anton Bruckners Sinfonisches Werk: Stil- und Formerläuterung* (Leipzig: Musikwissenschaftlicher Verlag, 1943).

[104] Georg Göhler, "Ernst Kurths *Bruckner*," *Neue Zeitschrift für Musik* 93.12 (1926), 682–83. Göhler concludes his review by exhorting musicology to remain an "exact science" and to keep distant from the paths taken in Kurth's book. At one point Göhler claims that Leo Funtek had already done everything, far more clearly and succinctly, in *Bruckneriana* that Kurth did in *Bruckner*. This is a gross exaggeration. Funtek's book is a mere 62 pages compared with Kurth's 1310 pages. It is true that Funtek foreshadows several of Kurth's leading ideas. But the scope of *Bruckneriana* is far more limited, and the analysis far less detailed, than that of *Bruckner*. Kurth acknowledges Funtek's insights in *Bruckner*, vol. I, 373 n. 2, 384–84 n. 1, 512 n. 1, and 1319.

Kurth complained to Halm about a different review in *Der Kunstwart* (summer, 1926), by Arthur Liebscher, who neglected all substantive questions, and mocked Kurth's prose based on phrases taken out of context (letter to Halm, February 21, 1927, 69.833/21). With sales flagging about six months after *Bruckner* appeared, sounding paranoid, Kurth imagined "the whole fight against Bruckner is focusing itself on me" (letter to Halm, June 13, 1926, 69.833/13).

addition to combatting misunderstandings of "linear counterpoint," also tried in *Beethoven* to clear up misunderstandings and unfair exaggerations about Kurth's ideas on form. [105]

Göhler might better have described Kurth's book as anti-Positivistic rather than as unscientific. As I have explained in this essay and elsewhere, Kurth's work is an outgrowth of anti-Positivistic reform that peaked in the 1920s. Humanistic reformers of that period attempted, not to destroy objectivity, but on the contrary through cognitive and intuitive means to reveal and rediscover essential aspects of "objective culture" that the apparatus of Positivistic-scientific methodology had either neglected, or obscured and overlooked altogether.[106]

In addition to charges of being unscientific, another obstacle to the appreciation of Kurth's *Bruckner* was the publication, during the 1930s and 40s, of the notorious *Urfassungen* of the symphonies.[107] Kurth was aware that the first printed editions might be corrupt – though he surely did not realize the extent – but chose to publish his book anyway in a time when interest in Bruckner's music was growing.[108] Kurth's formal analyses were based on heavily edited first editions and proved incorrect in light of autographs. Certain features of orchestration, register, phraseology, and other technical characteristics on which Kurth's interpretations relied did not exist, or only significantly modified, in the original versions. Some of Bruckner's "waves" thus have a different design than Kurth thought.[109] Once the authentic scores began to appear in the 1930s, Kurth might have revised *Bruckner*, but critical responses may have kept him from doing so. The publisher may also have hesitated because of the high cost of redoing so large a monograph. Finally,

---

[105] Halm, *Beethoven*, 125–27.

[106] As H. S. Hughes has observed of the generation before Kurth, "the young thinkers of the 1890's can be regarded as aiming at precisely the opposite of what they have usually been accused of doing. Far from being 'irrationalists,' they were striving to vindicate the rights of rational inquiry. Alarmed by the threat of an iron determinism, they were seeking to restore the freely speculating mind to the dignity it had enjoyed a century earlier" (*Consciousness and Society*, 39). On the anti-Positivistic spirit in the early 1900s, see above, pp. 7–9, and *EKATA*, 7, 16.

[107] Manfred Wagner distinguishes among the "versions" in "Zur Diskrepanz zwischen Urfassung und späteren Fassungen bei Anton Bruckner," *Österreichische Musikzeitschrift* 33 (1978), 348–57. Leopold Nowak differentiates between "original version" and "final version" in "Urfassung und Endfassung bei Anton Bruckner," *Bericht über den Internationalen Musikwissenschaftlichen Kongreß, Wien, Mozartjahr 1956* (Vienna, 1958), 449–51.

[108] Kurth, *Bruckner*, vol. II, 603n: "We must reckon with the possibility that entire sections of symphonies have been omitted in the printed scores as a result of misguided recommendations from Bruckner's students. Just how far this proves correct is impossible to determine until a *scholarly edition of the complete works* brings the original versions to light." Several Bruckner Societies were founded in the early 1920s in Germany and Austria, and Kurth may have felt that his book would help make the case for Bruckner's music.

[109] My annotations to Kurth's text point out discrepancies between Kurth's piano reductions, made from scores prepared by the Schalk brothers and/or Ferdinand Löwe, and modern scores, prepared by Robert Haas and Leopold Nowak.

Kurth's advancing Parkinson's disease may have prevented him from undertaking the project.[110]

The initial uncertainty and debate over *Bruckner*, whatever "damage" it may have done to Kurth's reputation, did not hinder interest in his ideas. Kurt Westphal's book on form (1935), for example, with its notions of an "evolutionary curve" and "evolutionary tension" (*Verlaufskurve, Verlaufsspannung*), derives largely from Kurth. Like Kurth, Westphal also considers the evolutionary curve an experiential phenomenon, an *"aural process"* (*Hörvorgang*), a "purely psychic reality. . .For the parts unfold their full qualitative effect only in the aural process."[111] More recently, Franz Brenn (1953) outlines a theory of dynamic form based on an "intensity curve" (*Intensitätskurve*) and distinguishes between exterior and interior form. The latter is a "representation of psychic life [*seelischen Lebens*]." Unlike Kurth, however, Brenn holds that interior form

> does not exist separately unto itself but rather only fused with the "exterior". . ."Exterior" form is also interior. Exterior form is the audible and demonstrable inner form. . .[112]

In our day, Wallace Berry (1976) discusses musical structure "as to its functional and expressive consequences within an 'intensity curve'. . ." Berry's language even resembles Kurth's when he characterizes musical structure as *"the punctuated shaping of time and 'space' into lines of growth, decline, and stasis hierarchically ordered."*[113]

---

[110] Kurth began to show signs of the disease in the early 1930s. Kurth's frustration with *Bruckner* is clear from remarks in a letter to Halm (69.833/13), cited above in note 104.

[111] Kurt Westphal, *Der Begriff der musikalischen Form* (Leipzig: Kister & Siegel, 1935; rep. Schriften zur Musik, ed. Walter Kolneder, vol. XI, Giebing: Katzbichler, 1971), 50, 65, 76–78.

[112] Franz Brenn, *Form in der Musik* (Freiburg, Switzerland: Universitätsverlag, 1953), 26, 29, 30–31.

[113] Berry, *Structural Functions*, 4, 5. There are numerous passages in Berry's book which, in style and content, sound like Kurth: "The affective value which inheres in isolated. . .sonorous events should not be overlooked or discounted in any comprehensive view of musical expression and experience. . .The primitive impact of the naked musical event. . .divorced from syntax, must be regarded as an aspect of musical effect which is far from adequately understood" (ibid., 16–17). See also Berry's summary statement about mounting and receding intensity (p. 26).

PART I

Grundlagen des linearen Kontrapunkts
(Foundations of linear counterpoint)

1

Polyphonic structure

The passages translated in our chapter 1 are from *Grundlagen des linearen Kontrapunkts*, 3rd ed., part 1, chapter 5 (pp. 58–63, 66–67); part 2, chapter 4 (pp. 142–45); and part 4, chapters 1 (pp. 361–69, 372–73) and 2 (pp. 374–82). In part 1 of *Grundlagen*, "Foundations of melody," Kurth proposes the idea that melody – and music generally – is sonically manifest psychic motion (pp. 4, 8). Based on that premise he distinguishes between interior and exterior music, similar to Arthur Schopenhauer's distinction between the noumenal and phenomenal worlds (p. 6), and interprets this inner/outer modality psychologically (pp. 4, 7, 8, 14). He goes on to theorize broadly about melody, about its genesis, understood holistically (pp. 14–16, 21–24); its essence, identified metaphorically as "kinetic" energy (pp. 9–12); about the relationship of such energy to rhythm (pp. 51–54); about various fundamental melodic phenomena (scale, leading tone, dissonance, chromaticism, pp. 39–51); and about the effect of melody on harmony, which leads to the notion of "potential" energy (pp. 68–96).

The first section translated below, "Approach to compositional technique," deals with melodic versus harmonic approaches to Bach's music. Kurth challenges contemporary, primarily harmonic interpretations of the music, and presents historical and psychological evidence to support his melodic-genetic view. He argues that harmony in Bach's polyphony is an equilibrium of horizontal and vertical forces. Melodic strands "get caught" in chords, which are thus imbued with potential energy (pp. 61–62). Part 2 of *Grundlagen*, "The Problem of Counterpoint," is a survey of contrapuntal theory and instruction methods, beginning with organum manuals and running up through texts of his day. The survey ends with a "Conclusion," translated below, in which Kurth summarizes his "Fundamental approach to the theory of counterpoint." The last section of translated passages, from part 4, "Polyphonic structure," chapters 1 and 2, is a group of short analyses dealing with two specific contrapuntal techniques (staggered melodic apexes, and harmonic enhancement of apexes). The analyses show the great subtlety of Bach's multi-linear textures.

APPROACH TO COMPOSITIONAL TECHNIQUE

The fundamental trait of contrapuntal design

[58] The interaction between dynamic tensions and a harmonic equilibrium,

between energy and tone, as manifest in the [single] melodic line, determines analogously the relationships in polyphonic music.

Just as the usual explanation of melody as a "series of tones in time" necessarily produced an ineffectual and meaningless concept that exhausts itself in superficial matters and ignores the genuine element of animation in melody, so too the interpretation of all compositional relationships generally can be referred to the determinative primal phenomena that engender musical activity before the actual compositional technique in its results, rules, and manifestations is established.

In the initial approach to compositional technique we tend to remain heavily dependent on notation. The majority of current technical terms for musical structure adhere to the notated image, [59] so that the structure is characterized as *vertical* and *horizontal*, according to whether the [analytic] summary takes the form of chords or linear progressions, i.e., simply according to the way the page is read.[1] Such terms have merely symbolic significance, translating actual relationships evident in musical events into more comprehensible geometrical relationships. These terms are useful because they illustrate more abstract concepts and facilitate the presentation.

In translating spatial relationships derived from the notation into *temporal* ones by distinguishing between the "simultaneity" and "succession" of tones, only a primitive differentiation of unrelated categories is achieved, however, since the bases of the structure are not simultaneous and successive tone relations but rather underlying processes that manifest themselves in these relationships. The two fundamental phenomena of musical hearing, harmonic and melodic comprehension, must themselves first be traced to determinative origins to which their internal laws are bound. Musical hearing and compositional technique are governed [60] by the interaction of two intersecting *forces*. Here, too, it depends above all on the question of how theory should conceive of the interplay of melodic and harmonic elements.

---

[1] [EK] While in the *terminology* for the technique of melodic polyphony the expression "counterpoint" has established itself today rather uniformly as a contrast to a harmonic structure, inconsistency still prevails regarding the meaning of the word "polyphony." As a rule, we speak of a polyphonic style with regard to a linearly designed structure, thus likewise in contrast to a chordal structure, although the term "polyphony" itself means nothing more than "many voices," hence indicating no contrast with harmony. Harmony, too, is associated with several voices, just as sometimes in the literature, if more rarely, the word "polyphony" is used in this more general sense of many voices, in contrast to one voice. (In the following discussions "polyphony" is always to be understood in the restricted sense of a many-voiced, *melodic* design, and analogously with the expressions derived from it.) Regarding the "vertical cross section," the designations "chordal" and "harmonic" style are no longer differentiated in any essential sense. Of the two concepts "harmony" and "chord," the latter is originally the more narrowly limited. Chord [*Akkord*] is to be understood as the *form* of the sonority, harmony as simultaneous sounding itself in general (strictly speaking nothing essentially different than many-voiced in general), but the two designations are interchanged today. "Tonality" is to be understood as the organizing of the chordal element in the sense of an attribute of unity around a chordal center (the tonic).

Concerning the force that underlies melodic hearing, it became apparent in connection with the single line that the usual theoretical approach completely negates that force and makes it dependent on harmony by deriving the melodic line and the intervallic design of its course *genetically* from harmonic relationships. From the outset, this deficiency caused the melodic course to be evaluated not as something *positive* but rather as a "disassembly," that is, merely as a displacement from simultaneous relationships into successive ones. It is eminently clear that, concerning the theory of polyphony, this viewpoint must lead to an analogous bias and distortion. Theory has come to evaluate harmony alone as the basis of the entire compositional technique, and to present melodic activity, even in polyphony, as something completely passive. The consequences for the theory of a linear-polyphonic design can readily be seen.[2]

From this standpoint, as in the case of melody, the polyphonic structure would be determined solely by forces that lie dormant in the chord, in harmony. Here, too, the union evident in the external notation was taken too narrowly as the point of departure. Melody and harmony are interpreted as *homogeneous* when they are *heterogeneous* elements, in principle two fundamentally different phenomena.[3] The transition from a horizontal to a vertical reading style (or vice versa) is entirely different from a transition in the superficial manner of relating tones to one another. It is the control of forces at work here, not a mere change of reading styles.

But just as the animated melodic process was characterized with the energy of movement representing the primary feature, the individual tones and their harmonic relationship representing the secondary feature, so too in melodic-contrapuntal polyphony things would be reversed were we to begin with chords, which show the vertical profile. *Melodically designed polyphony is no more a series of chords than a [melodic] line is a series of tones.*[4] [61] The musical activity in a composition is the opposite process: the vertically embracing harmony runs through

---

[2] [LR] Kurth had already lodged the same complaint voiced here in *Voraussetzungen*, 6–7. He elaborates in *Grundlagen*, 17–21.

[3] [LR] I discuss Kurth's interpretation of harmony and melody as "heterogeneous" elements in *EKATA*, 111.

[4] [LR] Over fifty years before Kurth published *Grundlagen*, Heinrich Bellermann responded to a similar tendency of theory to overevaluate harmony in polyphony: "Our music, as it evolved gradually since the thirteenth century, is *polyphonic* music. A large part of its effects depends on the simultaneous sounding of several concurrently led voices. Herein lies true polyphony, not however in a succession of ready-made chords (as is frequently done today in compositions, and is even recommended in instruction manuals). Rather, the chords are only the result of connecting several melodically led voices" (*Der Contrapunctus* [Berlin: Springer, 1862], ix: "Unsere Musik, wie sie sich seit dem dreizehnten Jahrhundert allmählich entwickelt hat, ist die *mehrstimmige* Musik; ein grosser Theil ihrer Wirkungen beruht auf einem gleichzeitigen Erklingen mehrerer nebeneinander geführter Stimmen. Hierin besteht die wahre Mehrstimmigkeit, nicht aber in einer Aneinanderreihung von fertigen Accorden (wie dies heutzutage häufig in Compositionen angewendet, ja sogar in Lehrbüchern anempfohlen wird), sondern die Accorde sind erst die Folge einer gleichzeitigen Verbindung mehrerer melodisch-sangbar geführter Stimmen."). Kurth shares Bellermann's insistence on a melodic basis for counterpoint, but does not share his enthusiasm for Fux's species method (see notes 15 and 17 below).

the current of melodically directed "unfoldments" [*Entwicklung*][5]; the linear progressions [*Linienzüge*], which represent the primary feature here, *become ensnared* in chords. Of course here, too, as with the simple line, the process of an equilibrium producing harmonies cannot always be consciously distinguished. The organization into chords and chordal relationships essentially occurs together with the conception of linear polyphony, especially when advanced musical training or when a natural aptitude for harmony is involved. However, the infiltration of the secondary feature is then simply placed closer to the origins [of polyphony], a fact which ought not to obscure the differentiation of the primary, compositionally fundamental process (the sustaining melodic energies of polyphony) from the secondary one (the organization of the linear complex into chords).

The historical development [of composition] agrees with this harmonic embracement of the primary linear progressions, which must be upheld as the animated process of linear, contrapuntal polyphony. For only the efforts toward the simultaneous linking of melodies led to the creation of chords. The harmony embracing the linear progressions began, in increasing measure, to consolidate the tones into chordal effects, to absorb them into chords, and gradually to emerge with autonomous effects that shine forth for their own sake, until the compactness of chordal music evolved out of this centuries-long process. Historically, what led to polyphony was the *will to multiply and heighten the melodic movement, not expressly the appeal of harmonic sonority*. The emphasis on sonority as the essence of the compositional design came only in a later stage of polyphony.[6] The forces that absorb the

---

[5] [LR] In the passages from *Grundlagen*, I have translated *Entwicklung* throughout as "unfoldment." When Kurth uses the word *Entwicklung* in discussions about Bach's counterpoint, he does not mean "development," a common translation of *Entwicklung*, in the sense of thematic or motivic manipulations. By linear *Entwicklung* Kurth means the process by which contrapuntal lines unfold dynamically during a piece. The work as a whole, then, exhibits an overall unfolding process, a *Gesamtentwicklung*. Rather than translate *Entwicklung* each time as "unfolding process," or even simply as "unfolding" – which as a gerund can be awkward in translation – I adopted the word "unfoldment." I am aware that "unfoldment" is not properly a word. However, it conveys Kurth's meaning succinctly and more vividly than other possibilities, such as linear "course," "evolution," or "progression," the last of which becomes confusing when Kurth speaks of a linear progression (*Linienzug*).

[6] [LR] Kurth specifies no time period when he says "a later stage of polyphony," nor does he explain what he means with "sonority." If sonority means triad, then "later stage" world perhaps mean Renaissance polyphony, from, say, around 1500 on. However, the development of counterpoint indicates that ordered sonorities, understood as interval progressions (*Klangschritte*), were essential to contrapuntal structure from its earliest beginnings. Kurth's claim for an essentially linear counterpoint, based on historical evidence, is untenable in light of the long, documented tradition of a *Klangschrittlehre* established in counterpoint treatises from the thirteenth century onward. Several scholars have investigated this tradition, most notably among them Ernst Apfel (numerous publications, going back to his dissertation [Heidelberg, 1953], as well as his more recent studies: *Grundlagen einer Geschichte der Satztechnik* [3 vols., Saarbrücken: Selbstverlag, 1974, 1976]; *Diskant und Kontrapunkt in der Musiktheorie des 12. bis 15. Jahrhunderts*, Taschenbücher zur Musiktheorie, vol, LXXXII [Wilhelmshaven: Heinrichshofen, 1982]). Carl Dahlhaus (*Untersuchungen über die Entstehung der harmonischen Tonalität*, Saarbrückener Studien zur Musikwissenschaft, vol. II [Kassel: Bärenreiter, 1968]) and Klaus-Jürgen Sachs (*Der Contrapunctus im 14. und 15. Jahrhundert* [Wiesbaden: Franz Steiner, 1974]; "Zur

tones into a chord enter into the various dynamic progressions of an originally linear polyphony only as an embracement [*Übergreifen*], which organizes the sonorities into certain forms but which is imbued with the continuous current of the melodic forces. In linear polyphony, the flowing movement is the main content and the animated activity, which the technique of counterpoint must also reveal. As long as we ignore the autonomous significance and energy of the line, interpreting it as a mere series of tones (themselves [62] mere harmonic representatives), it is natural that every attempt to achieve a theory of counterpoint must turn out as a harmonic-vertical compositional design, i.e., as a reversal of the relationships.

The effect of harmonic cohesion

Before I return to the question (to be treated in later sections) of how, based on the line and in opposition to the harmonic view, this process of penetrating the structure will be established as a foundation for the theoretical treatment of counterpoint, from the viewpoint of an approach to compositional technique deriving from active forces, it remains only to characterize the vertical element of structure, the phenomena underlying all *harmonic* hearing, in the most general summary possible, one which transcends the individual theoretical systems of harmony. Here, too, in the domain of vertical effects, *forces* are evident that determine our musical activity and, secondarily, manifest forms. An attraction prevails between simultaneous tones, a gravitational force that inclines toward consolidation in a particular chordal image, the consonant triad. A kind of *cohesion* exists between the tones in music. The consonant triad is the basis and the beginning of all further regularities only in a theory of chords. In that attraction between tones, however, an active force must be recognized that engenders the primal urge for relating the simultaneous, "vertically" oriented tones to one another, for absorbing the mass of the chord as a unit. Therefore even if we view the basic image of all harmony,

---

Tradition der Klangschritt-Lehre," *Archiv für Musikwissenschaft* 28 [1971], 233–70) have also contributed substantially to the early history of counterpoint. All of the discant and counterpoint manuals stressed proper movement among intervals as the basis of polyphonic writing. Composition may have been "successive" up until around the time of Pietro Aaron's famous statement in chapter 16 of *Toscanello in Music* (1523) about simultaneous composition. But the two-part framework, the basis for music in three and more parts, was established primarily according to well-defined principles of interval progression and not according to similarly well-defined linear principles – though creating good melody in all voice parts was emphasized. Regarding a "structural framework" (*Gerüstsatz*) as a basis for florid counterpoint in the thirteenth and fourteenth centuries, see Hans Heinrich Eggebrecht's discussion of the *Codex Calixtinus* and the "Vatican" treatise, as well as Sachs's discussion of "De floribus musicae mensurabilis" (Petrus dictus Palma ociosa), in *Die mittelalterliche Lehre von der Mehrstimmigkeit* (Geschichte der Musiktheorie, ed. Frieder Zaminer, vol. V [Darmstadt: Wissenschaftliche Buchgesellschaft, 1984]), 55–58, 236–40. Benito Rivera deals with harmonic versus contrapuntal views of fifteenth- and early sixteenth-century music in "Harmonic Theory in Musical Treatises of the Late Fifteenth and Early Sixteenth Centuries," *Music Theory Spectrum* 1 (1979), 80–95.

the consonant triad, as the primordial image of repose among harmonies (the potentiality of a cadence), still the harmonic repose of the chord itself represents an *equilibrium of forces*, a *result*. The absorption of the triad itself to become a consonance is based on lively activity that operates between the tones and that aims to unify them into a chordal whole, to integrate them into a certain basic harmonic form. Harmony is a play of forces [*Kräftespiel*] directed at this equilibrium.[7] As long as the gravitation prevailing between the tones does not achieve equilibrium in the triadic form, there exists in *harmony* the unresolved tension of *dissonance* [63] that stimulates further development, analogous to the way the concept of the *horizontal* tension-dissonance was derived from unspent energies of dynamic melodic phases.[8] Harmonic dissonance also consists in the continued influence of unabsorbed forces that stimulate further activity, particularly as a vertical equilibrium. And what is characterized as resolution in the chordal sense is the *release* of forces directed at the specific basic forms (the consonant triads).[9] Further, harmonic consonance, the vertical relaxation, does not therefore signify full musical relaxation, because the permeation of the harmony with unreleased tensions arising from melodic-kinetic energies comes into consideration. Harmonic dissonance, residing in the more *obvious* effects manifest in the harsh external impression, is merely experienced more prominently and directly than the unreleased tensions, which are rooted in purely psychological subconscious processes resulting from the fundamental melodic-kinetic sensibility.

The feeling of repose in the consonant chord misleads theory into beginning with an energy-free state of harmonic *repose* as the origin and ultimate basis, instead of discerning an equilibrium of forces rather than *primordial* repose in the consonant triad, even from an exclusively vertical-harmonic viewpoint – let alone the melodic-energetic relationships (to be discussed later) which come into play.

[7] [LR] With "cohesion," Kurth may have had Carl Stumpf's idea of "fusion" in mind. Kurth's cohesion, however, is more dynamic than Stumpf's fusion. Stumpf explains that, psycho-acoustically, two tones fuse because of an inherent similarity of the constituent tones, and because of certain "specific synergies" in the brain which cause the tones to be perceived as a fused unit (Stumpf, *Tonpsychologie* [2 vols., Leipzig: Hirzel, 1890], vol. II, 127–83 [on fusion, its gradations and laws], 184–219 [possible causes of fusion]). In order to explain the fused character of a triad, Stumpf posits the notion of "concordance," a kind of multiple fusion ("Konsonanz und Konkordanz," *Beiträge zur Akustik und Musikwissenschaft* 6 [1911], 116–50). Kurth, on the other hand, stresses the melodically engendered forces in the tones of triads, so that the ostensible repose of even a major triad is but a momentary "equilibrium," a reciprocal cancelling out, of opposing forces. My article "Ernst Kurth's *Voraussetzungen der theoretischen Harmonik* and the Beginnings of Music Psychology" (*Theoria* 4 [1989], 10–33), discusses Kurth's ideas on fusion, as well as those of Wilhelm Wundt and Theodor Lipps. See also *EKATA*, 109–11.

[8] [LR] Kurth explains melodic dissonance as unspent energy in *Grundlagen*, 46: "The concept of musical dissonance must be extended beyond the wholly unsatisfactory restriction to harmonic-chordal dissonance to the linear, 'horizontal' energy relationships, and dissonance should be understood more generally as the existence of any unresolved tensions. . ." Kurth discusses the notion of a dynamic, or linear, "phase" (*Bewegungsphase, Linienphase*) in Grundlagen, 11, 14, 21–23. See *EKATA*, 34–36.

[9] [LR] Kurth contrasts the word *Auslösung* (release) with *Auflösung* (resolution).

The interplay of contrasting elements

[66] If, according to Stumpf's formulation of the "fusion phenomenon," the *vertically* oriented cohesion effect constitutes *that relationship of* (simultaneous) *sensory contents (individual tones) "whereby they form a whole rather than a sum,"* then with regard to the other of the two structural forces – the basic process upon which *horizontal*, melodic hearing depends – the effect of kinetic energy can be characterized similarly as *that relationship of individual tones where* (in succession) *they form a whole rather than a sum*, the continuum of the line that arises from the melodic energy flowing over the individual tones.[10]

The two basic forces of musical perception, which according to the reading style are designated briefly as vertical and horizontal, have one thing in common: they counteract the autonomous significance of the individual tone in music. Each force strives in its own way to bring the individual tone under its influence, chordally or linearly. In musical activity the individual tone means nothing, its context everything; the individual tone unto itself escapes conscious awareness, which summarizes larger complexes. Apperception of the individual tone contradicts the essence of music; music always signifies activity, dynamism, while the awareness of the individual tone is, in itself, still merely acoustico-physiological hearing.[11]

The compositional treatment of musical materials, as well as its technique, is based on the dual tendency of these two fundamental forces, on the competition to absorb the individual tone into their sphere of influence, and on the fluctuating equilibrium between the two sensations of force.

An *oppositional* tendency thus characterizes the technical features of a linear-contrapuntal design and, on the other hand, of harmonic design. Their difference is profound; it extends to the very roots of compositional technique, which in the

---

[10] [LR] The idea of the whole being more than the aggregate sum is one of the central theses of Gestalt psychology. In the years just before 1917, when Kurth was writing *Grundlagen*, there was no established "school" of Gestalt psychology nor any extensive body of Gestalt-psychological writings from which Kurth might have derived his ideas. In the late 1800s, before the Gestalt movement got under way with Max Wertheimer's pioneering "Experimentelle Studien" (*Zeitschrift für Psychologie* 60 [1911]), there were a few authors who had written about holistic perception. Before Wertheimer, both Ernst Mach and Christian von Ehrenfels wrote about supersummative qualities of objects of perception. Mach spoke of a *Zeitgestalt* and a *Tongestalt* in his *Beiträge zur Analyse der Empfindungen* (1886, 104, 128), and von Ehrenfels spoke of "Gestalt qualities" in his essay "Über Gestaltqualitäten" (*Vierteljahresschrift für wissenschaftliche Philosophie*, 1890, 249–53, 258–62). Significantly, both men referred to super-summative properties in melodies to illustrate their points.

[11] [LR] The term "apperception" goes back to Descartes (*apercevoir*, *Traité des passions de l'ame*, 1649), but it was Gottfried W. Leibniz who explicitly distinguished between perception and apperception, the former meaning passive reflection, the latter active, conscious reflection (*Principes de la nature et de la Grace fondés en raison*, 1714?). Johann Friedrich Herbart used the term to mean that activity which organizes diverse, raw data of perception, resulting over time in an "apperceptive mass" (*Psychologie als Wissenschaft*, part 2, 1825). For Wilhelm Wundt, who gave the term its meaning for many early twentieth-century writers, apperception was the synthetic cognitive act (*Grundriss der Psychologie*, 1896).

harmonic view begins with the chord, and in the linear view with the *line as the unit and origin*. For if there is a desire [67] to penetrate the musical structure from two sides, then in both cases theory must begin with the sources from which flows the twofold play of forces in the music: with the force that tends toward a chordal consolidation of the tones, and with the energy that underlies linear shaping: the phenomenon of a unified melodic phase. Since a synthesis was attempted, based on these very sources, instead of a recognition and clear formulation of their difference, and because the two elements, line and chord, were approached by basing both on only one aspect, on the *harmonic* viewpoint, one had to stray ever further from really carrying out a dual penetration of the musical structure.

The *indissolubility* of the two forces, which intersect with one other in composition, became [for theory] the misleading element. Instead of seeing the play of forces, the reciprocal permeation and interpenetration between two heterogeneous elements, only the exterior of this indissolubility was seen. For no melodic design is conceivable where the dynamic progressions are able to free themselves to the point of complete independence from harmonic considerations, just as, conversely, currents of restrained motion lie beneath the smoothed exterior of harmony stabilized in triads.[12] The union of both fundamental forces of the com-

---

[12] [LR] Misconceptions of "linear counterpoint" and the resultant criticisms of *Grundlagen* led Kurth, in the preface to the third edition (1927, xiv–xvii), to clarify his view of the relationship between melody and harmony. The year before the third edition appeared, Kurth asked August Halm in a letter dated June 13, 1926 if he were willing to clarify his (Kurth's) position in order to counteract accumulated misunderstandings and so to prevent future, ill-informed criticisms. Halm agreed to help by addressing the problem in *Beethoven*, in progress at the time. In December of 1926 Halm sent Kurth the manuscript. Kurth responded a month later by suggesting some new wordings and pointed out that Halm himself had at one point inadvertently misrepresented Kurth's idea of linear primacy. Kurth admits that, based on psycho-dynamic processes, he had asserted linear primacy in general, but not as the exclusive basis of Bach's music in particular. The pronounced, mature linearity in Bach's music, Kurth says, necessarily goes hand in hand with his fully mature harmonic awareness: "Both determine and mutually enhance each other" ("Beides bedingt und steigert sich gegenseitig," letter of January 1, 1927, Deutsches Literaturarchiv/Schiller-Nationalmuseum, Protocol no. 69.833.19, p. 3). Kurth refers Halm to parts 1, 2, and 5 of *Grundlagen*, which stress the "interpenetration" of melody and harmony. The heavy emphasis on linear elements, he explains, was to highlight the interplay of horizontal and vertical elements, and so to counteract popular harmonic biases (e.g. in Richter, Jadassohn, Riemann, among others).

A neutral reading of *Grundlagen* does not square with Kurth's claims. Although he does often bring out the mutuality of linear and harmonic forces (pp. 66–67, 144–45), just as often he says that, conceptually, linear forces are primary and harmonic forces secondary (pp. 61, 144–45). He is also explicit about the line being the genesis (*Ursprung*) of counterpoint and, accordingly, about the line being the basis for contrapuntal theory and writing technique (143). For psychological and historical reasons, Kurth refuses to give melodic and harmonic forces equal prominence in the theory or practice of counterpoint. It will not do, in the face of reasoned criticism, to deny such an explicit conceptual foundation. Halm apparently recognized this. Responding to Kurth's letter, he wrote that, although he had not used Kurth's rewordings, he had used them to guide his revisions, and that he sensed there was indeed a difference between their views of Bach's counterpoint: "sometimes I tend to believe in the primacy of harmony" (letter of February 3, 1927, Deutsches Literaturarchiv/Schiller-Nationalmuseum, Protocol no. 69.562/1). Over twenty years earlier, on the very first page of his *Harmonielehre* (Leipzig: Göschen'sche Verlagshandlung, 1905 [orig. 1902], 5), Halm had in fact

position is, in the lively process, a struggle, a confrontation. And their union, producing artistic effects in the music, lies precisely in the *force* of this conflictive meshing of opposing, interactive elements. Theory must begin with this play of forces in the reciprocal cross-current and bring out the specific fundamental will of a compositional design if it wants to distinguish a chordally founded compositional technique from a melodic-contrapuntally founded one, techniques which are then completely different in their basic technical premises as well.

But the forces affect one another even more profoundly. Just as all melody is imbued with harmonic elements, so too not only counterpoint but also *harmony* and *chords* are imbued with dynamic tensions, which determine their musical effect and compositional technique. . .

Conclusion: fundamental approach to the theory of counterpoint

[142] For this reason, in the theory of counterpoint it is completely incorrect to take the union of linear and chordal elements as a point of departure.[13] Only by starting with a *separation* of the horizontal and vertical traits, instead of with the reciprocal interpenetration, and by resisting their union in musical activity is it possible to attain not only a pronounced linear polyphony but also a conception midway between a chordal and a contrapuntal compositional design. Following a tendency opposite to that of harmonic theory, we must begin with the *most extreme* linear structure in contrapuntal theory.[14] [143] A transition between a harmonic and a contrapuntal compositional type cannot be defined in any way. A transitional phenomenon is always too unstable to be a point of departure. It can be grasped only from the origin of the currents that infiltrate one another.[15]

---

stated clearly that he considered harmony primary. Nevertheless, Halm states, incredibly, that the differences are "insignificant" (*unwesentlich*), that he has given them no prominence in his revisions, and instead has emphasized their conceptual agreement.

[13] [LR] When at the beginning of this paragraph Kurth says "For this reason," he is referring to the thoughts that conclude the immediately preceding section. He has just argued that, historically, counterpoint is genetically linear, and that the theory of counterpoint ought to respect that genesis. The theory should not ignore harmony, to be sure, but it should not be harmonically *founded*. The last part of Kurth's historical survey of the evolution of counterpoint, from the Classical period onward, explains that conceiving melody as voice-leading connections in a pre-existent harmonic framework is different from conceiving it as anterior to, and reaching maturity in, a resultant harmonic framework: "As long as we speak of an *animation* of voices, we are still dealing with a harmonic structure. Rather than an *animation* of voices, an *essential individuality of the voices* prevails in counterpoint" (*Grundlagen*, 142; further: "Counterpoint does not *proceed from the chord* but rather *reaches consummation in the chord*," ibid., 444). The opening words of the present section ("For this reason") should be understood with these ideas in mind.

[14] [EK] Cf. the historical foundations, [*Grundlagen*], 126.

[15] [LR] Kurth criticizes Fux's approach to counterpoint in *Grundlagen*, 103–16. He blames the species method, applied with increasing orthodoxy in subsequent generations, for breaking down the sense of genuine complementary melodic lines as exemplified in the high Baroque period (Bach). Kurth argues that the

The origin of contrapuntal composition lies not in the chord but in the line. The theory and technique of counterpoint must therefore begin with the line. That denies, however, not only the explicit harmonic method but also the entire customary theory of counterpoint inherited from Fux, as has been discussed at length.[16]

The first condition for carrying out a theory of counterpoint is thus the abandonment of the principle "punctum contra punctum," which not only undermines the idea of linear unity, of a continuous melodic process, but simultaneously destroys the fundamental will of polyphonic-linear structure. The theory based on that principle of "note against note" produces a structure in which the lines are *linked to one another from the outset*, moreover *it even bases the structure and the linear unfoldment on this linkage* ("punctum contra punctum"), on *the negative element in the structure.* Logically, that is completely contradictory. The view that the point of departure for counterpoint is to link together individual tones of the lines and to construct from them a vertical harmonic framework generally seems to be a foregone conclusion for theorists today, above all because, historically, this procedure has been inherited from theory. But it is precisely a historical overview that permits theoretical independence [from past traditions] and a clear disregard for the [inherited] approach toward contrapuntal technique. The effort to produce simultaneous melodic lines is the original will that underlies polyphony from the earliest times but in theoretical treatment was intersected by the development that led to harmony, owing to a concentration on vertical phenomena. With the standpoint of connecting "note against note," instead of achieving the desired objective, we automatically come back again and again to harmony, since in that way the combining [144] of simultaneous tones is elevated from the outset to the be-all and end-all of the mode of composition. We ought not to start with that very element which, in the disposition of the structure, represents the inhibiting element, opposing free linear influences. Connecting one tone in one voice with one tone in another puts things backwards.[17]

problem starts with thinking of counterpoint as note against note. "First species," he claims, "is in reality a harmonic composition" (*Grundlagen*, 112, "Die erste 'Gattung' ist in Wirklichkeit ein harmonischer Satz..."). He complains of the rigidity and uninspired results of the method, and asks what redeeming qualities, if any, fifth species can have after a student has completed the "stupefying process" of mastering the other four (*Grundlagen*, 111, *Verblödungsprozess*). Of course any method may produce poor results if applied too inflexibly. Fux's method, precisely because it is so systematic, has perhaps too often been victimized by pedants, who have given it an undeserved bad reputation. Authors such as Heinrich Bellermann (*Der Contrapunctus*, 1862) and Heinrich Schenker (*Kontrapunkt*, 1910, 1922) hoped to lead toward a greater mastery and deeper understanding of counterpoint through the species method, not to lead away from those objectives.

[16] [LR] If, as Kurth has just said, dynamic progressions cannot free themselves entirely from harmonic "consideration," then contrapuntal composition must surely be rooted at least partly in such considerations. It might have been more prudent had Kurth simply argued ideologically in favor of equal emphasis on linear forces, based on the idea of a lively interpenetration of melodic and harmonic forces, and refrained from the genetic argument, which cannot be decided.

[17] [LR] At one point in his polemic against Fux, Kurth boldly asserts "The principle 'punctum contra punctum'

By contrast, it is necessary to comprehend fully the neglected problem in all of its simplicity. The crux of contrapuntal theory is *how two or more lines can unfold simultaneously in the most unhampered melodic development* – not by means of the harmonies but *despite* the harmonies. A technique adhering to this view stipulates above all an approach to *harmony* in the structure that deviates essentially from previous theory, harmony being interpreted as the *secondary* element in relation to the melodic progressions. Only with this approach to sonorities as embracing linear progressions can we proceed to the further claim that the sonorities grow to the fullest possible harmonic effects.[18]

---

is historically the end of a melodic mode of writing and the beginning of a harmonic one" (*Grundlagen*, 129). Kurth's dislike for the expression *punctum contra punctum*, elaborated at length in his critique of Fux (see above, note 15) grows out of a contempt for the "species" method. Basing counterpoint on interval compatibility, Kurth argues, is self-contradictory from the outset. Counterpoint is linearly conceived and cannot be harmonically produced through joining intervals in succession: "The shortsightedness of the old principle 'note against note' prevents the possibility of a genuine linear organization of the compositional technique" (*Grundlagen*, 113). Fux was merely a convenient choice for Kurth's polemic. His claim for a truly linearly conceived counterpoint, however, runs up against the tradition of teaching counterpoint by means of ordered interval progressions, as discussed in note 6 above. Furthermore, as Klaus-Jürgen Sachs explains, in addition to meaning literally note against note, *punctum contra punctum* may also have meant the contrapositioning of mensural values, allowing for two or more short notes set against one equivalent long one (Sachs, *Der Contrapunctus*, 31–32. Sachs criticizes Kurth for interpreting *punctum contra punctum* too narrowly.). Prosdocimus (*Contrapunctus*, 1412) describes two-part counterpoint as "melody against melody" and distinguishes between counterpoint in the "strict sense" (*stricte sumptus*), and in the "loose sense" (*large sumptus*), meaning perhaps a distinction between contraposing individual notes (strict) and contraposing mensural values (loose, i.e. florid). Prosdocimus limits himself to discussing the strict type since "it is the true meaning of the term counterpoint." More important to Prosdocimus than any "true meaning," though, is his pedagogical aim: to provide thorough training in the note-against-note style, since *contrapunctus large sumptus* will then be understood "immediately" (*Contrapunctus*, trans. Jan Herlinger [Lincoln, Nebraska: University of Nebraska Press, 1984], 29, 31).

It is clear from early counterpoint manuals and, more significantly, from the music of the time, that authors considered melodically well-designed, florid counterpoint the goal and that "strict" counterpoint (the *Gerüstsatz*) was intended as a pedagogical strategy, a stepping stone toward that goal. Some vertical guideposts were needed lest the counterpoint lapse into chaos. Just as Kurth tacitly assumes an ever-present harmonic framework for Bach's music, so too authors of counterpoint manuals from the earliest times assumed an ever-present melodic awareness in their readers.

In rejecting Fux and *punctum contra punctum* as a basis for understanding counterpoint, Kurth seems to have mistaken methodology for ideology. Unlike Fux, Kurth spends quite a bit of time developing an extensive ideology of melody and counterpoint. Furthermore, again unlike Fux, Kurth develops a number of *analytical* strategies but no *compositional* strategies. *Grundlagen* is an analytical guide, and is pedagogical in the sense of *analyzing* counterpoint. But by no means is it a practical guide for *writing* counterpoint, which requires a different pedagogical strategy (intervallic or harmonic skeleton).

[18] [LR] The essence of Kurth's argument is that, in order to understand and appreciate fully the significance of harmony in counterpoint, we must start with the lines and observe how harmonies are formed, in all of their volatility, from a linear confluence. Such a conception leads to a different view than starting with harmony as a given and observing how lines wend their ways in and out of chords. This latter conception leads to a less dynamic and, to Kurth's mind, inaccurate view, inaccurate not because harmony plays no role in polyphony – Kurth has said that melodic design is to some extent dependent on harmony – but because, conceptually and analytically, harmony is then disproportionately overvalued and melody correspondingly undervalued.

It follows from this line of thought that, with a divergent approach, a different *technique* in the structure must also result for the independent harmonic effects. A glance at the harmonic phenomena in Bach's melodic polyphony will reveal that a different image exists here than if it were a matter of a chordal conception. Bach's counterpoint can never be adequately explained, as current theory tries to do, by examining the series of chordally conceived sonorities from beat to beat, let alone achieving the technique for reproducing the style. His linear polyphony is not perceived chordally at all, nor is it designed for the sake of chordal effects. We completely overlook that *sonorities as resultants* appear completely differently than *sonorities as foundations*. Current theory does rightly register as progress the complete surmounting of the old principle of interval compatibility by mature harmonic clarity. But in the process it also committed the error of forcing the linear mode of composition onto the basis of a chordally founded design. It is clear that the equilibrium of all vertical phenomena in the sense of mature harmonic tonality is neither affected nor eliminated from [145] counterpoint when for harmonic formations another approach is achieved that interprets these formations as the secondary element. On the contrary, only in this way [i.e. in a linear view] does the harmonic fullness begin to achieve its special power and significance. It is not just the unawareness of pedagogy in basic stylistic and technical questions but rather one of the most pronounced signs of a decline in the power of musical imagination generally when it is insufficient to understand that linear polyphony can support a tonally mature and potent, resplendent harmony without being supported by it.[19] While the view emerging in the newer development of contrapuntal theory has its one-sided merits in placing the harmonic-tonal maturity at the forefront (only to lose sight, though, of the problem of counterpoint), it is necessary to put the achievement of mature tonal harmony in service of counterpoint, without placing counterpoint in complete dependence on a purely harmonic design, however. We must arrive at a technique that begins with the energy of the line as the formative power of the structure and preserves the horizontal current as the chief determinative content even in polyphony.

---

[19] [LR] Kurth added these last two sentences, from "On the contrary. . ." up to "without being supported by it," in the third edition (1927). The insertion is one of a number of such statements, in which Kurth responds to criticisms leveled at *Grundlagen* for overemphasizing purely linear aspects of Bach's counterpoint, without sufficiently acknowledging its harmonic aspects. Hermann Wetzel criticized Kurth along this line in his review of *Grundlagen*, published in the *Bach-Jahrbuch* (1917), 173–75. Kurth was quite perturbed by the appearance of Wetzel's review, not only because of its negative evaluation, but also because the *Jahrbuch*'s editor, Arnold Schering, who had repeatedly solicited Kurth to write the main article for the 1917 issue, tried to influence Kurth's decision by mentioning that a review of *Grundlagen* would appear in that issue. It was only under the pressure of Schering's repeated requests to write the main article that Kurth finally agreed, and he was surprised, and angered, that Schering had not warned him ahead of time about the tone of the review. Kurth explains the incident in a letter to August Halm, dated March 6, 1920 (Protocol no. 69.833, Deutsches Literaturarchiv/Schiller-Nationalmuseum, Marbach am Neckar).

Polyphonic structure

The acknowledged beginning for every theory of counterpoint is thus the *technique of the monophonic line*, which, as in all polyphonic art, is to be achieved primarily by taking Bach's melodic style as a model.[20] From there, based on the general approach to counterpoint defined so far, the way we will approach the polyphonic linear technique will be carried out in the subsequent discussion which, beginning with the technique of the monophonic line (part 3), leads from the basic internal formal properties of contrapuntal structure (part 4) to the actual technique of linking multiple lines (part 5). Placing the theoretical and, in the narrower sense, technical discussion of the linear structure – posited last as a result and requirement – only after the broader perspective of the style and technique of the linear design (sections 3 and 4) is a necessity that will become clear in the course of the presentation, but should be noted in advance as an orientation to the material. . .[21]

Staggering of apexes and intensifications

[361] The real contrast in linear shape lies. . .in the relationships among intensifications. Just as the individual voices supplement one another in complementary rhythms when one of them reaches points of repose or pauses altogether, so too one of the traits of contrapuntal design is the *staggering of linear apexes*. High and low points in the melodic unfoldment never coincide in a two-part structure, so that the start of an intensification begun in one voice always occurs at a point where the other voice is engaged in a development leading either to an apex or a tapering off. The following examples show how the peaks of the individual linear phases (marked with plus signs) are distributed in both voices over different beats.

Ex. 1.1 [K241] Inventio in A major, mm. 8–9

---

[20] [LR] Carl Dahlhaus criticizes Kurth for giving Bach's melodic style a genetically preferential, paradigmatic status against which other melodic styles are measured for their "purity." See Carl Dahlhaus and Lars U. Abraham, *Melodielehre* (Cologne: Hans Gerig, 1972), 33; and Dahlhaus, "Bach und der 'lineare' Kontrapunkt," 55–79.

[21] [LR] Kurth added the sentence "Placing the theoretical and. . ." up to "orientation to the material" in the third edition, perhaps as an explanation for why he delayed the technical-analytical discussions so long. Kurth's approach to the music was sufficiently new, as he himself recognized, that an extensive conceptual groundwork had to be laid out first before proceeding to technical analyses, lest these seem to be without foundation. In sketching out the contents of the book, Kurth hoped to prepare the reader for his point of view.

[362] The non-coincidence of linear apexes is especially significant where two voices move in identical note values (as in the following examples), so that rhythmic differentiation no longer enhances the impression of two voices.[22] Here the preservation of the polyphonic character lies above all in the melodic differentiation by means of staggering the intensifications. Intensifications running parallel up to, and coinciding in, their peaks would no longer be genuinely polyphonic.

Ex. 1.2 [K244] Clavier Duet in G major (BWV 804), m. 17

[363] The effort to avoid a concurrence of apexes is especially pronounced, for example, in the combination of similarly shaped, rapid, agitated lines from the Clavier Duet in E minor.

Ex. 1.3 [K245] Clavier Duet in E minor (BWV 802), mm. 29-30

However, when the apexes in this piece coincide, using the same motive, it is at the *low points* rather than at the high points that the curves diverge, so that ordinary parallel motion, which would contradict genuine counterpoint (the differentiation of two independent linear progressions) is avoided (low points marked with crosses).

Ex. 1.4 [K246] Clavier Duet in E minor, mm. 19-22

[22] [LR] Kurth gives a few examples of staggered apexes that I have not included here. One example is from Bach's fugue in E minor, mm. 5-6 and 24-25, from the *Well-Tempered Clavier* Book 1 (Kurth's Ex. 242). The other is from Bach's Fantasy in C minor (BWV 906), m. 33 (Kurth's Ex. 243).

Polyphonic structure 51

[364]. . .Parallelism between two voices does occasionally occur in Bach's polyphony, but it always signifies a tapering off in the actual polyphonic activity. It no longer indicates a fully expressed polyphony but rather a simplification aimed at reinforcing one linear progression with thirds or sixths which, aside from the fuller *harmonic* effect, approximates in a certain sense a plain unison passage.[23] (Occasionally in Bach's music, a short passage of octaves occurs in two voices that are, in other respects, contrapuntal – cf. the two-voice E-minor fugue in part 1 of the *Well-Tempered Clavier* – which of course merely indicates a dynamically reinforced monophonic passage.) Such parallelism in two voices in thirds or sixths, a weakening of the contrapuntal principle, is artistically applicable as a way of slackening off in service of the undulatory design. Such slackening is much like the occasional spinning-out [365] of a single voices, which does very often interrupt the polyphony. But such coincidences of apexes must be understood as a *deviation* from the fundamental nature of the linear-polyphonic character, which lies in the independence of the individual dynamic progressions. . .[24]

Bach, in his infinitely refined art of development, often brings *apparent voices* into play in order to achieve intensifications of this sort, namely by means of a transition from parallel motion [366] to a staggered apex with an actual voice.[25] The G-major Prelude from part 2 of the *Well-Tempered Clavier* [*WTC*], for example, begins in the following way.

Ex. 1.5 [K249] G-major Prelude, *WTC*, 2, mm. 1–2

[23] [LR] Calling passages in parallel thirds of sixths a "simplification" of an essentially bi-linear texture down to a reinforced single line is perhaps an exaggeration. To be sure, an extended passage in thirds or sixths is, texturally speaking, less complex than two independently led voices. Deciding just how much less complex depends, however, on context. Parallel thirds or sixths accompanying a leading melodic line in Brahms might be considered less complex, for instance, than a similar texture in the Clavier Duet cited in Example 1.4. There, parallel scalar passages complement surrounding ones that are largely in contrary motion, or those that alternate between contrary and parallel motion in quick succession, as in Example 1.3. See note 26 below.

[24] [LR] Kurth added the section from "Such parallelism. . ." up to "dynamic progressions" in the third edition of *Grundlagen*. He wanted to stress that dynamic linear principles shape the music in passages of parallel thirds and sixths, which might otherwise be viewed purely from the harmonic standpoint. Parallel intervals of this sort are for Kurth an intermediate phenomenon lying between genuine two-part polyphony and monophony.

[25] [LR] Chapter 3, on polyphonic melody, explains what actual and apparent voices are. Briefly, an apparent voice is an overriding melodic continuity composed of registrally highlighted, non-adjacent tones that are associated by virtue of their long-range stepwise relationships. An actual voice is the literal, note-to-note melodic development.

The voice in eighths running parallel with the apparent voice in the upper line undergoes an intensification later, by staggering its apex with the upper line, as in the second of the following measures.[26]

Ex. 1.6 [K250] G-major Prelude, *WTC*, 2, mm. 11–13

[368]. . .This staggering of apexes is one of the most essential formal laws of polyphonic design. It especially comes into consideration with linear behavior where, in *chordal* outlines, the undulations in both voices intersect one another. In designs of this sort the *peaks* of motions are always reached on *different* beats, for example:

Ex. 1.7 [K255] Inventio in A major, mm. 12–14

[26] [LR] In the third edition Kurth added the section from "Bach, in his infinitely refined art. . ." up to Example 1.6 (K250). Examples 1.5 and 1.6 were added in order to show how, in passages of parallel motion, Bach staggers apexes in conjunction with apparent voices.

[369] A radical contrast to chordal writing is immediately apparent here. If the curvilinear apexes and low points, respectively, were to coincide in the following way, for example, it would be purely harmonic writing.[27]

Ex. 1.8 [K256]

The voices would represent nothing but a rhythmically enlivened arpeggiation of chord progressions, and the contrapuntal character would be destroyed. The linear design asserts itself in full clarity, however, precisely amid such opposing tendencies of a harmonic character in that the voices preserve their mutual independence in their drive toward the peaks of their undulating motion. Bach's two-voice polyphony exhibits the jaggedly criss-crossed image of *intersecting* waves with their mounting up, ebbing away, and fluctuating overlap. . .

[372] Such a formal design serves the foremost principle of all linear contrapuntal technique: through an artful distribution of tension and relaxation in the network of voices, never to allow the internal dynamism to flag. Where one voice pauses in its motion, all the more energy must enter in the other.[28] Thus the same basic

---

[27] [LR] Curvilinear apexes are the melodic peaks in a series of melodic surges. Taken together, the non-adjacent peak notes form a "curvilinear development," or an "overriding line." Kurth discusses these phenomena in "Zur Motivbildung," 97–99, 104–5, 108, and in *Grundlagen*, 272–73, 276. Chapter 3 of this book provides translations of Kurth's work on polyphonic melody, which features overriding lines. See also *EKATA*, 67, 82–86.

[28] [EK/LR] Kurth remarks in a footnote that adding a voice to a *cantus firmus* precludes any real linear equality, as well as any genuine dynamic reciprocity and unity, among the participating parts. He points out that, in fact, asking students to add voices successively to a *cantus* opens the way for an undesirable homophonic conception of counterpoint, where one voice predominates. As an occasional supplementary exercise, such an assignment may be profitable, but certainly should not be used as a pedagogical mainstay. Kurth states, perhaps too idealistically, that students should learn to conceive polyphonically from the outset in order not to neglect the dynamic mutuality among linear strands that characterizes true counterpoint. He then criticizes textbooks that ask students to add a third voice to an existing two-part counterpoint, and in fact suggest that students save their two-part exercises for later expansion to three voices. Hugo Riemann believed Kurth was implicating his (Riemann's) text and sharply criticized *Grundlagen* for lacking pedagogical utility (Riemann, "Die Phrasierung," 39). In a reply to Riemann's review, Kurth countered that many texts of the day suggested expanding two-part into three-part exercises, and that he had no specific text in mind (Kurth, "Zur Stilistik und Theorie des Kontrapunkts," *Zeitschrift für Musikwissenschaft* 1 [1918], 181–82).

trait maintained for the monophonic line also distinguishes the older-style polyphony from the Classical-homophonic manner of composition: the trait of unflagging energy in polyphony confronts the prevailing tendency to fall into regular periodic points of repose. Generally, any place in polyphony contains an intensification; the linear structure is continually imbued with tension and forward motion. Something *restless* resides in Bach's counterpoint.

[373] This phenomenon of pervasive tension contained in the character of linear polyphony lies even in the distinctiveness of the melodic *lines* themselves, whose innermost nature is illustrated by the constant energy of their kinetic tension. Moreover, the heavy saturation with *dissonances in the harmonic regard* arises from the same basic characteristic of perpetually agitated restlessness as yet another hallmark of Bach's counterpoint. Over lengthy passages, often enough over their entire course, Bach's compositions avoid a full joining of all voices in a *cadence* on a *consonant* chord. When such a cadence does occur, an intermediate cadence in the context of the form as a whole is practically always intended, the demarcation of individual main sections, development sections, etc. Otherwise, however, within the broad compositional unfoldment, a continuous play of linked dissonances occurs. Where one dissonance resolves, be it a chordal dissonance (seventh, ninth), or a suspension or the like, another dissonance is already forming in one or several other voices. This is especially true of a composition in three and more voices. The two-voice composition is somewhat richer in consonant intervals, without forfeiting thereby any of its tension (occasioned by *linear* energy). In this respect we should consider the special technical feature of how, in Bach's polyphony, a conclusion on fully consonant harmonies is largely avoided in stressed places. A counterpoint that, throughout, simply leads smoothly into points of consonant repose at stressed places is a poor one. It lacks something most essential: the element of ever-driving restlessness. The vertical structural relationships encroaching on the voices – in all aspects subordinate to the fundamental linear trait founded on dynamic development – adapt to the driving restlessness by constantly forming dissonances. In Bach's style, suspension dissonances are even more common than the chordal dissonances of sevenths and ninths. Long passages of his compositions often exhibit uninterrupted suspension chains. This wealth of dissonance joins with the demand for the greatest *harmonic-sonorous* power and *fullness*, just as, above all, every individual *line* of the counterpoint, with its *apparent polyphony*, aids the effort toward the richest *fullness* of the musical structure.

THE INFLUENCE OF DYNAMICS ON HARMONIC RELATIONSHIPS[29]

Enhancement of apexes

[374] The entire polyphonic compositional design is mainly directed at *enhancing the shape* of all the individual lines. In addition to the aforementioned phenomena of complementary rhythm and staggering of intensifications toward apexes in the individual linear phases, this aim is served additionally by a certain meshing of the primary linear relationships and the vertical relationships impinging on them, which cooperate in Bach's music to highlight in the most artful way some characteristic features in the lines. The sonorities through which the linear polyphony passes are often designed so that they not only embrace the voices with the effect of full-sounding harmonies but also accord with the energies and tensions contained in the lines and heighten their expression. On the one hand certain dynamic progressions – especially directional reversals in the motions – and, on the other, dissonances which appear in the sonorities, affect each other reciprocally. If, for example, a regression in descending motion occurs after a linear ascent toward an apex, often the release of tension at the turnabout is vividly delineated by a collision in dissonances, which affect the turnabout. Or when the apex tone is extended, in the course of its duration there arises in the remaining voices a harmonic formation that allows the tension of a descending dissonance to flow into the apex tone and thus, owing to the harmonic effect, stimulates a turnabout. In particular, the shape of themes in polyphony is delineated in this way. In the theme of the "Chromatic Fugue," for example [375], the motive of measures 1–2 reappears at measure 3 in a motion which presses toward B♭ (m. 5) and there turns around.

Ex. 1.9 [K261] Chromatic Fantasy and Fugue (BWV 903), Fugue, mm. 1–8

Interlaced with other voices, that apex also encounters a dissonant collision, from which the motion rebounds.

---

[29] [LR] In the first edition, the title of the chapter partly translated here (*Grundlagen*, part 4, chapter 2) was "The Interaction of Linear Tensions and Dissonant Harmonic Formations" ("Ineinandergreifen linearer Spannungen und klanglicher Dissonanzbildungen"). That title became the first subheading in the third edition, and the original first subheading, "The Influence of Dynamics on Harmonic Relationships" ("Einfluß der Bewegungsdynamik auf die Zusammenklangsverhältnisse") became the chapter title in the third edition.

Ex. 1.10 [K262] Chromatic Fantasy and Fugue, Fugue, mm. 21–14

Analogously, the apex tone of the following theme from *The Art of Fugue* (Fugue 3) is subjected in the polyphony to a tension brought on by the harmonic setting, which forces a directional reversal and descending motion. [376]

Ex. 1.11 [K264] *The Art of Fugue*, Fugue 3, mm. 9–11

[378] Also in linear formations that do not represent the theme itself, linear shape and dissonance mesh in this way. In a linking passage from the fugue in B major (*WTC* 2), a broadly unfolding intensification arises in the highest voice from b′ to b″, whose apex acquires a descending tension due to the entrance of a dissonant formation (C#7).

Ex. 1.12 [K270] B-major Fugue, *WTC*, 2, mm. 68–72

Polyphonic structure 57

[380]. . .Dissonances that stimulate a turnabout [and] which arise only after the arrival of the apex are especially typical for apexes which are extended, by syncopation, beyond a heavily accented beat. The fugue theme from the Toccata and Fugue for Clavier in C minor [BWV 911] moves downward by step from the apex tone A♭ with a motivic figure. In the polyphonic setting, a dissonant second occurs each time before the downward motion. . .
[381]

Ex. 1.13 [K277] Toccata and Fugue in C minor (BWV 911), Fugue, mm. 46–49

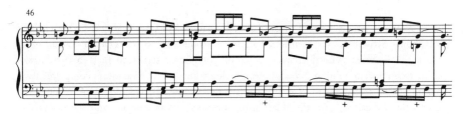

Such cooperation of energies arising from linear motions and from sonorities is often exploited as a means of heightened intensity in the compositional process, as occurs in the course of development sections. In the following theme from the [two-part] Invention in D major, the apexes (marked with crosses) are initially consonant with the other voice (e.g. in mm. 3 and 4).
[382]

Ex. 1.14 [K278] Inventio in D major, mm. 1–4

Later, however, at the turn toward the dominant (m. 13), the shape of the theme entering anew is significantly enhanced by the collision in dissonant tones at the turnabout points.

Ex. 1.15 [K279] Inventio in D major, mm. 12–18

2

Thematic and motivic processes

Our chapter 2 is a translation of most of part 4, chapter 4 of *Grundlagen*, 3rd edn., entitled "Polyphonic Structure." As mentioned in the introduction to our chapter 1, part 4 of *Grundlagen* discusses general characteristics of polyphonic structure (part 5 investigates specific techniques of joining two and more melodic lines). Part 4 examines complementary rhythm, special treatment of apex pitches (see our chapter 1), techniques of melodic and textural intensification, and the relationship between linear contour and harmonic dissonance. In chapter 4 Kurth explores "Consolidation and Dissolution of Thematic Motion," and proposes the idea of developmental motives (*Entwicklungsmotive*), melodic kernels that are "a kind of distillation of melody down to pure symbols of motion" (p. 436).

By thematic consolidation and dissolution (*Verdichtung, Auflösung*) Kurth means the process which a theme (for example a fugue subject) undergoes over the course of a polyphonic piece. Once stated, the theme dissolves into generic motivic shapes (developmental motives) during transitional passages (*Zwischenspiele*), and then crystallizes during thematic presentations (*Durchführungen*). Kurth's mode of thematic analysis implies a dynamic understanding of form based on the aforementioned general traits of polyphonic structure in the context of an alternation between thematic crystallization and dissolution.

CONSOLIDATION AND DISSOLUTION OF THEMATIC MOTION

The unfoldment of thematic presentations and transitional passages

[408] Without considering the special theory of form, in connection with the internal design and unfoldments in linear polyphony, there are yet three *general* formal concepts to be examined, which are deeply rooted in the technique of the linear design, and which actually represent a *transition* from polyphonic technique to the theory of form. Above all, they can be understood in their basic characteristics [409] only with regard to the nature of the art of linear unfolding. They are the familiar concepts of *exposition* [*Exposition*], *thematic presentation* [*Durchführung*], and of the *transitional passage* [*Zwischenspiel*].

These three formal concepts are mostly mentioned only with reference to the fugue. However, they pertain to all thematic-imitative technique and thus also to the smaller forms that do not otherwise exhibit fugue-like structures. The more the smaller forms, preludes, inventions, etc., approach thematic unification and economy [*Konzentrierung*], the more strongly the first two of these phenomena – exposition and thematic presentation – begin to emerge and differentiate themselves from the other sections. They can be characterized here in a very short summary. From the viewpoint of the dynamic linear unfoldment, particularly in its influence on formal phenomena, the technique in the so-called "transitional passages," on the other hand, attains to great importance, especially for the smaller forms, which are the basis of elementary contrapuntal exercises in the classroom.

In the most general sense, every intensified compositional process in a musical piece is called "thematic presentation." The term acquires its special meaning, however, in the context of imitative and fugal forms of counterpoint, where such passages are classified under the term "thematic presentation" and are characterized by the theme entering successively in all voices, in the midst of intensified modulatory and extensive contrapuntal treatment. The initial thematic entrance in all voices, with their gradual mounting to the full number of voices, is called "exposition."[1]

The exposition and thematic presentations are bound to certain more restricted conventions, especially to a certain change in key of the theme between the entrance in the tonic and in the dominant, only in the actual fugal form. With regard to the series of imitative entrances and the scale degrees for the thematic entrances, however, the exposition and thematic presentations in the smaller forms can be much freer. The main feature remains the appearance and counterpointing of the *theme itself*.

Concerning form, though, the "transitional passage" is the most interesting. It denotes the sections between the [410] exposition and [the first] thematic presentation in the fugue, or between the individual thematic presentations, and further those passages *within* the exposition or thematic presentation that lie between the

---

[1] [LR] I have rendered *Durchführung* as "thematic presentation." I realize the problems of this translation, but the German word (literally "leading through" or "carrying out") is not easily put into English. In German, depending on the type of piece in question, *Durchführung* connotes two different processes, both of which Kurth mentions. First, he uses *Durchführung* to mean "every intensified compositional process," for example, the motivic manipulations that typically follow thematic statements at the beginnings of Baroque pieces (e.g. in dance suite movements), or the analogous manipulations in development sections of sonata-allegro forms. Second, he uses *Durchführung* to mean post-exposition subject entries in fugues, where the subject appears, *intact*, in conjunction with different contrapuntal devices (stretto, augmentation, diminution, inversion). In contrast to the non-fugal *Durchführung*, then, which features motivic operations that fragment or transform themes, the fugal *Durchführung* features contrapuntal operations that present the subject as a whole, each time in different ways. In English, the fugal *Durchführung* might better be rendered as "entry group." Nevertheless, in order to avoid translating *Durchführung* in two different ways, I adopted the expression "thematic presentation," in the sense of developing the potential of a subject by means of contrapuntal artifices.

entrances of the theme itself. In a word, "transitional passages" are all passages where the linear formations do not consolidate into the referential shape of the theme as a whole. In the first case [between the exposition and first thematic presentation] they are usually more extensive, but there is no essential difference from the second variety. Transitional passages always serve the same purpose of unfoldment and are not constructed out of independent motives but rather are derived in the most diverse ways from thematic material. Their significance, and thus also their great [compositional] difficulty, lies in the linking of motions and intensifications, while exposition and thematic presentation have their difficulties more with respect to the special technique of thematic manipulation. Hence [we use] the term "transitional passage," which from the standpoint of purely thematic technique represents, of course, a pause in the manipulation of the germinal linear shape itself, whose label, however, does not suit its significance in every respect.[2]

The formal concept of a transitional passage is very unjustly restricted to fugues. For precisely in the smaller imitative forms, where passages marked by a return to the main theme are not distinguished from the whole piece, as are thematic presentational passages in fugues, the remaining broader, more freely spun-out unfoldments are often by far the greater portion of the pieces.[3]

The seeds of these formal concepts lie in the technique of unfoldment in the monophonic line, just as, in general, all internal design of polyphonic pieces represents a large-scale *expansion of melodic phenomena*. As with the monophonic line, sections in polyphony where thematic shapes predominate must be distinguished from those where thematic shapes increasingly dissolve into linear spinning-forth [*Weiterspinnung*]. These phenomena of thematic consolidation [*Verdichtung*] and thematic dissolution [*Auflösung*] are merely extended to the network of a larger number of voices. This contrast [between thematic consolidation and dissolution] comes into play in all polyphonic music, even though it acquires a special significance for the rules of the *external* formal construction only in fugues, since an imitative and, to a certain degree, motivically unifying technique [411] exists in all counterpoint, from the first beginnings and smallest forms. The sections of thematic presentation that stand out due to the entrance of the main theme correspond to those parts in the simplest monophonic forms where the main theme returns in clear profile after a cadence in the relative minor or dominant key, etc. The formal concept of the transitional passage, on the other

---

[2] [LR] As the following paragraphs show, Kurth's main concern is the transitional passage, the so-called "episode," which, he argues, has been unjustly assigned a secondary status in fugues. In Kurth's processive view of form, however, the transitional passage is essential to the dynamic-formal unfoldment, and thus co-equal with thematic presentations in importance. For this reason Kurth rejects the term "episode" (see below).

[3] [LR] These same ideas are presented in "Motivbildung," 113.

hand, is latent in those sections of the monophonic form where the theme dissolves into a spinning-out. The transitional passage is nothing but a spinning-out process that embraces the linear unfoldment of *poly*phony. The small polyphonic forms, just like the small monophonic ones, generally effect a return to the themes themselves after the chief modulations, after the transition to the dominant following the close of the first part, and very often even within the first part in the case of a turn toward the relative minor. The concluding parts, as well, are almost always characterized by the appearance of the themes.

The function of the transitional passage is the balancing of motions, the continuing of an initiated unfoldment, the subtle activity of balancing intensifications and gradual resolutions of tension. In lively activity, it assists in the interconnecting of motions, and in the linking of larger complexes within the form as a whole. It is based, therefore, on a highly developed sense of form, which transcends the purely technical problems of thematic presentations, the various ways of combining themes and motives imitatively and contrapuntally. Defining the transitional passage as an "episode," seeing in it only the idea of something "subsidiary" because it does not belong to the section of thematic presentation, was possible only from a point of view which, by clinging to the *external* view, created the prevalent theory of musical form, without having any further notion about the spirit of form. The harmonic-modulatory transition also plays a part in connecting individual parts of a piece. But such a transition is not, as many textbooks state, the only purpose of the transitional passage; its essential content resides in relationships of motions and intensifications, as is the case with all polyphonic phenomena, understood in their origins.[4]

---

[4] [LR] Kurth presents these same ideas in "Motivbildung," 113–15. His assertion that the "essential content" of transitional passages is dynamic (i.e. "balancing of motions") is essentially different from the views of his predecessors and contemporaries concerning the "episode." Writers on fugue have generally focused on the melodic content of episodes, which should derive, they say, from the subject or its counterpoint. Another concern is the length and frequency of episodes: lengthy episodes may produce an imbalance in the overall design, and too frequent episodes may overshadow the main thematic passages. Friedrich Wilhelm Marpurg addresses these issues in his *Abhandlung von der Fuge* (2 vols., Berlin: Haude und Spencer, 1753–54; rep. Hildesheim: Olms, 1970, vol. I, 151–52). Luigi Cherubini adds nothing new regarding these matters in his *Course of Counterpoint and Fugue* (2nd edn., trans. J. A. Hamilton [2 vols., London: R. Cocks and Co., 1841; orig. 1835], vol. I, 332–33). Siegfried Dehn recognizes that "the main interest of some fugues lies precisely in the episodes [*Zwischensätzen*]." By this statement, though, Dehn means the technique of "fragmentation" and "reconstitution" (*Zergliederung, Rückbildung*) of the subject in the episodes and subsequent thematic presentations (cf. Kurth's ideas of thematic "dissolution" and "consolidation," presented later in the present chapter). Salamon Jadassohn, whose various texts were widely used around the turn of the twentieth century, goes so far as to say that the "interludes" are "only. . . .connecting links between theme and answer, or between the principal groups of thematic entries" (*A Course of Instruction on Canon and Fugue*, trans. G. Wolff [Leipzig: Breitkopf und Härtel, 1887; orig. 1884], 101). André Gédalge, who devotes an entire chapter of his *Treatise on Fugue* to the episode, also stresses its melodic content (*Treatise on Fugue*, trans. A. Levin, ed. S. B. Potter [Mattapan, Mass.: Gamut Music Co., 1964; orig. 1900], 112–54, 233, 320).

If we survey the contrapuntal forms, from the smallest ones up to the fugue, the "thematic presentation" [412] no longer represents the basic content and the "transitional passage" a loosening [of thematic rigor]; conversely, rather, the free spinning-forth of the unfoldment represents throughout the basic sustaining current in which the individual passages consolidate into a more literal thematic content. Those are the "thematic presentations," and only when seen in light of these, from the particular viewpoint of the fugal technique, does that basic sustaining current represent a "transitional passage" where it abandons the literal theme. If the sustaining current with its undulations is not considered the essential element, we lose sight of all artistic sense in Bach's fugues; they become dry formal games, as the usual theories of composition and form inadvertently portray them. Nothing is more characteristic for Bach's fugues than the extraordinarily free treatment of the thematic presentations and the transfer of many of their major apexes and chief contents into the "transitional passages."[5]

Thus the *conclusion* of a transitional passage always prepares a thematically more consolidated section, and generally represents an intensifying development, with the thematic entrance acting as its resolution. However, the tension relationships can be arranged so that a thematic presentation, with its return to the actual

---

Kurth, in contrast to these authors, penetrates beyond superficial motivic elements to uncover the underlying dynamic quality and function of transitional passages. Motives extracted from a fugue subject are deployed in a particular transitional passage, not because of their intrinsic melodic-rhythmic interest or flexibility, but because their shape suits the dynamic function of the transitional passage as required by the momentary stage in the formal process. Furthermore, the participating motives are not just "fragmentations" (Dehn) but rather "distillations" (*Abklärungen*, see below), i.e. simplifications of the main thematic material, in order to maximize the effect of a particular transitional passage.

[5] [LR] The entire last paragraph, from "If we survey" on, was added in the third edition. Kurth apparently wanted to stress even more strongly than he had before that the transitional passage is an essential element in contrapuntal forms, and not merely "filler," a secondary event, an "episode." The transitional passage, as the "sustaining current," conveys us from one thematic presentation to another, and thus lies at the heart of processive form (see above, note 2). Kurth's emphasis on the dynamic function of the transitional passage leads him naturally to the idea of thematic consolidation and dissolution, discussed later in the present chapter.

Kurth's statement about fugue becoming a matter of "dry formal games" refers to the "academic" or "school" fugue, with its stereotypical tonal design filled out with a series of contrapuntal techniques applied to the subject. This mold-oriented view, often encountered in classroom texts, contrasts with Kurth's view of fugue as a dynamically unfolding process. For pedagogical reasons, nineteenth-century textbooks tended to reduce forms to comprehensible schemata. Hugo Riemann, though, often the implicit target of Kurth's criticisms, did recognize the dynamic function of transitional passages. In his *Katechismus der Fugen-Komposition* (2 vols., Leipzig: Hesse, 1890, vol. I, v), he said "the free transitional passages do not turn out to be connective links interpolated between principal sections of the fugue but rather occur in the principal sections themselves, rounding out the thematic entrances, acting as a foil for them, or also surmounting and crowning them" ("Die freien Zwischenspiele ergeben sich nicht als zwischen Hauptteile der Fuge eingeschobene Verbindungsglieder, sondern treten in die Hauptteile selbst ein, sich mit den Themaeinsätzen ergänzend, ihnen als Folie dienend, oder auch sie überbietend und krönend."). Kurth makes the same point about transitional passages surmounting and crowning thematic statements in the examples that follow presently.

theme, initiates an intensification completely anew. Accordingly, in such certainly less common cases the [preceding] transitional passage does not lead to an intensification but rather, on the contrary, to a slackening off (and, as a rule, with a harmonic cadence as well), for example:

Ex. 2.1 [K321] F#-minor Fugue, *WTC*, 2, mm. 7–9

The first tone of the soprano (c#′) is the end of the second thematic entrance in the exposition. Here, the transitional passage leads, in descending attenuation, to the third thematic entrance in the bass (end of m. 8). . .

[414] Very often, however, the apex of an intensification has not yet been reached at the end of a thematic presentation, i.e. at the end of its final thematic statement. In this case the entrance of the transitional passage does not signify a sudden slackening off or a noticeably distinct section. Rather, its function is precisely to continue the intensification up to its apex, and only afterwards to prepare anew for tension. This is once again decisive for the performance, which should not subside dynamically at the end of the thematic presentation. After the apex, which *first occurs in the transitional passage*, there is no closure and sudden regression toward the onset of renewed development but rather a gradual attenuation toward a low point and, subsequently, once again a gradual mounting of tension. Such a completion of an unfoldment that is not concluded during the main thematic passages indicates clearly the true nature of the transitional passage, which here, too, corresponds exactly to the concept of "spinning-out" in the monophonic line. Just as the main activity in the thematic presentation lies in the special demands of the thematic material, so the transitional passage facilitates the formal requirement of continued unfoldment and of a balancing of motions – a balancing where all initiated tensions achieve their fulfillment, are discharged in an apex. . .

[415] The transitional passage between the exposition and first thematic presentation in the C#-minor fugue (*WTC* 1), for example, is of the type introduced above (beginning at the bracket with the theme).

Ex. 2.2 [K323] C♯-minor Fugue, *WTC*, 1, mm. 14–20

The measures shown here begin with the last thematic entry of the exposition (soprano). The brief transitional passage initially carries the ascending motion yet one measure further [beyond the end of the soprano's statement], so that the intensification of the five thematic statements, climbing from low to high, first reaches its apex at the C♯-minor chord (with the soprano e″ [at m. 18]).

Such a continuation of a thematic intensification up to its culmination point in the subsequent transitional passage is very common (cf. the transitional passage in [Kurth's] Ex. 270 [mm. 68–72 of the B-major fugue, *WTC* 2]).

Finally, a third possibility is when a passage occupied with the main theme [416] already shifts into a regression at the end of the final thematic entry, but with the regression reaching its low point only later, in the transitional passage. Even then, the transitional passage is concerned, accordingly, with continuing and balancing motions. The developmental design of the unfoldment differs, however, from the second type: the beginning is an ongoing attenuation, with new intensifications arising only afterwards, for example:

Ex. 2.3 [K324] E-major Fugue, *WTC*, 2, mm. 20–27

[417] The first two measures shown contain the final thematic statement of the foregoing thematic presentation (tenor). First, the transitional passage continues the descending motion down to a low point (m. 23), and ascends from there up to the conclusion of the intensification at the end of measure 26, where the soprano enters with a new thematic presentation (in diminution).

All of these developmental dispositions of the transitional passage are equally valid for transitional passages located between thematic presentations, or within them, i.e., simply located between two thematic entrances in one and the same thematic presentation or exposition. The character of the transitional passage thus depends primarily on the basic characteristic of the theme, a characteristic which is always fulfilled only in the polyphonic development and unfolds in the large [dimension].[6]

The process of thematic dissolution in the melodic content of transitional passages

The function of balancing motions has yet a further effect on the *motivic content*, which is highly characteristic for the ultimate foundations of all linear and thematic formation. As already mentioned, the transitional passage in fugal forms is linked to the demand for thematic unity in the piece, and is taken up by motives derived from the theme itself. The transitional passage generally tends, however, to simplify the motivic features in a certain sense, in such a way that the features essentially agree with its particular function and formal tendency, with its *particular typical dynamic transitions*. If we look first at fugal forms, the motivic lines exhibit a [418] procedure best designated as a *generalization* of their dynamic progressions.[7]

We see here that the motivic formations, understandable only as clear derivatives of the theme, dissolve into more universal features that symbolize a very simple and vivid ascending or descending motion. Even if this procedure cannot always be observed being carried out fully in the transitional passages, the signs and tendency are still evident. Hence there arises the noteworthy phenomenon that *transitional passages in works of the most diverse kinds* and *of the most heterogeneous thematic content* evolve certain typical *motives*, which are *identical or at least very similar to one another*.[8]

---

[6] [LR] Theorists of the past, e.g. those mentioned above in note 4, would agree that the transitional passage depends on the "basic characteristics" of the theme. But in contrast to earlier writers on fugue, who point to motivic and rhythmic properties as basic characteristics, Kurth points to dynamic properties. It is the dynamic behavior of the subject, as disposed in thematic presentations, that influences the behavior of a transitional passage, not motivic content per se.

[7] [LR] The equivalent sentence in the first edition makes no reference to fugues in particular. See note 16 below.

[8] [LR] The following discussion, leading to Kurth's notion of "developmental motives," is a brief version of what became the "Motivbildung" article.

For example, in the case of ascending motives, such typical transitional motives include simple linear features such as the following ascending tone series, beginning on an upbeat and usually consisting of only four tones.

It appears mostly in sixteenth-note motion, or even slower, in the transitional passages of an extraordinarily large number of fugal works as the bearer of ascending unfoldments, e.g. . . . drifting through the various voices in the following transitional passage and carrying the entire surging motion of the piece upward.

Ex. 2.4 [K325][9] F#-minor Fugue, *WTC*, 1, mm. 28–29

subject entry

[420] Such a motive, reappearing countless times, is a simple motion into which any sixteenth-note line can resolve itself, no matter what theme it comes from. The ascending motive in Example 2.4 comes from the upbeat figure in the transition between measures 2 and 3 of the theme shown in [Kurth's] Example 26 [F#-minor fugue, *WTC* 1]. . .

In each instance, the transition motive [in Kurth's Exx. 325–29] – outwardly nearly equivalent, in its nature and *formal definition, however, identical* – arises out of other, *completely differently* shaped themes. It need not arise directly from the theme, however; rather, it can develop from the melodic material derived from the spinning out of the theme. Such a derivation from the most diverse motivic features embodies the most noteworthy element, which leads to the actual content of this characteristic motivic activity in the transitional passage. Only the flowing sixteenth-note (or eighth-note) motion remains from the original theme; and in

---

[9] [LR] As additional examples, not shown here, Kurth includes measures 45–47 from the B-major fugue, *WTC* 2; measures 71–73 from the A-minor fugue, *WTC* 1; and measures 27–31 from the fugue in the Chromatic Fantasy and Fugue, BWV 903.

the linear formation this motion adapts itself to a certain *dynamic expression*, which agrees with the formal meaning of the transitional passage, as for instance in the previous examples [421] of an ascending unfoldment or, as with further examples to be shown, in a descending or also intermittent, oscillating unfoldment. This formal function strives to manifest itself in very simple, vivid dynamic gestures that course through the polyphony. The motives become generalized by shedding *their individual cast*. Hence there is a relatively small number of such specific transitional motives, like the following ones.

There are climbing [*aufwärtsrankende*] formations, for example, similar to the simple, directly ascending motives in Example 2.4...as in:

Ex. 2.5 [K330] B-minor Fugue, *WTC*, 1, mm. 7–9

[422]...For *descending* unfoldments, the most common formation is the inversion of one of the simplest of the ascending motives, of the direct, diatonic line ascending over a fourth:

[423]

Ex. 2.6 [K333] Fugue, from Toccata and Fugue in F# minor (BWV 910), mm. 52–54

[424] In addition to the most concise dynamic gestures leading directly downwards, other figures, simple and vivid in their dynamic expression, are formed as typically recurring, specific transitional motives, e.g. for *more slowly descending motions*.

Ex. 2.7 [K335] Fugue, from Toccata and Fugue in F♯ minor (BWV 910), mm. 17–19

[425]. . .With the motivic formations symbolizing a slow ascent, as well as with those symbolizing a slow descent, a change-over into uniformly undulating gestures emerged already in those thematic formations that were characterized as an *oscillating theme*, and that also belong to the characteristic, most common forms of motion in transitional passages.[10] It is the linear formation, used by Bach in the most diverse works, whose lively expression resides in the lightly swaying and uniform motion, as though carried along in weightless flight. Transitional passages begin to approximate this motion especially at places where the ascending or descending unfoldment pauses intermittently and preserves an achieved pitch level for short passages (particularly in apex passages prior to the descending unfoldment, which often take on an ethereal quality owing to the motion of the oscillating theme). In its simplest and most rudimentary form [426] such preservation of a pitch level would be the continuity of one and the same fixed tone. But polyphony demands some vestige of motion and symbolizes the oscillating by means of a slight wavering around a medial pitch level, instead of by means of a voice resting completely on a sustained tone. This motion, which can likewise occur as a principal theme on its own, is formed primarily in broadly unfolding transitional passages, in oscillating lines such as:

---

[10] [LR] On our page 67 (beginning of Kurth's p. 421) Kurth alluded to oscillating motives yet "to be shown." The present discussion illustrates them. In part 3, chapter 5 of *Grundlagen* ("Characteristics of the formal development"), not included in this reader, Kurth offered some examples of oscillating motives (see the following note).

and similar ones, which resemble the dynamic expression of these gestures.[11]

. . .However, because in polyphony passages held for a time at one level always evolve into developmental and transitional passages, and likewise lead onward in a continuously flowing unfoldment, various interrelated hybrid forms arise between the unusually flexible form of *oscillating* linear motion, the *ascending*, as well as the *descending* motions. So, for example, in unfoldments that climb very slowly [there are] *ascending* motives [427] that lead upward only a step at a time, closely resembling the oscillating figures, in any case illustrating more an upward oscillation than the energy of a direct linear rise. . .

Ex. 2.8 [K336] Fugue, from Toccata and Fugue in F♯ minor (BWV 910), mm. 10–12

. . .[428] The same motivic figure appears in downward-oscillating transitional passages, transformed into a slowly descending motion.

In the same sense, there are typical, stately downward-oscillating motivic progressions:

or in sixteenth notes, e.g., as in the following measures.

Ex. 2.9 [K338] Fugue for Clavier in A major (BWV 950), mm. 52–55

---

[11] [LR] Kurth refers here to his pages 212–13, where he points out the oscillating character of the second subject of the C♯-minor fugue, *WTC* 1, measures 36–41, and to measures 27–30 of the B-major fugue, *WTC* 2.

[429] The way oscillating motion is introduced as a *theme* in the C♯-minor fugue (*WTC* 1, [mm. 29–41]) shows. . .how these linear formations in Bach's music are to be understood in their dynamic context, even outside of transitional passages, and how deeply they are rooted in the significance of dynamic processes. There, [the oscillating theme in the C♯-minor fugue, mm. 36–41] is preceded by the *ascending* line of a diatonic fourth, the same line that emerges elsewhere as the typical transitional motive [mm. 31–36]. In a manner that is as simple as it is ingenious, Bach elucidates the character of lofty oscillations in the subsequent theme [mm. 36–41] all the more by preceding it with that short and primitive symbol [the ascending fourth, m. 35] with its urgent, upward-bearing dynamic expression.

The understanding for the dynamics of the motion and for the urgent forces that lead to linear formation and spinning-forth in transitional passages must above all guide the instrumental performance. Essentially, the performance should be nothing more than an active creation [*Mitgestalten*] of the linear progressions and thus always a re-creation of them, according to their *formal energy*, and only with the intent of bringing out the varying ascending, oscillating, or descending dynamic forces – the purest shaping, almost emancipated from the notes. The performance must follow this [internal] dynamic unfoldment primarily regarding the external dynamics. Shaping the oscillating motions in particular requires the appropriate delicacy in the tone production on the instrument, as well as empathy with the character of the thematic formation. There is nothing more annoying than to hear these figures chiseled out in a loud, etude-like touch or rushed in tempo, which even with motives of ascending and descending oscillations is linked to the generally stately character of their dynamic processes. The best performance is the one that ignores the [individual] tones and actively shapes the linear motions.

The generalization of dynamic progressions

Within one and the same work, in the transitional passages the disintegration of thematic lines to become general progressions that merely serve the dynamic unfoldment [430] can, however, lead to ascending, oscillating, and descending formations *interweaving* variously with one another. For example, the motion of the oscillating theme in the B-major fugue from Book 2 of the *Well-Tempered Clavier* [mm. 27–30, Kurth's Ex. 20] leads to the formation of the ascending motive in [mm. 45–47, Kurth's Ex. 326]. Hence not only can the *same* typical *transition motives* be derived from completely *different themes* but also, conversely, *one and the same thematic line can resolve into different* simplified *dynamic gestures* of this type. To mention just one example, of the transitional motives cited above, the ascending upbeat line [in mm. 28–32 in the fugue from the Toccata and Fugue for Clavier in

F♯ minor (BWV 910)], additionally the motive leading downward in the opposite motion [Ex. 2.6], the downward-oscillating motive [Ex. 2.7], and the one ascending slowly by step [Ex. 2.8], are all derived from the same line, from the one in sixteenth-note motion, which counterpoints the theme (lower voice in m. 3 of the following example), and which itself derives from the theme (mm. 1–2).[12]

Ex. 2.10 [K339] Fugue, from Toccata and Fugue in F♯ minor (BWV 910), mm. 1–5

[431] Such ascending motivic motion need not always be linked to an overall intensification in the music. Often it can represent an upward-driving *counter-current* to a simultaneous downward-directed unfoldment in the other voices. In transitional unfoldments in polyphony, such progressions can undulate repeatedly in a more varied dynamic play of forces than with a uniform ascent or descent sweeping through all voices. A stately, gradual ascent or descent of the whole polyphonic complex, which appears most conspicuously in the rising or falling of the *uppermost* voice, results from this interplay of dynamic progressions. The following transitional passage illustrates a reciprocal undulation of two currents, each of which delineates with its motive the dynamic expression in the simplest conceivable form of an ascending line, beginning on an upbeat. (The [ascending sixteenth-note] figure [found in Ex. 2.12]

---

[12] [LR] Our Example 2.10, which reproduces Kurth's Example 339, differs considerably from the music given in modern editions. Specifically, at measure 4 the countersubject in Kurth's example (left hand in Ex. 2.10) differs from modern versions.

is derived from the beginning of the theme.)

Ex. 2.11 [K340] Sinfonia in D major, m. 1

Ex. 2.12 [K341] Sinfonia in D major, mm. 12–14

[432] An infinitely more powerful energetic process arises, *resulting from the interacting constituent drives.* It is easiest to see how powerfully captivating such an internal tension is when compared with an unimpeded unfoldment that flows evenly in all voices.[13] (Herein lies, incidentally, one of the great differences between Bach and his many imitators. They make the unfoldments too easy, too passive. Compare in this connection the contrapuntal pieces [433], perhaps the fugues, of Mendelssohn, Schumann, Brahms, Rheinberger, among others. Bach allows every global unfoldment to emerge clearly as a struggle, and often a very urgent resistance, against the local dynamic in the motives of opposing tendencies. This [technique] also agrees, characteristically, with his incomparably stronger harshness of dissonance. Imitators often manipulate such motives superficially and aimlessly, and without the feel for their primitive power.). . .

---

[13] [LR] Kurth added this paragraph, as well as two musical examples (nos. 342, 343) in the third edition, in order to illustrate how Bach, in contrast to later composers, greatly enhances the dynamism of a transitional passage by combining ascending and descending tendencies in various participating voices.

[436] This shows once again, from a different standpoint, how in the incomparably variable art of musical lines all transitions are illimitable, and how demarcation is not possible for even the simplest fundamental structures. It is a matter, not of demarcations, but rather of the form-building principle. Therefore it is unnecessary to expand this suggestion of a few basic motives into a longer enumeration. All of the linear formations mentioned, as well as similar ones, are gestures which simply express a particular formal energy. Out of them unfold the architecture and sonic perspective of the ever soaring voices and imitations.[14]

Since these generic motives illustrate linear energies that arise as a result of the force of the various unfolding intensifications and de-intensifications, they are better designated as *"developmental motives"* than as transitional motives, above all because they are of importance not only for the "transitional passages" but also for the entire contrapuntal unfoldment. If at first we consider their significance for the transition, there occurs here a kind of *distillation of melody* down to pure symbols of motion. If thematic presentation means thematic *consolidation*, then the transitional passage is thematic *dissolution*. That which remains of the original characteristics of the theme and its motives in this disintegrative process are those *absolute dynamic gestures, simplified down to an ultimate kernel* and thus possessing only the *most general* outline.[15]

It is here that *Bach's* personality, in its demonic depth, shines forth most forcefully from the work of art. In its most hidden inner power, it comes to the fore most strongly and purely in this generalization of dynamic gestures. An enormous impetus lies in the large unfoldments of his transitional passages, the liberation from the thematic content and shedding of the particular cast of a specific motivic shape, aspiring to the freest immaterial forms – dynamic expression released from all bonds. The transitional passage is an [437] etherealization into the incorporeal. The process of motivic dissolution in it is not an interruption of the thematic material but rather an *overcoming* of it.

The presentation led us to take fugal forms as a point of departure.[16] All of the observations made here on developmental motives and their compositional treatment can, however, be extended without restriction to all contrapuntal forms. In fugues, the contrast between individual and generic motivic outline is simply more conspicuous. The extension of the whole principle presented here to virtually

---

[14] [EK] See my *Romantic Harmony*, part 7, on the transformation of these most primitive motivic symbols of motion in other styles.

[15] [LR] This is a revised and enlarged version of a similar paragraph on the top of page 431 in the first edition. Kurth was trying to clarify the idea of consolidation and dissolution in order to make the idea of developmental motives more understandable.

[16] [LR] Kurth added this paragraph in the third edition. He apparently felt the need to be clear about using Bach's fugues in particular, rather than other works, as a point of departure for the study of developmental motives. Thematic consolidation is of course especially clear in fugues (subject statements).

all polyphony follows naturally from the fact that in all forms that are not fugal at all, or loosely fugal, the free developmental passages also predominate as the sustaining current of the spinning-out process. In every polyphonic work, we can trace how the lines resolve themselves everywhere into simple dynamic gestures. That among these the same few typical figures recur time and again follows from the simplest principle of all dynamics: certain most general motions, expressions of force, always remain as the ultimate substratum of all others.

But in yet another sense there is a connection with the most general traits of the shaping process. Viewed from another perspective, these developmental motives led back, of course, to the foundations where the logic and essence of thematic formation could be observed (cf. *Grundlagen*, part 3, pp. 214ff). Since melody is motion, a symbol of coursing energy, linear dynamics were to be understood as the basic feature of every motivic and thematic formation, dynamics whose simplest and most primitive manifestations reside in the developmental motives. Moreover, many themes of contrapuntal works of art do not, therefore, go beyond the general outline of such developmental motives, as oscillating motions, for example, illustrate especially often. Countless themes are thus only slight variations on the basic types of developmental motives, or they exhibit several of them, as demarcations here always dissolve into transitions.

And so the phenomenon of thematic dissolution, observable in the transitional passages of fugal forms, leads back [438] to the aesthetic and ultimate psychological foundations of linear art in general.[17] Thematic material, in transcending the most general dynamic forms, evolves toward an individualized outline, and its compositional treatment in the developed forms toward a renewed dissolution into the most general motives. The motive arises out of motion and dissolves back into motion. *The beginning and end of all polyphony is motion.*

---

[17] [LR] This is an expanded and revised version of a similar paragraph in the first edition.

3

Polyphonic melody

The present chapter contains excerpts from the most striking and, for the history of analysis, probably the most important chapter in *Grundlagen*: a discussion of polyphonic melody ("The Polyphony of a Single Line," *Grundlagen*, 3rd edn., part 3, chapter 8). Kurth devotes eighty-six pages to the topic, making the chapter by far the largest in *Grundlagen*. Kurth's discussion of polyphonic melody is historically important because it investigates large-scale melodic connections which in some cases resemble, superficially at least, the large-scale melodic continuities discovered at around the same time by Heinrich Schenker (see *EKATA*, 99, 101–2).

In describing such large-scale continuities, Kurth introduces the notion of the "apparent voice" (*Scheinstimme*, pp. 279, 282), consisting of registrally related, nonadjacent pitches. The "actual voice" (*Realstimme*, p. 302) is the note-to-note melodic development. The apparent voice may create an "apex line" (*Höhepunktslinie*, pp. 273, 275–76), or "rim line" (*Randlinie*, p. 289). Such lines consist of nonadjacent pitches called "rim points" (*Randpunkte*, p. 277). Kurth calls the resulting broad melodic continuities "higher-order linear phases" (*übergeordnete Linienphasen*, p. 272), or simply "overarching lines" (*übergreifende Linien*, "Zur Motivbildung," 98–99). They provide "curvilinear intensification" (*Kurvensteigerung*, p. 272) and thus are essential for creating and regulating dynamic form.

Kurth begins with some general remarks on polyphonic melody and illustrates the idea with a few introductory examples (pp. 258–60). He then examines a number of specific polyphonic-melodic techniques, among them implied and prolonged dissonances (pp. 268–69), the subtle emergence and disappearance of apparent voices (pp. 328–33), and the interaction between apparent and the actual voices (pp. 333–48). Kurth's chapter also includes the largest analysis in *Grundlagen* from a single work, two lengthy sections from the fugue of Bach's third solo violin sonata (pp. 313–22).

THE POLYPHONY OF A SINGLE LINE

Effects of fullness and technical means for heightening melodic tension in a single line

[262] An additional series of typically recurring stylistic and technical properties in Bach's melodic lines may be summarized from another point of view. In Bach's

monophonic linear progressions, even in extended monophonic passages (as for example in the complete movements for solo violin or cello), there is never a feeling of emptiness or insufficiency, which could easily arise given the relative acoustical sparseness of a continuously spun-out *single* line, compared with the fullness of mature polyphony. This is due to a certain, most remarkable melodic design which, besides embodying the enormous tension of melodic motion – the first and last basic requirement of all melodic composition and the outstanding trait of linear progressions – aims at *greatly magnifying the harmonic potency* in monophony so that it gives the impression of a musical work in which more than a single line participates. In Bach's melodies certain phenomena emerge, of which the simplest and most immediate derive from the requirement of forceful, clear expression of the *harmonic course*, and of approximations of chordal forms. Such roundings out of the line over harmonic contours counteract the sparseness of monophony. The thin, monophonic progression expands into more consolidated harmonic effects as soon as the linear course broadens out over chordal outlines. The harmonic impressions which play into the spinning-out of the melody enhance the brilliance and richness of the line. Because of their aforementioned constant alternation with diatonic passages, these harmonic impressions rise to even fuller effects.[1]

However, besides the fullness of harmonic effects, yet other systematic, technical means of melodic shaping are directed at the goal of evoking the impression of polyphony and a fuller texture by means of a single voice. Countless admirable, skillfully applied *allusions* to additional parts woven into the voice reach beyond the capacity of what can actually resound in the material of a single voice. There is a technique developed in Bach's lines such that *polyphony* is *latent* in the monophonic linear unfoldment [*Entwicklung*]. It suggests an aural comprehension and supplementation of musical procedures that are richer and more diverse than *actually sound* in the one voice.

Only a few details of the technical method need to be added here to the effect of fullness arising from the rounding out over chordal contours. (All of the technical phenomena which bring about the power and intensity of the harmonic effects are ignored in this context insofar as they belong to the domain of harmonic theory proper, a mastery of which is required here. The present discussion is limited to the linear unfoldments themselves, which strive against the rounding out into harmonies.). . .

[264]. . .In the rarer cases, where extended passages of music restricted to pure chordal contours appear in Bach's monophony, a melodic line is usually concealed

---

[1] [LR] The last section of part 3, chapter 7 in *Grundlagen* ("Manifestations of equilibrium in the *Fortspinnung*," Kurth's pp. 256–62), which immediately precedes the present discussion, shows how diatonic passages in Bach's monophonic works often alternate with arpeggiated passages. This alternation creates a sense of dynamic-formal equilibrium, according to Kurth. His Examples 79 and 80, measures 34–38 and 68–72 of the Prelude from Bach's C-major cello suite, illustrate this procedure.

Polyphonic melody 77

in these contours. Closer examination of such pieces that appear to consist only in harmonic outlines shows that continuities to be understood linearly begin to resound from this externally chordal design. If for example we examine the initial measures of the Prelude from the E♭-major Cello Suite [265], in the higher tones linear fragments and melodic continuities can be heard that arise between the apex tones in the [melodic] figure of each half measure, i.e., between every second and fifth eighth note of the measure.[2]

Ex. 3.1 [K86] Cello Suite in E♭ major, Prelude, mm. 1–15

Moreover, in addition to this uniformly undulating, implied upper voice a kind of bass line emerges, which begins with the nine-measure pedal-point E♭, and then starts to unfold further in a descending motion, D–C–B♭–A, etc. (Both unfoldments may be traced throughout the course of the movement. Particularly from measure 19 onward, a longer, descending, broadly spun-out bass line emerges, from measure 25 onward an ascending unfoldment in the upper voice.). . .

[268] Besides these allusions to chordal fullness, the line, in order to transcend the content of mere monophony, is also imbued with elements which heighten its tension by means of *implied* occurrences of *dissonance*, by means of concentrating

---

[2] [LR] Kurth gives the meter signature as common time. Modern editions show alla breve time.

the melodic energy at individual points that urge especially strongly toward a resolution. In part, it occurs very simply, in the same sense as harmonic effects, dissonances being implied in the linear path. This includes not only such melodic paths where the line moves in the shape of dissonant chords, e.g. of seventh chords, but rather also harmonic suspension effects.

Bach often achieves heightened tension with such allusions to harmonically dissonant tones by delaying the entrance of the resolution tone, prolonging its effect. The line first continues on independently and provides a resolution to the dissonant effect only after a time by touching on the resolution tone, for example:

Ex. 3.2 [K94] Cello Suite in D minor, Allemande, m. 20

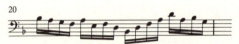

(Delay of the resolution of the tone a in the third beat)

[269] Because these chordally grasped dissonant tones are preserved in musical hearing beyond the immediately following parts of the line, they protrude from the linear continuity, and form among themselves a separate continuity with the tone that supplies the resolution. These unresolved tones *hang* until we hear their continuation. . .

Such effects of hovering dissonances also touch on the technique of implied polyphony by means of certain projected points which, in jutting out, together form a new line. Similar suspension effects are in the following example.

Ex. 3.3 [K97] Cello Suite in G major, Allemande, mm. 13–14

(Here, the linear path implies a chordal dissonance [g' as a seventh in A–C#–E–G], used to imply a suspension effect in the next measure.). . .

Implications of polyphony in the single line

[272] In addition to these two manners of concentrating tension melodically, by hovering suspensions and by restraining the effects of leading tones, increases in purely melodic tension may be achieved when a sudden, aurally striking interruption of a specific [melodic] direction occurs. This direction is then resumed and

continued only after an intervening passage, so that the tone with which the linear progression was initially severed is preserved in our hearing and then is connected up with subsequent tones – as in the case of hovering suspensions in the line.[3]

Continuities external to the whole linear image are thus formed between the individual tones, and in an artful manner an intensification leading to an apex often results from these continuities...

In this way Bach makes far-reaching connections of many individual tones in the line to form a larger progression, unfolding in one breath and in continuous tension. An overriding linear phase [*übergeordenete Linienphase*] (implied by longer note values) embraces several phases of the monophonic spinning-out process itself, established in part in the technique of *curvilinear intensifications* [*Kurvensteigerungen*].[4] Indications of independent continuities external to the line already came up in those cases where melodic lines or bass lines emerged out of passages that moved in chordal contours. Just as the course of the melodic line is determined by kinetic tension, so such projected points belonging to these continuities extend the feeling of unity [273] across larger passages, and in this way significantly heighten the tension of the entire line. These differentiated continuities are developed into effects of the most diverse type...

In the following example there is a...line emerging independently in a rapid ascent (c#′–d′–e′–f′–g′) and a slower descent (g′–f′–e′–d′–c#′).

---

[3] [LR] "Motivbildung," 87–98: "The protruding apex of an individual wave is held fixed and unconsciously linked with the next apex, which appears as the continuation of the first one. In this way unfolding lines of a higher order arise, ascents or also descents of larger proportions" ("Der herausragende Gipfelpunkt einer einzelnen Wellung wird festgehalten und unbewußt mit dem nächsten verknüpft, der als seine Fortsetzung erscheint. So entstehen Entwicklungslinien höherer Ordnung, Steigerungen oder auch Senkungen größerer Proportionen."). In *Musikpsychologie*, 255–65, Kurth explains the psychological mechanism that permits such a mode of hearing.

[4] [LR] With "curvilinear intensifications," Kurth alludes to the discussion on page 251 of *Grundlagen* (Kurth's Ex. 70, mm. 22–24 of the Prelude from Bach's G-major Cello Suite), which exhibits a technique similar to the one illustrated in our Example 3.4. Kurth cites the subject of the E-minor fugue (mm. 1–6), *WTC* 2, as an example of directional interruptions that assist in creating an "overriding linear phase." The notes of the "phase" stretch from e′ to e″. Kurth discusses curvilinear developments in "Motivbildung," 97–99, 101, 104–5, 108–9, 119. In the article, he uses various terms for the tones composing overarching melodic continuities (*Kurvenhöhepunkte, übergreifende Höhepunkte*), for the long-range lines (*übergreifende Linien, übergreifende Züge, Entwicklungslinien höherer Ordnung*), as well as for the technique involved (*übergreifende Gesamtentwicklung, übergreifende Steigerungsentwicklung, Kurvenentwicklung*).

Heinrich Schenker cautions against identifying overriding melodic continuities by singling out pitches based on registral criteria alone: "The highest tones of the upper voice tend to tempt and attract our curiosity, and because they are the highest tones they are also forever thought to be tones of the Urlinie" ("Resumption of Urlinie Considerations", *Das Meisterwerk in der Musik*, vol. I, 188; the translation given here is from Sylvan Kalib's dissertation, "Thirteen Essays from the Three Yearbooks *Das Meisterwerk in der Musik* by Heinrich Schenker: An Annotated Translation" [Ph.D. diss., University of Chicago, 1973], vol. II, 135). While Schenker would probably agree with Kurth's interpretation of Example 3.4, he would disagree with many of Kurth's overriding lines. I discuss a few such disagreements in *EKATA*, 83–84 (Exx. 4.8, 4.9), 85–86 (Exx. 4.11, 4.12), and 101–2.

Ex. 3.4 [K107] Cello Suite in D minor, Prelude, mm. 43–48

[283] Concerning the *performance* of monophonic unfoldments in Bach's music, in the shaping of the melody the technique of these projected notes should not lead to the demand for highlighting them through special emphasis. In a correct performance, which follows the unfoldment of the linear phases, the proper measure of accentuation for such projected points comes about on its own. Distinguishing them from the surrounding context hardly requires consciously bringing them out. On the other hand, the performance that follows the unfoldment of the melodic line guards against fabricating arbitrary continuities between points merely according to the external notated image, points which, given their dynamic status within the linear unfoldment, should not at all be highlighted and brought into connection in the same sense [as points in genuine overriding lines]. Rather, the special quality and appeal of this phenomenon lies more precisely in the fact that, in addition to the actually sounding voice, such implied apparent voices ought not to be brought out from their characteristic obscurity. They can better be emphasized by means of agogic subtleties in performance, by slightly *lengthening* such tones beyond their strict metric value and further, in sensitive melodic playing, by striving to imbue the broader melodic continuity arising from the linear course with special melodic expression. . .

Richness of apparent polyphony in Bach's melodic lines

[302] In. . .many of the examples cited, often not just two but frequently several simultaneous voices arise, and this polyphonic impression is continuously enhanced by a uniformly applied rhythmic meshing of the voices involved. The various means for achieving the allusion of polyphony arise in rich variation, artfully interwoven with one another. Bach hears [*empfindet*] so polyphonically throughout that he compresses a complete polyphonic network into his monophonic line. When in the process two voices of the apparent polyphony, or an apparent voice and the actual voice, meet in one and the same tone or intersect at the same tone, we

hear these common meeting points of the voices as though sounded doubly, since they are included by both linear progressions simultaneously – a phenomenon which likewise contributes to the expansion of the musical activity in monophony.

[303] Cooperation of various types of implied polyphony lies for example in the following lines. . .[5]

Ex. 3.5 [K165] Violin Sonata no. 3 in C major, Allegro, mm. 21–30

[304] In the low register a pedal-point develops on g, which is sounded variously on more accented parts of the measure and, intermittently, also on the unaccented, final sixteenths (mm. 22 and 24). It continues as the bass line, a–d', starting at measure 27. Above this pedal, there is an upper apparent voice which, from measure 25 onward, evolves from weakly emerging, undistinguished beginnings (mm. 21–24) into a magnificently unfolding contour of a lyrical melody.

Ex. 3.6 [K166]

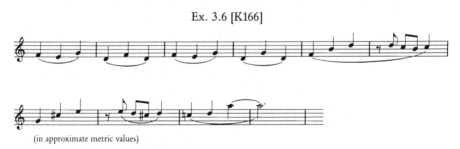

(in approximate metric values)

---

[5] [LR] In addition to the passage shown in Example 3.5, Kurth cites excerpts from the Gigue of Bach's G-major Cello Suite (mm. 16–20) and from the Gigue of the D-minor Violin Partita (mm. 32–34) to illustrate the intersection of actual and apparent voices. He does not mark the tone where the voices meet in any of the examples. In our Example 3.5 (K165), the meeting points are the first sixteenths in measures 22 and 24, where the actual voice crosses d' in its scalar descent just as the apparent voice touches on that same tone, and then skips to f' (beat 2) and back to d' (beat 3).

[312]. . .Recognizing, then, that the entire technique of the monophonic line is directed essentially far more at the (implied) expansion of linear energy than at the rounding out in harmonic effects, a noteworthy confirmation of this fact can be seen where, in monophonic pieces, [313] Bach resorts to chordal supports by exploiting the technique of double stops, as in individual movements of weighty tempo from the works for solo violin or cello. There, it can be clearly observed how even these chords by no means introduce mere harmonic effects into the music but rather aim chiefly at simulating linear polyphony by means of a brilliant technical device. A chord enters, for example, such that it incorporates the line as an apparent upper voice and allows it to continue as an apparent lower voice, or vice versa.[6] This is a *simulation* of several participatory voices insofar as the whole developmental progression of the movement is still sustained by the technique of spinning out a single line. The following measures from the Allemande of the Cello Suite in C minor, for example, illustrate such a case.[7]

Ex. 3.7 [K180] Cello Suite in C minor, Allemande, mm. 23–26

Here, the first chord allows the line to appear as an upper voice, whereupon the line, emerging out of the chord, continues as the lowermost voice, as if in another instrument. Then a chord enters at measure 25 such that the continuation [of the line] appears to issue from a new voice, an inner voice, and then at the next chord once again from the original, uppermost voice, etc. Such cases can be observed everywhere in connection with double stops.

---

[6] [LR] This whole discussion, including Example 3.7 (K180), was added in the third edition (from "Recognizing, then. . ." up to the end of the paragraph). The added example and accompanying analysis are intended to show that there are places where Bach introduces chords – here through double stops – that are not conceived purely harmonically. Rather, the chords imply a multi-linear texture, as described in Kurth's analysis. Both when chords are expressed explicitly (double stops), and when implicitly (arpeggiations as "rounding out over chordal contours"), Kurth offers interesting linear interpretations.

[7] [LR] Modern editions of this Allemande show Bach's scordatura tuning for the cello's A-string, to be tuned down a step to G. Kurth takes the scordatura into account in his version, reprinted in our Example 3.7, and rewrites notes played on the A-string a step lower. Consequently, the sixteenths B♭, A♭, and G in measure 1 of Example 3.7 appear in modern editions as C, B♭, and A, respectively. Likewise, the A♭s on beats one and three of measure 24, as well as the A♭ on beat one and the G on beat three of measure 25 (Ex. 3.7) are all notated a step higher, as three B♭s and an A, in scordatura versions. Further, like Kurth's Example 180, our Example 3.7 shows B♭ as the lowest note on beat one of measure 25. Modern editions show low G.

Polyphonic melody

The monophonic episodes from the C-major Fugue for Violin

[313] Motivic play, imitation, taking a motive through different apparent voices in a varied form, augmentations and diminutions, inversions and the rich technique of polyphony are often implied in a single line. That is what produces its concentrated power.

[314] One of the mightiest polyphonic developments found in all of Bach's monophonic works contains the following fragment from the Fugue (mm. 165–87) of the Sonata [no. 3] for Violin in C Major.

Ex. 3.8 [K181] Violin Sonata no. 3 in C major, Fugue, mm. 165–87

[315] The first four measures of this transitional passage allow the preceding, powerful apex of a fugal thematic presentation to fade out in a gradual de-intensification. From the second half of measure 168, a rapidly ascending sequence outlined in full chordal contours leads to measure 171; the third skips highlight

a lower ascending line (b–g, c′–a, d′–b, e′–c′, f′–d′), and a higher one (d′–f′, e′–g′, f′–a′, g′–b♭′, a′–c″).

At measure 171, reached as the apex of [the preceding] development, an extremely interesting passage of apparent polyphony begins. An acquaintance with the beginning of the fugue, with the subject, is necessary for understanding it.

Ex. 3.9 [K182] Violin Sonata no. 3, Fugue, mm. 1–8

(Chorale theme "Komm, heiliger Geist, Herre Gott")

The subject reappears, latently, in measures 171–74 of the line shown in Example 3.8. [316]

Ex. 3.10 [K183a] Violin Sonata no. 3, Fugue, mm. 171–74

(The initial tone, g′, appears here as though held for the whole measure, reinforced by the complete G-major harmony. The *syncopated* entry of the peak tones in the subject – a′, g′, f′ – heightens the melodic tension.) The motive from the subject [e′–f′–g′] appears in diminution beginning at measure 174 (labeled with a downward-pointing bracket in Ex. 3.8) after it had already appeared in measures 172 and 173 in inversion (labeled with an upward-pointing bracket).

Ex. 3.11 [K183b]

Observe here that the descending form of the motive (mm. 172–73 at the upward-pointing bracket) represents nothing but an abbreviation of the second measure of the subject.

Polyphonic melody 85

Ex. 3.12 [K183c]

Measures 172 and 173 are thus performed most correctly with a strong agogic lengthening of the first and highest tone of the motive, in such a way that the sixteenth note, a′, approximates a quarter note, as in the subject.

Ex. 3.13 [K183d]

Accordingly, in Example 3.10 the eighth-note figure from the second measure of the subject, highlighted by means of larger print for the main notes of the subject, is also faintly suggested.

The line is also designed so that the ascending motive (downward-pointing bracket, from m. 174 [Ex. 3.8] onward) flows into the highest tone, touched upon each time at the last eighth of the measure, so that it appears as a sustained tone approximating the value of a half note.

Ex. 3.14 [K184] Violin Sonata no. 3, Fugue, mm. 174–75

[317] Interlaced rhythmically with this [implied] half note, the same motive appears intermittently as a lower rim-voice [*Randstimme*] (labeled with plus signs). It ascends up to the root d″ in measure 179, likewise from measure 183 onward [on the third and seventh eighth notes of each bar] in slowed motion: e′–f♯′–g′–a′–b′; it continues in an ascending line up to the entry of a new thematic voice (m. 186). Additionally, another apparent voice, running along a third higher and consisting of the tones e′–f♯′–g′ (labeled with plus signs) sets out in measures 182–83 [m. 182, sixth and seventh eighth notes; m. 183, first eighth note]. This motive ascends further to a′ on the fifth eighth note of measure 183, then on the first and fifth eighths of measure 184, through b′ and c″, up to d″ of measure 185 – a line which is, therefore, imitated a third lower in stretto by the previously

designated apparent voice, so that the latter reaches the apex d″ at the beginning of measure 187.[8]

Moreover, above this network the upper rim-points [*Randpunkte*] form a series of ascending thirds [in mm. 174–78, fifth and last eighths in each measure] (f′–a′–c″–e″–g″), thus representing a separate apparent voice (also effecting a certain harmonic fullness), where, as mentioned before, each of these tones implies the values of a sustained half note due to repetition.

In measure 179, analogous to measure 171, the fugue subject starts anew on d″, sustained for a whole measure and reinforced, with the contours of the complete D-major harmony.

Ex. 3.15 [K185] Violin Sonata no. 3, Fugue, mm. 179–82

Analogously, the action of the descending and ascending motive from the subject (upward and downward-pointing brackets) ensues here again, and ultimately, from measure 182 onward, the line labeled with asterisks ensues, which leads to a g″, the tone at which a new thematic voice enters in measure 186.

[318] Linked with all of this rich apparent polyphony of motivically artfully interwoven voices is *yet* another *implied counterpoint of the countersubject* of the fugue, the chromatic lower voice (a′–g#′–g♮′–f#′–f♮′–e′, etc.) counterpointing the subject at the beginning of the fugue (see Ex. 3.9, m. 5). It is found in the monophonic line (Ex. 3.8) from measure 172 onward *as a lower rim-line* (c#′–c♮′–b–b♭–a) *with the subject*, and, analogously, along with the subject from measure 180 onward (g#′–g♮′–f#′–f♮′–e′).

No less polyphonic and yet completely different from these passages is another monophonic transitional passage from the same fugue (beginning in m. 245).[9]

---

[8] [LR] Kurth's discussion of the two lines in stretto is confusing because he uses plus signs to identify both. The first of the two enters in measure 182, with e′–f#′, and continues with g′–a′, b′–c″ on the first and fifth eighths of measures 183–84, and ends on the first eighth on measure 185 with d″. This first voice is "imitated a third lower," starting in measure 183 with e′–f#′ on the third and seventh eighth notes, and continuing with g′–a′ in measure 184, likewise on the third and seventh eighths. The remainder of the imitative voice leads through a′ (m. 185), b′–c″ (m. 186), and ends on d″ (m. 187), the same pitch that the first voice ended with two bars earlier.

[9] [LR] Kurth says "beginning in measure 247," but his Example 186 begins with measure 245.

Polyphonic melody

Ex. 3.16 [K186] Fugue, mm. 245–74[10]

[319] A broadly designed ascending linear unfoldment spanning twelve bars begins in measure 245; first, from measure 245 onward, the motive from the fugue subject (labeled with plus signs), is continued in an ascending sequence up to the

---

[10] [EK] The wedge symbol (like the asterisk and cross) indicates tones of a coherent line and is thus not to be understood here as an accent mark.

first tone of measure 250 (d″), and from there on, the upper rim-line (likewise labeled with plus signs) carries the ascent further up to the c‴ of measure 256.[11]

The main subject of the fugue (marked with crosses) is present starting at measure 255 (indicated by the larger printed notes).
[320]

Ex. 3.17 [K187] Fugue, mm. 255–58

Along with this subject, the chromatic countersubject (c‴–b″–bb″–a″, labeled with asterisks) starts with c‴ in measure 256, the apex of the long ascending upper apparent voice. At the same time, though, the thematic motion e″–f♯″–g″ in measure 256 is the continuation of an ascending lower apparent voice which begins faintly in measure 249 with a pedal point g′, and moves upward beginning at measure 252 (a′–b′, etc., labeled with downward-pointing wedges), growing ever more prominent up until the transition into the theme [at m. 255].

A different motivic activity begins in the second half of measure 258. The upper rim-line a″–b″–c‴ (labeled with plus signs) begins thematically and continues as an ascending line up to the apex g‴ in measure 263 (so that the tone a″ in m. 258 belongs to two lines, to the end of the countersubject's chromatic line, and to the line beginning the ascending motive, at the asterisks and plus signs). Further, from measure 259 onward the ascending motive derived from the theme appears in eighth-note motion (labeled with a downward-pointing bracket [in Ex. 3.16], the highest tone having the value of a half note, implied by the two attacks).

Ex. 3.18 [K188]

The inversion of the motive, a″–g″–f″, b″–a″–g″, c‴–bb″–a″ (labeled with an upward-pointing bracket) is rhythmically interlaced with this ascending motive. Beginning at the apex tone g‴ of measure 263, there is once again a falling motion in the upper rim-line (f‴–e‴–d‴. . .), out of which the fugue subject develops in measure 265 as an apparent voice (the initial tone c‴ emerging again starting at m. 264).

---

[11] [EK] An extension to a four-note series is even implied as well. The motivic apparent voice e′–f′–g′ in measures 245–46 continues and concludes with a′ at the beginning of measure 247, upon which a new series begins with f♯′, peaking in measure 249 with b′.

Ex. 3.19 [K189] Fugue, mm. 265–68

Here also, from measure 266 onward, the chromatic countersubject is set against the subject in implied counterpoint as a lower apparent voice (f″–e″–eb″–d″, continued down to g′ [m. 271], labeled with asterisks [to the end of the countersubject in Ex. 3.19, and all the way down to g′ in Ex. 3.16]). At the same time, the inversion of the [ascending eighth-note] motive is rhythmically interlaced in eighth notes with the subject (labeled with a downward-pointing bracket [in Ex. 3.16, mm. 266–69]).[12]

Ex. 3.20 [K190] Fugue, mm. 266–67

Beginning at measure 270, this descending motion is assimilated and continued by the actual voice.

Ex. 3.21 [K191]

Thus in the first transitional passage (Ex. 3.8), the fugue subject appears both times as the upper voice, the *countersubject as the lower* (mm. 171ff and mm. 179ff). In the second transitional passage (Ex. 3.16), however, the main subject appears first, conversely, as the lower voice (mm. 255ff), and the chromatic countersubject above it as the *higher voice*; at the entrance of the second subject (mm. 264ff), the subject again lies uppermost. These apparent voices are thus designed in *double counterpoint* (i.e., invertible through reversal).

---

[12] [LR] The motive to which Kurth refers is the four-note ascent in eighths, first encountered in Example 3.8 (mm. 174–78), and then in Example 3.16 (mm. 259–63). The inversion of that motive appears in Example 3.16 (mm. 266–69), shown partially in Example 3.19, and illustrated in Example 3.20.

Yet with all this richness of interacting voices in a concealed apparent polyphony, nothing contrived resides in these lines of Bach. The magnificent melodic unfoldment, full of great momentum and supreme beauty, hardly leads one to suspect all of the most artfully implied polyphonic content. [322] The two monophonic episodes from Bach's C-major fugue for solo violin (Exx. 3.8 and 3.16) are among the greatest wonders of melodic art. Actually, they are not episodes but rather truly *monophonic fugal thematic developments*.

The evolution and dissipation of apparent voices

[328] The *rise* of such emergent apparent voices and, likewise, the way they *recede* are among the most exquisite refinements of Bach's entire linear art. Their emergence out of the actual voice and their disappearance often occurs so imperceptibly that, even to the experienced eye, the accessory voices seem to blend together when we try to trace them back to their origin, or up to their ultimate confluence into the main current of the actually sounding voice. Their beginning and ending can scarcely be determined. The art of evolving [the accessory voices out of the actual voice] is particularly great here; often they slip by in the course of the actual voice without our becoming aware of how they entered and where they faded out.

Very often this blurred emergence of apparent voices, aurally unclear and indistinct, originates in the aforementioned characteristic of implying individual tones of an apparent voice through the motion of an actual voice over the contours of a complete chord whose roots are the implied tones, instead of through the tones themselves. This is particularly the case when, even within the implied chord, the tone in question does not even occur in the octave range in which the linear continuity would belong.

Hence in the following example, the vestiges of an apparent voice fade into the implied harmonic outlines.

Ex. 3.22 [K199] Violin Sonata no. 1 in G minor, Presto, mm. 119–29

[329] The ascending lower rim voice (marked with a bracket), evolved out of a motive of two tones, extends from a to f♯'. Its inception is to be understood as g, which, without actually being sounded, rings out from the G-minor contour traversed by the actual voice in measure 120; g rings through all the more strongly because measure 120 is preceded by the implied dominant chord (m. 119). Similarly, the apparent voice heads toward g' (m. 127), which is only implied by the outline of G-minor harmony. The context alone permits the particular tone to be heard in measures 120 and 127 (first g, then g'), both times in a register that the actual voice does not touch on at all. (Only in m. 128 does the motion pass briefly through the g' expected within the linear context.). . .[13]

[330] It is also typical for an apparent voice to dissolve in *syncopated* tones, for example:

Ex. 3.23 [K201] Violin Partita no. 1 in B minor, Double 2, mm. 44–48

Here, the actual voice contains a latent descending line. Running through an entire octave, from e″ to e′, it begins with an upper rim tone and ends in lower rim tones, thus intersecting the unfoldment of the actual voice. Metrically, its initial tones, e″–d♯″–b′–a′–g′, are the first ones in groups of sixteenths; its continuation to f♯′ and e′ occur in the waning force of syncopated metric placement. . .

[332] The initial tones of no less than five such apparent voices develop out of implied pedal points in the following four measures [from Bach's solo violin sonata in A minor].

---

[13] [LR] In connection with a passage from the Allemande of Bach's D-minor Cello Suite (mm. 11–12), Kurth observes that when a leading-tone resolution is displaced downward by an octave, our ear supplies the expected resolution in the proper octave (Kurth's Ex. 103, *Grundlagen*, 270–71). Although he says our ear supplies the resolution, Kurth is no doubt thinking of the tendency of a low cello note (in his Ex. 103, an A) to produce a strong first overtone, the resolution note, a. This phenomenon does not apply to Example 3.22, since of course the g″ in measure 127 does not produce any "undertones."

Ex. 3.24 [K204] Violin Sonata no. 2 in A minor, Allegro, mm. 43–47

[333] In whole notes, a lower rim line leads from the isolated g, implied for two measures as a quasi-pedal, crossing over a and b, up to c′ (marked with plus signs). From the last quarter of measure 43 onward, a pedal effect on c″ emerges out of repeated attacks – at first fleeting then more accented – and continues, from measure 45 onward, in a chromatically ascending line, c♯″–d″–d♯″–e″ (marked with asterisks). In the meantime, three descending apparent voices emerge, entering imitatively, each arising from an implied pedal: in measure 43 from a repeated f′, in measure 44 from g′, and in measure 45 from a′. With each of these three tones, which constitute the beginnings of motivic apparent voices, notice how the implied pedals arise initially from very fleeting [pitch] references, then by means of constant repetition, becoming ever clearer. Notated in the approximate values, as implied, the latter three apparent voices arise within the four measures in the following arrangement.

Ex. 3.25 [K205]

The entire actually sounding voice is permeated with a richly spun net of interwoven apparent voices. Counting the actual voice, these four measures exhibit an implied six-voice polyphony – an uncommonly delicate, veiled web of implied lines, each consolidating itself after imperceptibly subtle beginnings, [and] vanishing once again after flickering briefly.

The interaction of apparent voices and the actual voice

[333] When an apparent voice has established itself clearly, it is frequently significant enough to be incorporated into the main voice. That is to say, regarding the

motivic profile, the actual voice turns out to be a continuation of an accessory voice previously latent within the actual voice. In this way, such obscured linear progressions [334] come to light. The reverse process – the continuation in an apparent voice of a motive first presented in the actual voice – occurs often as well, for example:

Ex. 3.26 [K206] Violin Partita no. 2 in D minor, Allemande, mm. 28–31

The descending motion latent in the upper rim line from measure 28 onward (marked with plus signs) continues on in the actual voice at measure 30 (marked with a bracket), and also in a more energetic rhythm, in sixteenths, whereas the apparent voice has advanced each half measure.

Ex. 3.27 [K207] Violin Sonata no. 3 in C major, Allegro, mm. 3–9

[335] The bracketed motive in the actual voice at measure 4 [of Ex. 3.27] appears as a lower rim voice (+) at measure 8 in doubled note values, and as an upper apparent voice at measure 6 as well, inverted and augmented...[14]

[342] This phenomenon of the transition of motives and specific types of motion from the apparent voice into the actual voice shows most clearly that, with monophony, Bach actually imagined polyphonic activity in which, motivically, all voices take part. Hence in the following example, first the main voice and then an apparent voice participate in a broad linear curve.

[14] [LR] The motive in the apparent voice at measure 6, though similar to the bracketed motive in measure 4, does not match it exactly.

Ex. 3.28 [K216] Violin Sonata no. 3 in C major, Allegro, mm. 88–96

[343] In measure 88 there is an ascending line up to g''' in the actual voice, and from there an apparent voice descending in whole notes: g'''–f'''–e'''–d'''–c'''–a''–g''–, and continuing in quicker motion: e''–d''–c''–b' (marked with plus signs). e'''–d'''–c'''–a'' are implied pedal-like tones. Beneath this voice, from measure 89 onward, there is a voice d'''–(mm. 89–90)–c'''–b'' (up to here resounding as pedal-like tones), continued and sequenced in quicker values from measure 93 onward. Both apparent voices together yield the following sketch (in approximate values).

Ex. 3.29 [K217]

(The d'' at the beginning of m. 94 is implied by its lower octave.)[15]

The lower voice of the implied parallel thirds in the last two measures represents the continuation of the preceding descending sequence, the upper voice representing the accelerated continuation of the slower apparent voice, marked with plus signs. . .

[15] [LR] See note 13 above.

Polyphonic melody

[344] A descending line (marked with plus signs), formed partly by the actual voice, partly by an apparent voice, runs through the following monophonic structure.

Ex. 3.30 [K220] Cello Suite in D minor, Allemande, mm. 14–15

[345] Furthermore, [there is] a descending apparent voice (marked with asterisks).[16]

In the following example the motion of an actual voice dissipates in an apparent voice (as, for example, in [Kurth's] Ex. 210).[17]

Ex. 3.31 [K222] Cello Suite in C major, Gigue, mm. 105–08

In the first measure [there is] a descent to F in the actual voice, which continues with E–D–C as an apparent voice from measure 106 onward.

[348] In such artful dissipation the final transition of linear unfoldments often recedes very gradually into outlines that can no longer be clearly distinguished, into a faint suggestion of small and minute flickering apparent voices or motives. Bach's compositional means attain to such profoundly concealed subtleties that precisely the most sophisticated ones resist formulation in systematic technical phenomena. Therefore, this threshold where accessory voices are in the initial stage of evolution, or dissolution, requires a specially trained sense for the polyphonic implications residing in Bach's monophonic line. Often, the ultimate artistic effects can only be felt and, if extracted in delimited forms, they dissolve into vagueness. Every technique of art, in its ultimate and minutest facets, recedes from that which can be presented conceptually into a domain where more latent stylistic and artistic intuition determines the [musical] treatment more than does the conscious and calculating intellect.

---

[16] [LR] This example is discussed in detail in *EKATA*, 97–98, Examples 4.35 to 4.39.

[17] [LR] Kurth's Example 210 shows measures 32–47 from the Presto of Bach's Sonata for Violin in G minor. In discussing that excerpt, Kurth points out a descending apparent voice running from measure 35 to measure 46, where each note of the apparent voice (first note in mm. 35, 37, 39 and 41) is followed by a sixteenth-note descent in the actual voice.

PART II

Romantische Harmonik und ihre Krise
in Wagners "Tristan"
(Romantic harmony and its crisis
in Wagner's "Tristan")

4

Details of Romantic harmony

This chapter contains excerpts from *Romantische Harmonik und ihre Krise in Wagners "Tristan"*, 3rd edn., part 3 ("From the cadence to the alteration style of *Tristan*"), the largest section of the book, and from part 4 ("Paths of harmonic development"). Parts 1 and 2, the background for parts 3 and 4, interpret Romantic harmony psychologically, present the psychological bases of Romantic music in general (part 1, "Foundations"), and give a thorough analytic account of the *Tristan* chord and its various resolutions, enharmonic transformations, and symbolic meanings (part 2, "The first chord"). Part 3 presents specific harmonic techniques by expanding on the analytic findings of part 2, and parts 4 and 5 show the escalation of early nineteenth-century practices into those of the late nineteenth century.

The passages translated here deal with harmonic "contrasting" and "shading" (part 3, chapters 3 and 4, "Heightened harmonic coloring," "Harmonic shading," pp. 150–51, 153–55, 159–67); with melodic and harmonic alteration of chords, and distorted root progression (part 3, chapter 5, "The intensive alteration style," 183–86, 189–91, 199–201, 205–6, 210–11); and with "absolute" chords and chord progressions, including mediant progressions (part 4, chapter 2, "The interior dissolution of color in romantic harmony," 262–70, 270–77, 297–99, 301–5).

Readers should keep in mind that, for the most part, Kurth's analyses in *Romantische Harmonik* examine local-level harmonic details. These details often have broader implications, some of which Kurth explores in other portions of the book. In the passages translated here, he focuses on local events that define the harmonic idiom of the middle and late Romantic periods. In order to explain unusual chords and chord connections, Kurth relies heavily on single or multiple chromatic neighbor-note displacements of diatonic chord notes, as well as on single or multiple chromatic alterations of the chord notes themselves. For example two seemingly distinct chords that appear to form a progression may be "identical," as Kurth says, when one is a multiple neighbor-note displacement of the other (Ex. 4.15); or when a chord is "shaded" by lowering one or more of its notes by a half step (Exx. 4.4 and 4.8). Kurth classifies such local-level techniques as melodic and harmonic alteration, respectively. Our chapter 5 contains discussions of some larger-scale harmonic procedures.

Effects of color contrasts

[150] The subtle sense for the relationship between tonal practices and dynamic processes manifests itself with the Romantics at times clearly in the harmonization of melodies, for example [in the harmonization of] the following motive from Wagner's *Siegfried* (Act 3, Scene 1).

Ex. 4.1 [K65] *Siegfried*, Act 3, Scene 1 [Schirmer, 245]

Nothing could express that relationship better than these harmonies (excerpted from the "Sleep-Motive") which ascend with the chord in sharps and reverse directions at the chord in flats. The descent thus coincides with a darkening toward a chord which contrasts sharply with the first one owing to the downward-directed tone tendencies. The *vivid form* of the *movements* of the *motive* corresponds to the change of the *harmonies*, i.e., to the dynamic tensions concealed in their succession. In this whole scene between the Wanderer and Erda, note how the tonal usage in the harmonization of this motive is carried out in various ways, always descending with strongly subdominant shifts. (Even the *external* dynamic markings prescribed by Wagner – the alternation of crescendo and piano – go hand in hand with the tonal shift.[1])

---

[1] [LR] By "subdominant shifts" Kurth means progressions that explore "flat-side" harmonies (those on the descending circle of fifths with respect to some starting point), e.g. a progression from G-major to Eb-major harmony. Dominant shifts explore "sharp-side" harmonies (on the ascending circle of fifths), e.g. G-major to B-major harmony. See chapter 6, note 48. Kurth's point about ascending in sharps and descending in flats as signs of a coordination between direction and tonal shifts is intuitively clear, based on the passage he cites in Example 4.1, and on the surrounding music around that excerpt. There are many places, however, where local textual influences may affect harmony. In the same scene, where the Wanderer sings "daß du erwachest" (Schirmer, 243), the music ascends in flats before shifting to sharps (notably at the word "erwachest"), and immediately afterward, at "aus sinnendem Schlafe," the ascent begins in sharps and then switches to flats (again, notably at the word "Schlafe"). In other passages, where Kurth's proposed correspondence between direction and harmony do not hold up, it is harder to establish an unequivocal textual motivation. Direction and sharp/flat harmonies do not always corroborate one another so handily in *Götterdämmerung*, for example in Act 3, Scene 3, just after Hagen's demand "Her den Ring!" (Schirmer, 314–15), or a little later in the scene, at Brünnhilde's declaration "Denn der Götter Ende dämmert nun auf" (Schirmer, 330–31), where one might expect such correspondences. It would be far too confining, and artistically shallow, for Wagner to coordinate harmony and direction in such a superficial way. I doubt that Kurth intended any fixed correspondence. He is just pointing up the significance of such correspondences, when they do occur, in order to bring out the interaction of dynamic, harmonic, and dramatic elements.

The connection of music with words in particular, primarily in the lied and music drama, demonstrates how strongly the Romantics, with all of the heightened and erratic shifts into the dominant and subdominant region, were guided by attendant sensations of luminescence and darkening in the harmony. A fluctuation in both directions, with its unstable, iridescent harmonic luminescent effects, as well as unilateral abrupt shifts toward one of the contrasting tonal areas, appear everywhere directly connected with poetic and visual impressions.

[151] The effect is highly poetic, for example, in the following shift to the luminous D-major and G-major chords, from Act 1 of *Siegfried*, which are abruptly thrown into relief against the muted, shadowy key of the forest – an ingeniously simple impression of the bright surface of the stream, where "sun and clouds, e'en as they are," appear "in the water's sparkle" (From Siegfried's narrative in Act 1, "Then I came to the limpid stream. . .").[2]

Ex. 4.2 [K66] *Siegfried*, Act 1, Scene 1 [Schirmer, 33]

The nature poetry in the *Nibelungen* is full of such effects. See, for example, the many shifts between light and shadow in *Siegfried*, Act 2. Or note in Siegmund's monolog from *Walküre* (Act 1) the shift into a flat key at the words "Nächtiges Dunkel. . ." and immediately afterwards the brightening toward G and D major at the words "Wärme gewann ich und Tag" [Schirmer, 40–41]. . .

[153] As befits the whole general atmosphere, natural elements in *Tristan* are enhanced and refined to yield the most delicate impressionistic moods. Hence the following [154] passage (from Act 1, Scene 2), in the context of C major, exhibits a strongly subdominant shift, which over four measures is contrasted with the dominant. Light and shadow set each other off.

---

[2] [LR] Notice, too, that the shift to the "brighter" harmonies is accompanied by neighbor-note motion in whole steps (A–B in the tenor, D–E in the soprano), which contrast with the half-step neighbors during the "dark" harmonies. Further, the bass remains inactive during the dark section (pedal) but becomes active during the bright section (fifth leaps).

Ex. 4.3 [K70] *Tristan*, Act 1, Scene 2 [Schirmer, 21–22]

The cadential gesture with the dominant and *minor* subdominant. . .is expanded here such that measures 2–5 [of Ex. 4.3], as a group unto itself, represent a subdominant excursion [*subdominantische Ausweichung*]. (The harmonic linkage could perhaps be reconstructed by reinterpreting the second chord, C: V, as the dominant of C minor, followed by c: VI; this chord is understood as f: III, whereupon VII, i, and VI follow in F minor; the latter [the D♭-major triad] is interpreted retrospectively in C major as the Neapolitan chord, etc.)[3] The transition from the first to the second [155] measure already demonstrates how the sudden, powerful effect of the transformation to a gloomy atmosphere issues entirely from the poetry and imagery of the text setting. The sudden turn toward the A♭-major chord, as a color effect (a glance into the dusk of the distant sky) is, in an impressionistic sense,

---

[3] [LR] The harmonies in measures 2–5 make more sense if they are interpreted in A♭ major (I, V, vi, IV) rather than in C minor. A♭ major is just as "dark" a subdominant excursion as F minor.

the guiding creative idea. It is especially clear that this shadow effect, projected into the soft harmonies of divided violas and cellos, is the essential content of the harmonic design because Wagner reinforces this effect and highlights its surprising, unmediated quality more intensively by introducing a move toward a six-four cadence. After the first C-major chord (six-four) and its dominant, the six-four cadence causes us to expect a C-major chord in the second measure all the more and, consequently, to feel the darkening shift in the A♭-major harmony.

HARMONIC SHADING

[159] In the brief passage presented at the beginning of this section ([Kurth's] Ex. 37), the chromatic alteration of individual tones, as a means of simple *shading*, was already evident.[4] That is a phenomenon which pervades harmony everywhere especially since Wagner's *Tristan*, although even there it is not really new. Following the harmonic progression [shown] in [Kurth's] Example 37, it was already pointed out how c♭' and g♭ in measure 11 result from the downward push of the motivic motion passing through the inner voices. More noteworthy than the c♭' is the g♭ on the third quarter; for the c♭' appears simply in the chromatic motion [160] between c' and b♭. With g♭, on the other hand, a lowering of an actual chord tone occurs, which is not motivated by half steps surrounding on both sides. The linear progression [*Linienzug*] would preserve its descending character even if it passed through the chord with g. The linear motion that lowers g to g♭ is an intensified expression of the whole dynamic tendency, to which the overall harmonic setting immediately yields.[5] Furthermore, it is the darkening of the harmony and the whole mood. The lightly descending motion lowers the tone and mutes the harmonic color, which is darkened by a faint shadow that drifts over E♭ major. Thus when an ascending or descending motion asserts itself so strongly that it permits the occurrence of a tone altered in the direction of the motion (as here, even producing a lowered chordal third instead of the major form), typically it is a manifestation of that shading of chords which arises due to the pure *energy* and *volitional direction* of a motion, and no longer due to the uniform chromaticism of an *ongoing* linear motion. In their origins, both phenomena are

---

[4] [LR] Kurth refers here to his Example 37, on page 100 of *Romantische Harmonik*. The example is taken from *Tristan*, Act 1, Scene 1, starting six measures before Brangäne's entrance ("Blaue Streifen"), near the beginning of the scene (Schirmer, 6–7). The example ends at the words "Kornwalls grünen Strand," with a deceptive cadence on a "half diminished" chord on C. Kurth is concerned with measure 11, which contains a c♭' and g♭ instead of the expected diatonic counterparts, c' and g.

[5] [LR] While it is true that the g♭, as an altered chord tone, is striking, it is prepared motivically several times prior to the spot Kurth singles out (e.g., at Brangäne's first words, in the lower voices of the accompaniment). The c♭', on the other hand, although it is not an altered chord tone, contrasts with the many c♮s in the Sea-Motive, and thus stands out clearly.

of course related, since historically the former [shading] first developed from the basis of chromatic passing formations, analogous to the whole idea of alteration in general.

The real hallmark of this technique of harmonic shading, however, is the *pliability* with which originally tonal chords in late Romanticism accommodate individual tones to the manifestation of a simple direction. It is the reaction of harmonies to the slightest energetic tensions. Not only a significant pervasion of music with chromatic and other neighbor and passing formations but also a still more powerful urgency of hidden, sub-sonic dynamic forces in musical perception had to come first, before the weakened and loosened harmonic surface adapted its tonally determined chordal forms in unlimited *flexibility* to the flowing dynamic will that guides tones upwards or downwards. The harmonies of the high Romantic style become so sensitive that, like a light, thin and extraordinarily sensitive film, they instantly stretch as the current ebbs and flows. Even a slight wisp darkens and discolors them. A slight darkening often depresses the whole mood [161] with a single chromatically deviating tone, and can at times evoke wonderful shadings of faint melancholy, especially in *Tristan*. The most subtle brightening effects, however, are also induced by the reverse process of raising a tone.

It is above all through Wagner that, with this type of harmonic modification, a means of casting light and shadow over the music is utilized everywhere, be it only in the most subtle hints. The following measures from *Tristan*, Act 2 [Scene 2] could be mentioned as a characteristic example which permits this phenomenon to come to the fore clearly and intensively.

Ex. 4.4 [K74] *Tristan*, Act 2, Scene 2 [Schirmer, 180]

First, C major darkens into minor (with the underthird, A, coming in, a harmonic effect...likewise with a certain dusky impression, and one which Wagner in particular often utilizes). The downwards-shading alteration continues into the next measure, by seizing on the tone g♭'. (The resulting g♭' remains stationary as f♯', and the harmonic formation arising from this chromatic lowering, A–C–E♭–G♭ (=F♯), enharmonically reinterpreted, is led as g: vii, to g: V [162], with the bright major chord on D, in unique resonance, illuminating again the heavy atmosphere of flashing and fading in these measures. The tone b♭' in measure 3 is a passing note, rising in the melody from a' to c" on the one hand, and intended as a descending passing note [b♭] from c' to an a in the harmony on the other.)

But even very simple, non-modulating passages based on straightforward progression, and otherwise not affected by intensive alteration, undergo characteristic modifications by means of such chromatic shadings.

Purely technically, it is nothing but a manifestation of alteration. For here, too, a tendency tone [*Strebeton*] was created at a place where no chromatic connection occurs naturally. Nevertheless, harmonic shading is an especially noteworthy offshoot of the extensive alteration technique, one of its refined consequences applied, above all, in service of unique *artistic coloring effects*. It is not so much a matter here of the distortive, destructive effects of alteration but rather of a *luminescent* and *tinting* element. This manifests itself technically as well: first, because when more than one tone is modified, the chromatic deviations are applied only in *one* specific direction, only upward or downward throughout, and moreover because, much more than otherwise, such harmonic shadings affect alterations in the form of consonant or only slightly dissonant chords. For in this way the darkening or brightening effects are sensed all the more purely, i.e. not overpowered by strong harmonic dissonances. Nonetheless, this [lack of dissonance] is not a prerequisite of shading effects, and they can be found, though more rarely, in connection with strong dissonances as well. Third, it is a matter of those alterations that very early *dispense with* the *link* to a *specific* chromatic *continuation*, namely not only with the link to an individual voice – which of course the entire practice of alteration abandons rather early in instrumental music – but with the expected continuation to the appropriate adjacent chromatic tone altogether. That is a process which affects the remaining alteration techniques only in the period after Wagner, about which we will yet speak (part 6). Here, rather, the darkening and brightening effect, as the actual content [163] of the phenomenon, comes primarily to the fore. The tensions that arise with such chords vanish under the domination of these more harmonic and sensuous color impressions, and no longer have control and power over the continuation of the modified tones. A clear hint of impressionistic effects arises, if only to a greatly varying degree.

Nevertheless, it is dynamic tensions that first cause not only the chromatic modification of tones but also constitute the unique shading effects themselves. The sensations of light and dark in music originate in dynamic tensions. Everywhere it is inner *dynamic* processes that are reflected in apparently purely harmonic impressions, radiate outward upon them and are decisive in harmonic coloring. Instead of saying shading, one could be equally correct in saying dynamic shading – one of the countless pieces of evidence showing how, as the ultimate and most general fundamental process, harmony reaches out everywhere to transform energetic phenomena into sensuous ones. Those energetic processes do not bring about the overall phenomenon of color as such – which as a purely sensuous manifestation is immanent in all harmonic effects – but rather bring about only one *component* of harmonic tinting, namely that element which resides in its characteristic impressions of luminescence and shading, as they radiate all harmonic coloring in the richest variations and illimitable nuances.

Here the significance of *will* as such for the psychology of all musical hearing becomes clear from a new perspective. For what these effects of luminescence and shading amount to, penetrating deep into the harmonic color, is not at all actually *kinetic* motion in the larger melodic current but rather the mere *urge* toward motion, as evident in chromatic alteration. The relatively minuscule chromatic modification effects a far more intensive sensation of upward or downward tendency than many an ascending or descending melodic motive, no matter how turbulent. And this is so precisely because of its tension, which presses onward in a certain direction as it emanates from individual tones [and spreads out] over the entire chord (as "potential energy"). Here, in the luminescent harmonic effects, something emerges that was already recognizable as a fundamental trait [164] of alteration in general (see [Kurth's] p. 48). The *will toward motion* is always much more profound in its influence than that tension process which finds *fulfillment* in melodic motion. *Romanticism* above all had to sense this and lead to important consequences by penetrating behind all things, with its cosmic sensibilities, right down to the operative tension-laden forces.

If as a result of vigorous fluctuation between the two dominant regions the richly colorful expansion of harmony was based on more concealed dynamic tensions that permeate both harmonic *progressions* and harmonic relationships, then harmonic shading, as a manifestation of alteration, illustrates the influx of dynamic tensions into individual chords, as well as into their coloristic impressions. Shading is also one of the most common and simplest means of *modulation* involving alteration. Its meaning should be sought, however, not in this purely technical facet, but rather in the artistic tinting effect which, conversely, finds *expression* in those special technical possibilities of modulation (transition by means of simultaneously or successively applied alteration of individual tones). It is precisely examples like the one given in Example 4.4 [K74] which show, above all, how the play of fluid dynamic currents allow the harmony to shimmer in endlessly rich luminescent reflexes.

One of the most glorious color diffractions of this sort arises, for example, in the grand naturalistic atmosphere at the end of *Rheingold*, at the procession of the gods across the rainbow into Valhalla. In the plea of the Rhinemaidens sounding from afar, a slight alteration in the upper voice changes the repetition of the motive.

Ex. 4.5 [K75] *Das Rheingold*, Scene 4 [Schirmer, 217]

[165] The passage is to be understood as a tonal excursion [*Ausweichung*] to C minor. Tonally, the first four chords are c: III–VI–V–VI; at the repetition, the dominant chord, resolving deceptively to the A♭-major chord, has its seventh, f″, lowered to f♭″.[6]

---

[6] [LR] Georg Capellen analyzes the G–B–F/F♭ sonorities as two versions of an altered V9 in A♭ major ("Harmonik und Melodik bei Richard Wagner," *Bayreuther Blätter* 25 [1902], 22). A modern view might analyze them as contrapuntal chords, neighbors to a governing A♭ harmony.

Kurth may have invoked the C-minor "excursion" because the G–B–F/F♭ sonorities, with B♮s, would have been difficult to explain as altered VII7s in what is otherwise clearly A♭ tonality. Another reason for invoking a C-minor excursion may have been to contrast the present Rhinemaidens' sorrowful plea with their first, joyous outbursts of "Rheingold" (Scene 1), which appear in C major (Schirmer, 33, 36). With C major as the point of reference, Kurth's C minor, in addition to being in the "dark" subdominant orbit of A♭ major, contrasts effectively with the earlier C-major passage. Analyzing Example 4.5 in C minor would mean, however, that a passage just previous, where the Rhinemaidens begin pleading for the gold (Schirmer, 216), would have to be analyzed analogously. There (Schirmer, 216), Kurth's excursion is even less likely. The strongly articulated E♭–A♭ bass line throughout the entire passage contravenes an excursion into C minor. Kurth's questionable excursion notwithstanding, the F–E♭ neighbor motion in the uppermost voice does possess a subdominant quality, which is then strengthened (darkened) by the shift to F♭–E♭. Wagner himself singles out the Rhinemaidens' motive as an example of one that undergoes numerous transformations, depending on the dramatic context, throughout the *Ring*: "One would have to follow this uncommonly simple theme. . .recurring in manifold alliance with almost every other motive of the drama's wide-spread movement – through all the changes it receives from the diverse character of its resummoning – to see what type of variations the Drama can engender. . ." ("On the Application of Music to the Drama," trans. William Ashton Ellis in *Richard Wagner's Prose Works* [8 vols., London: Routledge and Kegan Paul Ltd., 1887; reprint New York: Broude Brothers, 1966], vol. VI, 187; originally in *Bayreuther Blätter* 2 (Nov., 1879), 323). Heinrich Rietsch points out the harmonic contrasts between the two version of the Rhinemaidens' motive in *Die Tonkunst in der zweiten Hälfte des neunzehnten Jahrhunderts*, 2nd edn., rev. and enl. (Leipzig: Breitkopf und Härtel, 1906; orig. 1899), 61–62.

The kinship between chords altered through shading and dominant and subdominant excursions is clearly illustrated, for example, when harmonizations of a single motive, which are distinguished by such key changes, are compared with one another, e.g., in the following two cases. The first motive (Ex. 4.6) is taken from the beginning of the *Tristan* Prelude (m. 17), and the second motive (Ex. 4.7) from the end [of the Prelude] (m. 94).

Ex. 4.6 [K76] *Tristan*, Prelude (m. 17)   Ex. 4.7 [K77] *Tristan*, Prelude (m. 94)

The first harmonization derives from the main key, A minor, the second one from the final cadence of the Prelude moving toward C minor. If the two harmonizations of the motive are set side by side, as they occur in this key change, the strong fading effect [in the second version] becomes immediately apparent, which, compared with the first version, is evoked by the chromatic lowering of F♯ and a to F and a♭. And the harmonic tinting resulting from the rich color of major [harmony] shading into gloomy darkness emerges in connection with the sharp turn toward the subdominant (the relationship between the keys A minor and C minor). It is the descending effect which again does not reside in the visible, traceable course overall, i.e. in connection with entire lines, but rather in the tone tendencies themselves, which radiate the harmonic character as a whole. Thus from this perspective as well, the aforementioned connection between tonal shifts and dynamic processes becomes evident.

[166]. . .Hence, veering sharply out of major chords into harmonies with a chromatically lowered third and fifth is particularly characteristic for music of the high Romantic period. Further, the underthird. . .is also added. So, for example, in the following measures from *Lohengrin*, where the major form [of a chord] on A first slips down to the tones c″ and e♭′, the underthird F simultaneously comes in as a root underneath this transformed harmony.

Ex. 4.8 [K78] *Lohengrin*, Act 1, Scene 3 [Schirmer, 92]

The effect here is of a striking harmonic darkening, additionally, though, of a sharp downward jolt, in the sense of energetic perceptions of harmony. The tone modification resulting from alteration induces the modulation from D major to B♭ major.

This technique is related to yet another special harmonic progression that soon became very common and a stereotypical form. In origin, it is based on a dominant–tonic cadence, e.g. E7 to A major or A minor. This A-major or minor chord occurs, then, in the form A–C–E♭, with harmonic shading of the fifth and, in the case of a major chord, shading of the third as well. Wagner's, and Bruckner's works, too, are full of such progressions, for example in *Tannhäuser*, Act 1, Scene 4 [167].

Ex. 4.9 [K79] *Tannhäuser*, Act 1, Scene 4 [Schirmer, 68]

Here, too, the shading is determined by the whole artistic context and mood: a certain touch of melancholy as the thoughts of the returning singer wander over past events and into distant reaches.

THE INTENSIVE ALTERATION STYLE

Basic characteristics and individual components

[183] In the broadest sense, alteration is understood as any chromatic modification that deviates from the tonally established foundation. Still, in theories of harmony the concept often exhibits very different applications and extensions. Style studies tend to speak of notated alteration only where more radically distorted chord forms occur. But a designation of that sort is neither definable nor exact since the chord *forms* alone are not decisive, and harmonic formations that are actually quite simple can also arise due to alteration. The evolution of energetic harmony shows how the linear element seeps into its most minute and concealed channels, how from the simplest harmonic phenomenon and the most straightforward cadences onward the path toward alteration is already prefigured [184], and how that path is already initiated starting from the very first chromatic deviations that merely go beyond the "diatonic" complex. The evolution of harmony also shows how, in the full expansion of harmonic relationships, from the simple applied dominants onward, there is a hidden connection, a deep-seated relationship to the technique of alteration, which is why alteration historically goes hand in hand with the ever-growing delight in the color of such broader and more restless tonal circumscriptions. Likewise, an intensive chromatic animation of voices always emerges simultaneously with the intensive style of chordal alteration as one of its immediate precursors.

For the concept of alteration, in its internal as well as in its historical development, this animation permits a differentiation between two separate and very essential stages. For a chord is already set in relief, distorted, altered, when a chromatically moving voice passes through it with a raised or lowered tone. Contrasting with this original and broader, more primitive sense of alteration, which clearly characterizes any deviation in melodic lines, is another phenomenon that, strictly speaking, must be designated as *chordal alteration* – namely the chromatic modification that enters *freely* into a chord, without the necessity of previous linear motion, and creates an impulse pressing toward subsequent harmonies. The transition from melodic to harmonic chromaticism, from kinetic to potential energy in chords, is expressed in these two phenomena. The fact that, in instrumental music, this requirement soon and naturally was liberated from its link to the same voice – so long as the resolution appears in the subsequent harmony – is a phenomenon that was likewise promoted by the energetic tension in the chordal fusion network spreading out over the harmony as a whole.

Chordal alteration had to expand into a broader development the moment artistic feeling was directed more at the interior dynamics than at sonic harmony, and sought in the individual tone less the sounding of tones than the quivering of psychic energies. The character of the leading tone permeates the entire harmonic style, [185] its restlessness the entirety of musical perception. Alteration, in its intensive stage of evolution, is characterized by the disintegration of all normal chordal forms, but also by the progressive dissolution of all chordal and tonal relations. Its chordal shapes, ever newly transformed and limitlessly transformable, arise most vividly. Along with this diffraction into the variegation of harmonic color, the distortion of the harmonic formations engenders the unrestricted, ever new possibilities of dissonance, which were a great torment for the classically trained ear of Wagner's contemporaries, perhaps even more so for their greatly anxious theoretical conscience.

Hence, harmonies arise that are always evolving and transforming, that yearn urgently to break out of themselves from within. They allow no feeling of calming to arise but rather only the awareness of active will. Although the phenomena of alteration were already familiar to much earlier periods – with Bach and, a hundred years earlier, with Schütz, even intensifying and becoming internally fortified, pointing toward Wagner – for the high Romantic period, alteration was destined to become the dominating and most fitting expressive form of harmonic sensibility. The total, unfettered release of dynamic energies, stirring up and storming through harmonies, often as though shredding them, characterizes the fully escalated alteration style, and provides evidence of the terrible force that produces music such as that of *Tristan*, in its full, powerfully concentrated uniqueness.

From the technical point of view, the chordal alteration style exhibits three *components*, all of which however merely illustrate the influence of the basic idea of alteration: the chromatic modification of *chord tones*, *neighbor-note insertion*, and third, closely associated with these two, *chromatic chord progression*, i.e., the principle of stringing chords together based on pure chromatic progression of all or of individual tones, and no longer based on tonal relationships. This principle will be discussed in closing. In the Romantic style, all three components of alteration occur extensively in connection with enharmonic procedures. The idea of reinterpretation, too, was actually an old one but was applied here with a purpose and power that opened up for the technique of alteration new avenues and possibilities for expansion.

On the technique of neighbor-note insertion and its connection with chordal alteration

[186] Just as distinctions [between melodic and harmonic alteration] were necessary from the first chord of *Tristan* onward, unlike the first of the three components enumerated [alteration of chord tones], neighbor-note insertion is not based on

creating a leading tone that chromatically modifies a chord tone but rather on creating an (upper or lower) neighbor note that strives toward a chord tone and is forced into the chord as a *foreign* tone (such as the g♯' in the first *Tristan* chord, which is wedged into the chord as a neighbor note to a'). Neighbor-note insertion is thus the interpolation of foreign tones that strive *into* the chord, just as the chromatically altered tones of the first variety strive *out of* the chord. The two phenomena are thus opposites in a certain respect. Nevertheless, they are not usually found strictly apart from one another, and both are generally termed alteration since the distortion of the harmonic image with tension tones is common to both. . .

[189]. . .Consider the famous introductory chord of Schubert's song "Am Meere".

Ex. 4.10 [K93] *Schwanengesang,* Part 2, no. 12, m. 1

The first harmony is a threefold neighbor-note insertion to the C-major chord. Or:

Ex. 4.11 [K94] Schumann, "Abendmusik," *Bunte Blätter,* op. 99

The striking chord in measure 2, uniting E and e♭', is intended as F–A–C–E♭, like the subsequent chord. Accordingly, c' and e♭' are the fixed pivots [*feste Angelpunkte*], E and g♯' the chromatic neighbor-note insertions to F and a'. . .

[190]. . .Often, in a chord permeated by neighbor-note insertions, one and the same tone strives in *two* directions *at once* in the manner of a leading tone, for example in the following measures from *Die Meistersinger,* Act 2, Scene 5.

Ex. 4.12 [K96] *Meistersinger*, Act 2, Scene 5 [Schirmer, 287]

The chord in measure 2 that follows the C-major chord is the dominant form, F–A–C–E♭–G, emerging clearly toward the end of the bar. Initially, a neighbor-note insertion, b♭ to a, appears, and further the tone F♯, as a freely entering neighbor note, in a dual sense: directed upward to g′ in the upper voice, and also in the inner voice (at the second quarter), actually as g♭′, striving downward to f.[7]

It is common in Wagner's music for the same tone to have two directional tendencies, and this phenomenon indicates the kind of compression of forces alteration is capable of producing in a chord. The reverse process also occurs with the escalation of the alteration style: replacing a chord tone with its two neighbor notes.[8] A chord like the aforementioned one in particular, from *Meistersinger*, shows the special capacity inherent in such tension harmonies which makes acoustical dissonances tolerable to the musical ear. These [acoustical] dissonances simply pale in their effect generally, when attention is diverted away from them toward the completely different energetic tension effects.

The first chord of the following motive arises from a fourfold neighbor-note insertion. [191]

Ex. 4.13 [K97] *Götterdämmerung*, Act 1, Scene 2 [Schirmer, 88]

---

[7] [LR] The Schirmer piano-vocal score shows G♭s in right and left hands, while Kurth's example (reproduced in Ex. 4.12) shows two F♯s.
[8] [LR] In *Voraussetzungen der theoretischen Harmonik* (1913), 133, Kurth uses the term "disalteration" (*Disalteration*) to describe the splitting a chord tone into its two neighbors. He provides several examples (pp. 134–46).

The chord encloses the resolution harmony, E7, with tension tones, three lower ones and one acting from above. Since Wagner, more contemporary development [of harmony] intensifies these neighbor-note formations to great expressive power. . .

[199]. . .The following harmonies, for example, whose highly distorted tonal underpinnings can again ultimately be illustrated very simply, show how strongly the intensive alteration style transfers the bulk of all harmony to tension tones, and how their effect is characteristically often expanded and reinforced. All of the alterations issue throughout from the enchanting visionary character of the song setting.

Ex. 4.14 [K104] Hugo Wolf, "An den Schlaf," *Mörike-Lieder*, 3, mm. 17–24

[200] Following the simple, though sonorous, enharmonic transition out of A♭ major, the first measure of the E-major section is a V7, with g♯′ as a suspension to f♯′. Then, in the second half of the bar [m. 18], a formation appears that is only apparently a new chord. In reality, it is a multiple neighbor-note distortion of the same chord, as the return to that chord in measure 19 indicates. e′ is a neighbor-

Details of Romantic harmony

note displacement of d♯′, c of b [bass], and the voice leading of the piano setting in particular – the entrance of e by a fourth leap in the tenor – simulates a genuine chord progression.[9] Escalations in the overall tension effect come into play here as well, an effect that hovers throughout as a highly charged musical force field. First, there is the way the suspension resolves to the f♯′, which is not only delayed and very foreshortened but also comes at the moment when the remaining voices exhibit tension-inspired distortions, so that the actual chord is thus "withheld" throughout, i.e., it does not sound completely anywhere in the measure. Tension formations occur everywhere. Note also the voice part, which maintains the root B, and so permits the tension-inspired distortion of the chord to be felt particularly intensively in the c of the bass. Measure 19 begins similarly and leads to a resolution of the suspension in the piano part only on the final eighth. Here again, however, the voice part introduces the resolution tone f♯″ earlier, reinforcing the strain of the suspension. An old law, according to which the *resolution* is not supposed to sound *simultaneously* in an upper voice during a *suspension*, is superseded in the *later Romantic period*, owing precisely to the desire for heightened *tension effects*. Once again, it is these effects that overcome the very harsh *harmonic effect* [201] from which that age-old inherited rule arose. Measure 20 is a I, with a suspension a♯′ headed upward and, again, a very brief resolution. In measure 21 [on beat one] a freely introduced formation suspending the chord in the second half of the bar appears in the external form of a diminished seventh chord: f×′ and a♯′ are leading tones to g♯′ and b′, [and] c♯ is a whole-step suspension from above to b; i.e., the harmony is again tonic.[10] The subsequent measures exhibit stronger tension images. Both measures 22 and 23 have the same harmonic basis, C♯–E♯–G♯–B,

---

[9] [LR] Interpreted harmonically, the pseudo-chord in the second half of measure 18 would be E: ii with lowered fifth, in second inversion. In the slow tempo (*Sehr ruhig*) we might attribute the sonority more independence than Kurth does, and thus hear it as a pre-dominant, especially since it moves to V. The harmonic figure in measure 18 is thematic for the piece, occurring in measures 1–2, 5–6, 9–10, 13–15, 22–23, etc., in different keys (A♭ major, B minor, D♭ major). In each case the figure begins with tonic, or local tonic, harmony, with its third uppermost, moves to a neighbor chord and then back to the tonic. In all instances prior to measure 18, Kurth's neighbor chord might be considered more than just a neighbor-note collection because both the bass and tenor in the accompaniment leap back and forth, simulating a chord progression, the second chord in each case being subordinate to the first. Measure 18 represents an intensification of the figure. There, the first chord is a dominant seventh (E: V7). The second chord has a clearer neighbor function due to the stepwise motion in all accompanimental parts save the tenor, which leaps a thematic fourth (cf. the fourth leaps in the bass in mm. 1–2, 5–6, 9–10, expanded to a minor sixth in mm. 13–15). Still, because of the slow tempo and the aural conditioning by chord progressions in measures 1–2, 5–6, etc., we might hear measure 18 as a progression, too, though Kurth's interpretation is intellectually and aurally clear. The chord in the first half of measure 22 is not so easily explained tonally (E: I7 with lowered third?). Like the sonority at the head of measure 21, the one at the head of measure 22 is a neighbor chord, as Kurth suggests.

[10] [EK] Measure 21 can be explained in yet another way, F×–A♯–C♯–E as an interpolation (VII) to the G♯-minor chord, i.e. to III, but with a deceptive resolution to its under-third chord, I (see part 4, chapter 1 on this typical deceptive cadence following an applied dominant [*Romantische Harmonik*, 249–58, particularly 255–58]).

appearing in each case at the close of the bar, and have the function of an applied dominant (V7) to the chord of measure 24, II (F♯–A–C♯). In the first half of the measures tension formations appear, the recognition of which is hindered by the simplified orthography. G [bass] is actually F𝈫, a freely introduced tension neighbor to G♯, e′ [alto] (d𝈫′) to e♯′, and d″ [soprano] to c♯″ (observe also the highlighting of the tension chords by means of the external dynamics). Again, the voice heightens the tension in measure 22 by sustaining the d″, unresolved, over the brief resolution to c♯″ in the piano setting (the voice having pitted the resolution tone against the tension tone of the bass in m. 18). In measure 24 there are also two suspensions, with the voice part touching on the resolution f♯″ before the piano part, and simultaneously with the suspension e♯″. Thus the harmonic progressions are surprisingly straightforward, but the tension effects are an overpowering network of forces that envelops and completely pervades them.

Distortion of harmonies and harmonic progressions

[205] As all of the examples given here and in part 2 demonstrate, the chromatic modification of a chord tone and neighbor-note insertion, in addition to distorting the external harmonic image, also cause the relationship between tension chord and resolution chord to simulate entirely different harmonic formations than they actually are, if traced back to their basic progression. This [simulation] occurs mainly because tension chords often correspond to [harmonic] forms that are elementary and, moreover, imprecisely simplified in their notation, i.e., they are not notated according to the leading-tone function of the individual tones. Just as, in part 2 (chapter 1), the various harmonizations of the main chromatic motive of *Tristan* indicated, the tension chords in Wagner's music, in relation to the resolution chords, are almost always dominants or subdominants, or are identical [to the resolution chord].[11] The alteration style goes far beyond this practice only after Wagner, especially from Hugo Wolf onward, and effects an intensive distortion of the basic relationships in the most varied, basic harmonic progressions. For in the alteration style of *Tristan*, one characteristic, already touched on briefly, is based on the remarkable phenomenon, particularly in the case of simpler harmonic *forms*, that complex, remote relationships emerge everywhere in harmonic *connections*, and that, by contrast, the stronger harmonies distorted by alteration can be derived from very simple underlying progressions.[12]

---

[11] [LR] Kurth calls chords "identical" when a single harmony is unfolded over two sonorities. See *EKATA*, 137, 178–80.

[12] [LR] The idea that complex, chromatic progressions derive from "simple" diatonic ones goes back to treatises from the first half of the nineteenth century. Wason discusses the historical background in *Viennese Harmonic Theory*, 23–25. The chief source of this viewpoint after 1850 was Simon Sechter's *Grundsätze der musikalischen Composition* (3 vols., Leipzig: Breitkopf und Härtel, 1853), vol. I: *Die richtige Folge der*

Details of Romantic harmony

[206] The succession of two chromatic Love-Motives in these measures, for example (shortly before the end of Act 2), exhibits identical tension chords that simulate other harmonies and harmonic progressions.

Ex. 4.15 [K109] *Tristan*, Act 2, Scene 3 [Schirmer, 214]

The first chord is like the one in the second measure, E♭7, only with a leading-tone insertion, E [bass] (actually F♭) to E♭. Similarly, the third and fourth measures are identical; G [bass] appears as a tendency tone to F♯. Additionally, the notation [in m. 3] is confusing, since b♭ is notated instead of a♯ (presumably in the context of the previous E♭7), and it simplifies the overall appearance of the harmonic notation here in accordance with the chord *form* as such, which could also be misleading.[13] Here again, the chord form coincides with a diminished seventh chord, without however coinciding with its meaning and inner dynamics. Notably, the effect is completely different as well, namely [it is] the specific character of alteration. . .

[210]. . .The two chords in the following "Fate-Motive" from *Walküre*, for example, are also apparently, i.e., according to the sound, very remote: according to the external form, a D-minor chord preceding a dominant seventh on C♯.

Ex. 4.16 [K114] *Walküre*, Act 2, Scene 4 [Schirmer, 172]

Grundharmonien; see Wason, 53–54, 59–60). Sechter was the point of departure for Anton Bruckner, Karl Mayrberger, Cyrill Hynais and other authors who tried to adapt Sechter's teaching to the chromatic practices of the late nineteenth century (Wason, *Viennese Harmonic Theory*, 80–83, 90–95, 99–111).

[13] [LR] This example is discussed in *EKATA*, 179–80. Kurth might have pointed out the voice exchange, between the tenor and soprano parts in the piano setting, as further support for his reading of one harmony being expressed by each chord pair. In light of the "identical" chords in Example 4.15, we might ask why Kurth did not analyze the *Tristan* Prelude's celebrated first chord pair similarly, where the tenor and soprano voices also execute a voice exchange. William Mitchell interprets the *Tristan* cadence in just that way ("The *Tristan* Prelude: Techniques and Structure," *The Music Forum*, vol. I [New York: Columbia University Press, 1967], 162–203). The augmented-sixth sonority, F–B–D♯, resolving to an E7 harmony in the Prelude's opening measures was apparently too familiar a pattern and, in Kurth's ear, too strong a harmonic progression for him to claim that the two chords were "identical."

As the notation indicates here, a completely different interpretation is the basis. The first chord is a tension distortion of the second one, is in fact tonally identical with it. D is a neighbor-note insertion, from above, to C♯; likewise a in the uppermost voice is a neighbor-note insertion to g♯, so that here too the first melody note of the motive appears as a dissonant, non-chordal tension tone. Thus the only new note joining the second chord is the seventh, b.[14] It is remarkable that, in the very last measures of *Walküre* (from the tenth measure before the end onward), the motive undergoes a transformation and occurs twice such that the first chord does in fact appear as a D-minor chord, followed by a second chord that is no longer C♯7 but rather an E-major triad. The effect is thus also completely different; the D-minor chord, a harmonic effect symbolizing the melancholy in Wotan's last, painful glance back at Brünnhilde, intrudes into the sustained E-major harmony of the "Magic Fire." This occurs not merely as a potent turn toward the subdominant within the surrounding E-major [tonality] but rather also due to the absolute character of the key of D minor itself. The character of alteration, as it initially occurred in the first motivic chord, D–E♯–A, is neutralized here, and the harmonic shape itself is consolidated. The original tension formation is converted into something harmonic, and the transformation of this motive reflects nothing else than the most general, basic genetic and historical process of all music.

[211] Accordingly, the alteration viewpoint not only greatly simplifies root relationships among chords, often surprisingly so, but also has the power to allow the tonal coherence of music to dissolve everywhere by permitting any chord, no matter how simple, to be interpreted as a tension formation, to change completely its fundamental [tonal] relationships. . .

---

[14] [LR] The Death-Proclamation Motive (Ex. 4.16) has been discussed extensively. Wason explains Bruckner's interpretation, taken down by one of the composer's students, Friedrich Eckstein (Wason, *Viennese Harmonic Theory*, 79). Werner Breig gives a modern-day account of the Death-Proclamation-Motive in "Das Schicksalskunde-Motiv im *Ring des Nibelungen*: Versuch einer harmonischen Analyse," *Das Drama Richard Wagners als musikalisches Kunstwerk*, ed. Carl Dahlhaus (Regensburg: Bosse, 1970), 223–34.

Kurth's analysis agrees with Bruckner's, as does Josef Schalk's ("Das Gesetz der Tonalität II," *Bayreuther Blätter* 11 [1888], 383–85). Schalk, though, views the bass D as a chordal ninth (f♯: V7), which resolves correctly in the next bar. Analyzing both the bass D and soprano a as neighbor-note displacements of C♯ and g♯, as Kurth does, means of course that they cannot resolve simultaneously lest parallel fifths result. Hence the soprano resolves before the bass and skips to the seventh, b, as the tenor takes over g♯ by means of an affective diminished-fifth leap. Georg Capellen gives an interesting quasi-phenomenological interpretation of the harmonies in his "Harmonik und Melodik bei Richard Wagner," 21–22. After criticizing Hynais's analysis, Capellen explains that an analysis must reflect our processive hearing of the sonorities. As our ear encounters D–E♯–A, given the previous harmonic-tonal context, we hear the sonority as a D-minor triad. Once the shift to the C♯7 harmony occurs, we reinterpret D–E♯–A retroauditively as a suspension chord delaying the V7 in the key of F♯ minor. According to Capellen, an analysis that truly reflects our hearing should account for both aspects of the sonority.

THE INTERIOR DISSOLUTION OF COLOR IN ROMANTIC HARMONY

The effect of the absolute progression

[262] Along with the harmonic evolution characterized by the emergence of tone fusion beyond the triad and ninth chords, leading to new types of technical procedures, there is yet another phenomenon in the mature Romantic period that emerges from the heightened feeling for harmonic sensuousness – nowhere more pronounced than in Wagner's music – and that assumes crucial significance for the broad evolutionary paths of harmony. This phenomenon must be understood primarily in connection with its continuing evolution, since it seems to exhibit nothing noteworthy or unusual in its simpler and original forms. It does not affect the structure of harmonies but rather the structure of harmonic *connections*, and there leads to destructive processes. Compared with these destructive processes, the harmonic progressions mentioned in the previous chapter, arising directly from chord formation and deviating, in part, from the tonality (deceptive cadences in conjunction with applied dominants), are merely preliminary phenomena of relatively minor significance, and do not lead to extensive dissolution.

A harmony for its own sake is subject to a *threefold* contextual influence. *First*, its musical effect depends on its relationship to the central tonic harmony, on its "tonal function." The same chord appears with an entirely different effect depending on whether it assumes the role of tonic, dominant, or any other close or more remote position in the overall key. [263] Accordingly, the overall key is to be understood with reference to a complete piece, or only to a tonal fragment. Since such fragments become ever shorter and more fluctuant in the development of Romantic music, the overall tonal orbits to which this type of chordal effect is referred narrows as well. *Second*, the effect of a chord also depends on the relationship to the immediately preceding chord. The relation to the immediately preceding chord confronts the relation to the tonic. This last phenomenon, the luminous effect of an individual progression, the appeal resulting from the *collision* of two chords, is concealed in simple tonal music, [is] more suppressed and inconspicuous in the overall effect of the harmonic context, being more absorbed in the tonal structure of the total complex. In other words, in the context of simple tonal music, the relation of a harmony to the tonic is more significant than the relationship in the progression of two successive chords individually, even though that [local] relationship always influences the effect of a newly entering chord as well. *Third*, besides these two *relative* aspects, [i.e. besides] the relationship to the central tonic and to the immediately preceding harmony, the effect of a chord is influenced by its sonic appeal as such, by its *absolute* effect. This effect, too, is never completely suppressed, and to a certain degree is always evident along with the two aforementioned aspects, but in simple tonal music it remains suppressed by the relative relationships.

While it is in the nature of tonality that the effect arising from the relationship to the central tonic is the first and fundamental one, the second as well as the third function [*Wirkungsmoment*] can be stressed. The unmediated effects of progressions, as well as ultimately the specific absolute sonic appeal, can be highlighted. If a development of this type is initiated in music, it naturally indicates a loosening and dissolution of the embracing, uniform sense of tonality. The first of those functions is constructive, in the sense of the tonal structure; it has a binding, centralizing effect. The others are destructive, having an isolating, destructive effect. The focus on individual effects neither comes about suddenly nor completely displaces the embracing harmonic-tonal feeling, [264] just as the emphasis on the absolute effect of a chord as such still does not exclude the participation of the other two functions, although it can lead to that point in its intensification. Each stage develops from the soil of the previous one, whose hallmarks thus carry and support it. All these processes that converge to highlight individual effects are based on gradual transitions, are intertwined, and are by nature illimitable. The harmonic colors well up from within, and so gradually engulf and destroy the unified tonal outlines. A pervasive process was bound to take hold in harmony as the individual progression gained in significance, even without reaching the ultimate consequence – the total disruption of the original embracing tonal unity. When a harmonic style reaches the point of highlighting the effect inherent in the unmediated collision of two chords as a specific effect in itself, we then have a phenomenon that, in its content and significance, lies on the same evolutionary path as the third evolutionary stage, the highlighting of an individual chordal, sonic quality as such, and prepares the way for it as well, as a preliminary step in the escalation toward the absolute individual effect.

The unmediated effect inherent in the succession of two harmonies is thus to be designated a progression effect [*Fortschreitungswirkung*]. The emphasis in harmonic practice shifted to [that unmediated effect] only after a certain diffraction into varied colors of individual stimuli was initiated in the general artistic expressive will. And, in connection with this, as always, the heated energetic sensibility had already led to the abundance of color stimuli that characterizes the Romantic spectrum. It is also clear that the highlighting of individual progression effects was associated initially and more commonly with the more conspicuous, *harsh* and, accordingly, usually tonally more complex harmonic successions, less with the simplest progressions, in which this effect is of course also present, if more discreetly. It is based on the relativity of *two* successive harmonies, not yet on the absolute effect of *one* harmony as such. Although it is, accordingly, *inherently relative*, I call it the *absolute* progression effect when such an individual harmonic succession is thrust *outward* – i.e., in relief against the surrounding context [265] – as a characteristic sonic appeal as such, as the unique effect of connecting two harmonies. Here, an internal evolutionary path of ever increasing significance is initiated early in the Romantic period, a path which has its psychological origin in the delight in the sonic appeal itself.

The destruction process and its countereffect in tonality

It is self-evident that the evolution [of the dissolution process] begins within the structure of uniform tonality and remains at first inconspicuous in its effects. Thus even though the evolution, in its escalation, is a highly significant aspect for the history of style as well as for music psychology and theory, it was until now ignored by theory, inasmuch as theory limited itself to verifying and reconstructing the embracing tonal continuity, even in cases of harsh progression effects asserting their autonomy. Such work did fulfill a necessary and essential need. In a biased view, however, only the one facet of the phenomenon was considered: its roots in the soil of tonal uniformity, the binding forces. It is also necessary, though, to keep these aspects in mind regarding further evolution, to recognize in them the seeds and the driving forces of growth in a much more complicated harmonic technique that reaches into new realms. Harmony, in *all* of its manifestations, has two sides which theory must examine and trace to their psychological foundations: a retrospective side, leading back to the beginning and essence, and a prospective side, tending towards autonomous liberation. The evolutionary path, in its beginnings, must therefore be followed within tonally uniform contexts, long before those contexts are breached and burst by the emergence of the absolute progression effect. Both sides, a clinging to the fundamental structure of tonality and an initiative toward its expansion and dissolution, can be observed in the new Romantic style in full inner life, and in the most intense evolution, at their most critical stage in *Tristan* – effect and countereffect.

In the first expansions of the cadence by means of applied dominants, and more yet by means of intensified shifts toward both [266] dominant regions, the effect of individual progressions already presses ever further to the fore. The development diverting attention away from the embracing tonal effects toward the individual ones is already clearly prefigured particularly in the collision of harmonies from remote tonal regions, and here, too, it was brought out how intensive light and color effects arise in connection with all of these expansions. Thus, to recall just one of the examples cited in that context, observe how poignantly the harmonic shift from G7 to the A♭ major chord in Example 4.3 [K70] is *isolated* for its own sake as an affective and coloristic impression. . .[15]

It is clear from this procedure that the actual content of the [compositional] conception lay in the progression effect as such, not in a tonal continuity with a central, fundamental harmony. . .For the theoretical conception it follows from this fact that the phenomenon underlying the progression is grasped at its core, and the isolating effect of the progression acknowledged, even when tonally unifying continuity embraces it. As explained, this process of course greatly expands the tonality. . .[267] A proof of how the musical characteristics of the leitmotif are transferred to this chromatic progression is also evident in the way its *progression effect* even occurs motivically, *as such*, in the course of the work, at the vague allusions to the idea of death, e.g., in Act 1, Scene 4, after Brangäne's question, "wolltest du fliehn? Wohin soll ich dir folgen?" at the progression E♭7–E7 in the orchestra, before Isolde's answer.

Ex. 4.17 [K160] *Tristan*, Act 1, Scene 4 [Schirmer, 62]

---

[15] [LR] The example, in *Romantische Harmonik*, 154, is from *Tristan*, Act 1, Scene 2 [Schirmer, 21–22], where Brangäne sings "das ist der Herrin Will'." Kurth also calls attention to the so-called Death-Motive (Kurth's Ex. 54, *Romantische Harmonik*, 132; Schirmer, 16, mm. 5–11), where an A♭-major chord collides with A major. He analyzes the progression in C minor, starting with a VI. He calls the following A-major harmony an "intensive dominant effect" but does not label it. He assigns roman numerals iv, V/V, and V to the remaining chords. Kurth characterizes the passage as typical of the *Tristan* music, which regularly circumscribes the tonality without actually stating tonic harmony.

We might interpret the A-major sonority as a contrapuntally modified D♭-minor chord, D♭(=C♯)–F♭ (=E)–B♭♭(=A), where the B♭♭ is a dramatic appoggiatura to the chordal fifth, A♭ (NB the relationships, expressed in reverse here, of the G♯–A appoggiatura figure in the Love-Motive, given enharmonically in the Death-Motive as B♭♭(=A)–A♭. Love and Death intersect in G♯/A and B♭♭–A♭.

Other authors who have analyzed the Death-Motive include Schoenberg ("Brahms, der Fortschrittliche," *Stil und Gedanke, Aufsätze zur Musik*, trans. Gudrun Budde, ed. Ivan Vojtech, Gesammelte Schriften, vol. I [n.p.: Fischer Verlag, 1976], 40; "Brahms the Progressive," *Style and Idea*, ed. Leonard Stein, trans. Leo Black [New York: St. Martins Press, 1975], 403); Georg Capellen ("Harmonik und Melodik," 19–20); and Heinrich Schenker (*Harmony*, ed. Oswald Jonas, trans. Elisabeth Mann Borgese [Cambridge, Mass.: MIT Press, 1973], 107).

(Also, just one measure later, G7 to G♯7.) The death symbol also flickers when, in Act 1, at the end of Scene 3, [268] nothing but the highly significant, eerie progression B♭7–B7 occurs between Brangäne's allusion to the love potion ("Den hehrsten Trank, ich halt' ihn hier") and Isolde's reply, "Du irrst, ich kenn' ihn besser. . ." [Schirmer, 54]; similarly, in the next scene, the chromatic progressions accompanying the equivocal words of Tristan, who is prepared for death: "Los den Anker, das Steuer dem Strom!" [Schirmer, 87], etc. The idea of death also appears in the harmonic change from A♭ major to A major at Isolde's narrative (Act 1, Scene 3), "Den als Tantris unerkannt ich entlassen, als Tristan kehrt er kühn zurück" [Schirmer, 37], and elsewhere. Thus a similar phenomenon, observed earlier with a single harmony (the first chord of the Prelude), manifests itself here in *Tristan* with a plain harmonic progression operating in and of itself: the rise [of a progression] to the significance of a leitmotif.

Technically, however, a case like this one is highly characteristic for the autonomy of the absolute progression effect precisely because it shows, on a small scale, how an enormous expansion of the concept of tonality takes place as long as a [tonal] uniformity still embraces all of the erratic, remote progressions. For the absolute progression effect is one that issues from tonality itself, and lay dormant within it all along. . .

[269]. . .With the escalation of the Romantic character of art, in addition to the effects of *chromatic* progressions, those of *mediant* progressions of all types increase greatly. Shifts of harmonies whose roots lie a major or minor third above or below one another, unlike those previously discussed mediant progressions that belong to *one* key, direct our attention to their harsh and multi-faceted appeal. The Romantic delight in color also extends to unmediated harmonic progressions whose roots are separated from one another by diminished fifths, augmented fourths, and other *altered* intervals. Such shifts appear early, often like a wedge driven abruptly into an otherwise straightforward series of harmonic connections. Hence a rift opens up on the series, a rift that is then bridged by a returning progression, or by a broader coherence. [270] Early Romantic music is already full of examples of this type. . .[16]

[275] Many motives. . .are based on the unmediated, absolute effect of tonally remote progressions. The [following] ecstatic harmonic progression resounds at the waving of the Grail in Wagner's *Parsifal*. [276]

---

[16] [LR] As examples, Kurth cites, among others, an excerpt from Berlioz's song "Au cimetière" (*Nuits d'été*, op. 7, no. 5), measures 9–15, where the harmony cycles from D major through B♭ and F♯ major, and then returns to D major.

Ex. 4.18 [K168] *Parsifal*, Act 1, Scene 2 [Schirmer, 91]

In Act 3 [Scene 2], the Grail-Motive, harmonized tonally at first. . . .is intensified to yield harmonic progressions whose colors diffract into the most glaring spectrum.

Ex. 4.19 [K169] *Parsifal*, Act 3, Scene 2 [Schirmer, 276]

[277] The roots of the first two chords proceed by a diminished fourth (E♭–B), the others by thirds, so that the octave is completed in descending equal steps: E♭–B–G–E♭. The supernatural strangeness of these harmonies lies throughout in the effect of the connection itself. Wagner especially loves to symbolize everything magical by means of the absolute effect of unfamiliar harmonic connections, e.g., the magic of the Tarnhelm with its disjunctive mediant shifts in *Das Rheingold*, or the related Magic-Potion-motive from *Götterdämmerung*. . .

The absolute harmonic effect

[297] It is in the nature of the process by which individual harmonic effects become autonomous that the absolute effect of progressions leads to the *absolute* effect of *harmonies*. Since the relativity of the effects is reduced to ever smaller dimensions and details, music naturally arrives at the effect of a harmony as such. Aside from opening chords, such a harmonic effect can of course never be separated from the effect of the progression. For no matter how clearly a harmony is elevated to autonomy and protrudes from the surrounding context, its effect is always influenced at least by its relationship to the preceding harmony, even if its tonal relationship is neutralized due to the complete dissolution of the key. Nevertheless, as was stressed earlier, a convergence alone toward the absolute harmonic effect still does not occasion a complete overcoming of the harmonic effect that results from its large-scale tonal relation.

Some of the examples cited already show that an extensive dissolution of harmony into progression effects leads to a focus on the individual sonority. In Brangäne's "Wachtgesang," for example, the absolute character of the harmonies, which shine forth as a special coloristic effect, is latent in the potent harmonic shifts.[17] The style of *Tristan* thus appears as a crucial turning point in the historical evolutionary curve because it not only highlights the absolute progression effect to the point of creating a fluid play of colors but also initiates yet another culmination that, with the exclusive appearance of all of these elements, later leads to an impressionistic form of expression.

On the one hand, the absolute harmonic effect is tied to the special qualities of the harmonic *form*, with unique effects of fusion. On the other hand – and this is above all the case with forms of the consonant triad – it goes back to the unique character of the whole *key*, as always represented most clearly by its tonic chord [298]. (It is in the nature of the phenomenon that it is mostly linked to particular instrumental colors.) The first case, where harmonies strive for an absolute autonomous effect based on their unique *form*, becomes more common in music only from about Wagner's later works onward. The introductory motivic chord of the *Tristan* Prelude illustrated such a case.

But one should not overlook that the absolute character of a *key*, too, only emerges from established relationships that were originally mutually dependent. For its effect did not emerge from, and establish itself as a result of, the absolute

---

[17] [LR] Kurth refers here to *Romantische Harmonik*, 285, where he first mentions the "Wachtgesang." The passage in question is in *Tristan*, Act 2, Scene 2 (Schirmer, 169–72), where Brangäne first warns the enraptured lovers of the approaching dawn. Kurth is calling attention to chord progressions such as G major – C♯ major – A minor (Schirmer, 170, mm. 6–9), G♯ minor – D major (Schirmer, 171, mm. 1–2), and others in the passage cited. The progressions accompanying Brangäne's plea "Habet acht!" are particularly striking, where D major harmony moves via chromatic voice leading to F♯ major harmony (Schirmer, 171, mm. 10–11).

acoustical pitch level of a tonic triad, but rather as a result of its position in the constellation of keys. The ever greater, luminescent intensification in the transition to more remote sharp keys, [and] the opposing internal dynamic process in the transition to flat keys, bring about the association of a specific character with a key as such. . .[18]

[299]. . .A passage in *Tristan*, for example, such as the one in Act 1 (Scene 5) at Tristan's words "War Morold dir so wert. . .", shows how the darkening of flat-key shifts leads naturally to flat-key chords that, taken in the absolute, act accordingly as individual dark tintings. The instrumentation, too – an alternation isolating low woodwind harmonies from pizzicato strings – shows that the chords here are introduced as coloristic accents as such.[19] The inseparability of the absolute progression effect from the absolute harmonic effect manifests itself very clearly in passages of this type. Observe, for instance, the emergence of the absolute harmonic effect of the E♭-minor chord in the following measures.

Ex. 4.20 [K185] *Tristan*, Act 2, Scene 1 [Schirmer, 113; Dover orchestral score, 225–26]

Here, too, right after the first of the quoted chords (full orchestra), and the second (strings), the E♭-minor chord is emphasized in dark woodwind colors. . .[20]

---

[18] [EK] C major is perceived as the middle and foundation for two reasons. First, in the historical sense the C major region is the homeground and point of departure of harmonic development in sharp and flat keys; the church modes already revolve around this center. Further, though – and this is by far more significant than the historical development – C major signifies again and again the origin and central starting point of musical sensibility for individual development, starting from the beginnings of musical training. This position establishes itself and determines not only the character of C major itself but all other keys as well. The effect of E major, for example, depends on the way it distinguishes itself essentially from C major. The whole absolute character of a key, reflecting back to C major, is thus not given in the nature of music but rather in the particular course of [music] history and pedagogy.

[19] [LR] Kurth is referring to a passage found in Schirmer, 77 (mm. 15–18).

[20] [LR] While the E♭-minor chord is striking to be sure, effectively highlighting the word *Späher* ("spies"), and does protrude locally, the subsequent harmonies clarify its meaning. Depending on how broad a context we consider, the chord is either an altered dominant preparation in B♭ (B♭: IVb) or, looking further ahead (Schirmer, 114), it might be analyzed on a higher level as a cadential six-four chord, moving to a V7/V in the key of E♭ major/minor. The full impact of an absolute chord, i.e. its aurally jolting effect, depends primarily on the immediately preceding chord or chords, as Kurth has said. The subsequent music generally integrates the seemingly deviant chord into a broader tonal context.

[301]. . .[I]f the fragmentation into separate absolute chordal colors is traced beyond Wagner, many such passages would be misunderstood artistically as well as technically the moment the autonomy of the individual effects is ignored as the fundamental trait. A chief hallmark of this development, from the beginnings of the Romantic period up to the present, is that those individual absolute effects occur ever more rapidly and with greater iridescence. This [development], too, is a symptom of inner harmonic seething. Confronted with such a technique and mode of perception, it is necessary to guard against applying a schematic of tonal reinterpretation where it would only be used with rigid pedantry, as a formula, and would not suit the creative content, which gradually yields a wholly different principle of coloring. Theorizing does not mean forcing things into norms that are already making way for other norms. Rather, it is a matter of recognizing the logic of the ongoing developments, according to which former norms are superseded. Otherwise theory loses its basic purpose and, caught in a biased view that no longer suits the premises, [302] is capable of seeing only confusion where, in reality, not the musical style but the viewpoint is confused. The following passages are also cited as isolated indications of how harmony in the period after Wagner often dissolves into individual impressions of chords that become symbols of harmonic colors [*Klangfarbensymbole*].

Ex. 4.21 [K188] Richard Strauss, *Salome* [Boosey and Hawkes, 6]

The cold A-minor chord. . .is an absolute harmonic effect that, with its coloristic and affective content, is motivated by the word "tot". . .[21]

---

[21] [LR] Here again, as with Example 4.20, the subsequent harmonies (after Ex. 4.21, A7 and D minor) help to explain the jolting A-minor chord.

[303] In the following passage from the same work, the individual tones of a melodic motive are accompanied by chords that are to be registered simply as harmonic impressions regarding their own tonal color as well as their form [i.e., their intervallic structure].

Ex. 4.22 [K190] *Salome* [Boosey and Hawkes, 173]

[304] The form [of the chords] arises as an autonomous fusion stimulus, which is why the dissonant chords dispense with all resolution. Additionally, the harmonic progression moves around a stationary pedal-like c'... Further, passages like the following are a fragmentation of tonality into individual harmonic reflexes of the same type [as in Ex. 4. 21].

Ex. 4.23 [K192] Richard Strauss, *Elektra* [Boosey and Hawkes, 34]

All of this illustrates not only the extraordinary proliferation of coloristic ideas but above all also their convergence in a new formal principle that transforms this [local] harmonic scintillation into large-scale contexts. The *technique is based not merely* on *the individual colors* but rather *primarily on the flux of colors*. Everywhere, the technique appears in connection with the highly fluid melodic gliding of harmonies into one another, just as the *alteration style* promoted [the harmonic flux] from the other [i.e., the sensuous] side.

[305] Even if it is characteristic that this Romantic phenomenon, too, is motivated and promoted to such a large extent by dramatic elements, still it is by no means limited to the joining of music with poetry, and also arises from the modified character of the music itself.

The dissolution into colors in the Romantic period extends yet further, to individual *tones*, just as it did to individual harmonies. Hence it also prepared the way for a type of musical perception that employs the tones and fusions of tones simply as color qualities, and surmounts the original structural principle of the harmonies – everywhere processes leading first to an *atomization* of music, from which music in turn amasses new possibilities.

5

Broader dimensions of Romantic harmony

Having covered many local details in parts 2, 3, and 4 of *Romantische Harmonik*, 3rd edn., in part 5 ("Paths of tonal development"), Kurth broadens the harmonic perspective to embrace larger units. Already in part 3, chapter 5 ("The intensive alteration style") he widens the harmonic context by examining "extratonal" progressions and introducing the idea of "basic pillars." When each sonority in a series of chords is viewed as a neighbor-note displacement of its successor, the result is a chromatic progression, which generally leads to a logical tonal goal, i.e., to a basic pillar ("Chromaticism of chord connections," pp. 219–28; see *EKATA*, pp. 181–85). In part 5, chapter 2, Kurth stretches the harmonic-tonal compass yet further in an investigation of sequences ("Paths of melodic innovation"). He analyzes a few short sequential passages (Exx. 5.4, 5.5, 5.6), and describes several large-scale sequences, one of which spans the first and second scenes in the first act of *Tristan* (pp. 342–43, 353–55).

One of the largest and most celebrated analyses in *Romantische Harmonik* is of the prelude to Act 1 of *Tristan* (part 5, chapter 1, "Paths of harmonic expansion," pp. 318–27). Robert Bailey translates the analysis in *Prelude and Transfiguration from "Tristan and Isolde"* (New York: Norton, 1985, pp. 196–204). The only other extended analysis in *Romantische Harmonik* is of the prelude to Act 3 (pp. 314–18), which is translated below. In both analyses Kurth demonstrates that, despite many exceptional harmonic turns and tonal detours, the music of the prelude to Act 3 nevertheless expresses a single key – quite straightforwardly in light of the basic pillars.

CHROMATIC CONNECTIONS OF HARMONIES

[219] The third component of the alteration style, chromaticism of chord progressions, is intrinsically related to the two previously discussed components.[1] Generally speaking, [such chromaticism] is caused by harmonic connections brought about simply by chromatic movement of single tones, or of all tones, such that this continuation of the individual chord tones can take different directions simultaneously. Hence, due to alteration, a special technique arises for con-

---

[1] [LR] The three components of the alteration style are, according to Kurth, harmonic alteration (chromatic modification of chord tones), neighbor-note insertion, and chromatic progression. He lists these in *Romantische Harmonik*, 185. Harmonic alteration and neighbor-note insertion are discussed in my chapter 4.

necting harmonies, which breaches the tonal principle in chord progressions. As long as it is a matter of chromatically modifying chord tones and of neighbor-note insertion, for the affected tones it is still a question of semitone voice leading [220], and that means that this component [chromatic progression] cannot be strictly differentiated from the ones discussed earlier. . .But this principle [of chromatic progression], which arises directly from those aforementioned phenomena, attains much greater independence, influences even unaltered tones and chords, and allows chromatic continuation of individual, or of all tones, to occur by perceiving them as leading-tone tendencies to the upper or lower adjacency [*Nachbarstufe*]. Thus all original meanings of a harmony may appear overturned with respect to its progression. For example chromatic movement induces progressions of this type:

Ex. 5.1 [K124] *Tristan*, Act 2, Scene 2 [Schirmer, 144]

Every chromatically led tone acquires a leading-tone function in relation to a tone of the following chord, so that a supple intermeshing is produced in such chromatic progressions. . .

[221]. . .Thus arise not only the most diverse and colorful extratonal chord *connections* but also, in the chromatic movement of voices, chord *forms* that cannot be explained tonally and did not arise tonally.[2] [222] Here again, there is an overlap between this technique and the two aforementioned components of alteration. . .

[224] Compared to [the] fluid, often insipid progressions of his predecessors, *Wagner* intensifies chromaticism in harmonic progressions to the greatest power. The harmonization of the "Tantris-Motive" in *Tristan*, for example, is based on the same principle.

---

[2] [LR] Rudolf Louis and Ludwig Thuille mention chromatic progression in their *Harmonielehre*, 276–77, and provide a primitive instance in their Example 288. The Appendix of the book comments on excerpts from the music of Peter Cornelius (Ex. 7, p. 350), Hugo Wolf (Ex. 10, p. 352), Richard Strauss (Ex. 32, p. 365), and Chopin (Ex. 34, pp. 367–68). The comments on Example 13, from Strauss's *Till Eulenspiegel* (p. 334), uses the expression "extratonal chromaticism" (*aussertonale Chromatik*, p. 355). Kurth seems to follow August Halm's description of chromatic progression (Halm, *Harmonielehre*, 100).

Ex. 5.2 [K130] *Tristan*, Act 1, Scene 3 [Schirmer, 34]

[225] The beginning and end of this two-measure structure exhibit a tonal connection, VI and V in A minor. The second chord, by contrast, results from the chromatic contrary motion of the voices, a process expressed tangibly in the notation. Wagner notates the harmony which, externally, is an F♯ chord, with b♭' in the descending motivic voice and, at the same time, with A♯ in the ascending bass. (See the motive in its longer chromatic extensions.[3]) Such notation reflects clearly the primal instinct for *linear* motions. For when the melody has a b♭' together with the F♯ major chord, it is not the convergence on the notated chord that is essential but rather the melodic course of the main voice. If we pursue this motive in musical perception, the chord does not in fact sound consonant at all because the melodic tension in it is not absorbed. Of course, as was emphasized already, the enharmonic technique has its other side, too, and is sometimes decisive for the opposite effect. For the frequent incorrect notation is expressly intended to simplify the chord as a whole [and] is then, conversely, an expression of the embracing sensuous fusion and absorption of all melodic elements in the fullness of the chord.[4]

As long as it is a matter of tonally closed continuities, as here, and not of modulatory transitions into other keys, the convergence of the voices into tonal chords, as into basic pillars of the passage, must always be examined at the endpoints of such passages, as well as at certain intervals.[5] Occasionally, when harmo-

---

[3] [LR] The meeting of b♭' and A♯ in the same chord illustrates what Kurth was describing in the second sentence of this chapter, about individual chord tones going in different directions simultaneously (see above, p. 130). Some longer examples of the Tantris-Motive may be found in Schirmer, 31–32, and at *Vivace* on page 33. The Tantris-Motive merges with a variant of the Love-Motive on page 31, at "im Sterben lag," when Isolde starts to recount how she healed Tristan.

[4] [LR] Kurth discusses the effects of enharmonic phenomena on harmonic alteration in *Romantische Harmonik*, 62–72 and 211–19. When he says that the enharmonic technique can have the "opposite effect," he means that, in contrast to his Example 125 (*Romantische Harmonik*, 220), where a seemingly consonant chord is actually dissonant, enharmonic phenomena can occasionally turn an otherwise dissonant chord into a less dissonant, or even quasi-consonant, chord.

[5] [LR] "Basic pillars" is my translation of *Grundpfeiler*. Elsewhere, Kurth calls such basic pillars "framing pillars" and "framing chords" (*Romantische Harmonik*, 317 [*Gerüstpfeiler*], 375 [*Gerüstakkorde*]). Kurth hears the main harmonic connection in Example 5.2 as VI–V, thereby reducing the status, not only of the apparent F♯ major chord, but also of the ii7 in the second measure. Given the clear B–E skip in the bass, it seems likely that Kurth

nies that cannot be interpreted tonally result from chromatic voice movements, it becomes clear how, in an internal dissolutive process, the original tonality of chord progressions disintegrates into a chromatic streaming of voices. These pillars and buffers disappear, however, where instead of tonally closed contexts a tonal transition arises, which often results in extended, purely melodically determined intermeshing of harmonies.⁶

In such abruptly disjunctive harmonic progressions, the meshing of ascending and descending linear tensions often engenders a succession of tonally remote chords and thus a distinctive iridescence of flashing and fading harmonic colors. Such is the case in the splendid, authentically Romantic symbolization of a dream-like suspension of the senses in the "Sleep-Motive" from *Walküre*.

Ex. 5.3 [K131] *Walküre*, Act 3, Scene 3 [Schirmer, 297–98]

[226] Apparent deviations from chromaticism as the foundation for harmonic connections occur here because chromatic-melodic progression is not bound in all cases to one and the same voice but rather continues as a line only ideally, insofar as only chromatically related tones are contained in the chords.⁷ The bass voice

---

heard a ii7–V harmonic progression, rather than hearing the ii7 as a neighbor-note chord to V. By reducing Example 5.2 to VI–V, in addition to distinguishing between chromatic passing and diatonic structural chords, Kurth had also distinguished between diatonic chords of greater and lesser weight.

⁶ [LR] See *Romantische Harmonik*, 366–72.

⁷ [LR] Kurth meant that the chromatic voice leading may migrate among parts, and thus only be implicit, rather than remain in a single part, making it explicit. For instance, the eb″ in the first chord of Ex. 5.3 (right hand) appears to continue with f♯″. Ideally, however, the eb″ continues with d♯′ (left hand) and then, chromatically, with d′.

in particular deviates often and acquires in part the character of chordal bass notes. In this way, the bass points up another phenomenon that goes hand in hand with such chordal chromaticism and arises from it: the formation of sensuously luxuriant chordal effects, especially mediant progressions, which, except for chord progressions whose roots are chromatically related, are always the most prevalent. Everywhere, Romanticism exploits the ability to hear one and the same phenomenon in two and more ways; it is fond of this coexistence [227] and its indefiniteness. . .

There is yet another technically noteworthy phenomenon in the last example. Here, too, it is clearly discernible how the free, continuous flow of the harmonic progressions caused by chromatic voice leading always seeks a certain stability and restraint in tonal continuities. The chord progressions turn repeatedly toward authentic [*dominantische*] cadences, initially at two-measure intervals. The first two-measure group leads into the beginning of measure 3 [of Ex. 5.3] with such a cadence (E major); similarly, the next two-measure phrase leads into the C-major chord of measure 5 with the dominant-like effect of the diminished-seventh chord B–D–F–A♭. From the sixth to the seventh measure, the two-bar cadential motion leads to the G♯ major chord by way of the (imprecisely notated) diminished-seventh chord F𝄪–A♯–C♯–E, and the motion is again evident at the transition from measure 8 to 9 as a cadence from the dominant-like diminished-seventh chord on D♯ to the E-major triad. In these straightforward cadences, we recognize how the free harmonic flux repeatedly seeks to stabilize and anchor itself on firm ground. The particular significance of such dominant-like cadential transitions moving toward continuation emerges later especially with Wagner's *sequential* technique.

If we look more closely at these two-bar dominant-like cadential motions, however, and at the chords into which they converge, they again exhibit a genuinely Romantic peculiarity. The initial chords in measures 1, 3, 5, 7, and in the last measure, are major chords on roots A♭, E, C, G♯, [and] E. Thus together they form mediant progressions (A♭ and G♯ being enharmonically equivalent) consisting only of descending major thirds. Moreover, the harshness of the *mediant progressions* in the harmonies acquires an appropriate complement in the harmonic *forms*, the chordal third appearing in the upper voice throughout, as is characteristic of Romantic harmony. The uniqueness of Romantic harmony emerges radiantly everywhere in Wagner's music.

The intensive alteration style, with all of its components, is nothing but the complete saturation of all harmonic-tonal foundations with subsonic dynamic forces. [228] The chromatic principle of chord connection shows this process at its height by illustrating an acquiescence of the tonally organized harmonic surface, as well as [illustrating] the reciprocal flux among its individual elements, its chords, under the upsurging pressure of the underlying energetic currents. It is the dissolution of tonal relationships due to the energy of tone tendencies. For [harmonic] forms, as for harmonic progressions, the highly developed alteration technique boundlessly expands the musical possibilities, and everywhere ruptures the stable structure. Everything surges and flows.

Historically, the evolution at this point reaches precisely the opposite stage of music of the end of the sixteenth and the beginning of the seventeenth century. There, as a rule, euphonious consonant harmony prevailed, shading off into dissonant formations only in local details. Here, in the high Romantic period, tensions are the rule, consonant harmonies the exception.[8] Even these [occur] as points of repose only in isolated cases, mostly as new initiatives toward constantly resurgent restlessness (whereby it must also be considered that a large portion of externally consonant chords must also be understood as tension chords, and from the outset cannot lay claim to the significance of points of repose). But it is not only through alteration that music is subject to this general permeation with dissonance.[9]

PATHS OF MELODIC DISRUPTION

The sequential technique of the Romantics

[333] While the whole play of harmonic light and color, which initiates the expansions of harmony, results from the escalation of all potential energies, the influences of kinetic energy also increase greatly throughout. Melodic phenomena in the most diverse forms also disrupt and destroy [334] tonal continuities. While an *organic* disintegration and dissolution from within was observed in the case of potential energy, the flowing linear force produces *disruptions* that simply sever the tonal development. Sequences and their derivatives are the most common manifestation in which this [process] occurs.

Their great significance is that they are used more and more widely and innovatively in the Romantic period, especially because of Wagner's influence.

---

[8] [LR] In contrasting the predominantly consonant harmony of the decades around 1600 with the predominantly dissonant harmony of the late nineteenth century, Kurth overlooks how early seventeenth-century composers, particularly Monteverdi, exploited dissonance for dramatic effect. One of the chief issues in the Artusi–Monteverdi controversy was the "proper" use of dissonance (see Claude Palisca, "The Artusi–Monteverdi Controversy," *The Monteverdi Companion*, ed. D. Arnold and N. Fortune [New York: Norton, 1968], 135–42, 153–57).

[9] [LR] This final sentence, about dissonance in Romantic harmony originating in sources other than alteration, is a brief, suggestive transition to part 4 of *Romantische Harmonik*, "Paths of harmonic development," where Kurth discusses certain harmonic procedures that contribute to the style of late Romantic harmony. He covers, among other things, chords beyond the triad and the effects of thirds as chordal building blocks in general, deceptive cadences, absolute progressions, absolute chords, and mediant progressions. These procedures were discussed in my chapter 4.

But from technical viewpoints, too, sequences undergo freer extensions, which indicate a profound influence of melodic elements in the whole tonal development and design. A sequence arises whenever a particular melodic fragment is repeated such that each time it moves up or down by a certain interval. If those movements no longer occur as "tonal sequences" – that is, if the individual repetitions no longer occur in the same key – then the harmonic continuity is breached and a movement of whole harmonies by a certain interval simply sets in. The extratonal sequence arises. It was also called "mechanical," because melody and chords are simply transposed completely unchanged, while in the tonal sequence the relative intervallic relationships must undergo certain modifications in order to conform to the prevailing key. While the expressiveness [of the tonal sequences] is justified solely from the purely technical standpoint, the most powerful effect is typical precisely of the [extratonal] sequences which prevail with the Romantics. But even with the tonal sequence, a *melodic* factor is already the bearer of the harmonic development: the constant stepwise ascent or descent. The melodic energy is the primary feature, the impelling content that causes the manner and order of the harmonic progressions, the only difference being that it does not yet destroy the structure of the tonality. The harmonic foundation holds the sequential motion at bay.

Accordingly, the sequence evolves from the isolation of defined melodic elements, just as the absolute progression results from the isolation of harmonic phenomena. The connection between the two, already touched on in the previous section, is obvious.[10] All sequential segments begin [335] with a wrenching effect [*Rückungseffekt*], and the shorter the segments become, [and] the quicker these wrenchings follow one another, the more prominent and colorful these progressions become. The melodic energies that well up from below prevail over the principle of tonal connection and sweep the harmonies along with them. Sequences are a series of undulations that disrupt the harmonic surface of the music.

As with the individual tones in a melody, in a sequence entire melodic phrases are seized by a dynamic progression and are swept along as unified structures. Hence the sequence could be defined as a melodic progression [*Melodiezug*] that consists not of tones but of whole motives and, moreover, out of motives with their entire harmonic networks. For this reason, though, it is generally a matter of only very simple forms of motion, usually only uniform ascents or descents in which the motive being sequenced moves upward or downward, since this overall motion can be traced beyond the fragmentary dimensions of the sequence motives. Every motive is a unit, specifically the unit of a tension process. And it was inevitable that Romanticism adopted this type of unified structures in even greater

---

[10] [LR] Kurth refers here to a large section in his chapter on "The interior dissolution of color in Romantic harmony" (*Romantische Harmonik*, 262–97). Parts of his discussion are included in our chapter 4.

measure than did Classicism. Often a melodic segment that, in continuous flux, emerges out of the context without previously having been a motive, is seized by the sequences and in this way *becomes* forged into a motive, i.e., into a closed dynamic unit.

Compared with tonal connections, a shift into sequences generally signifies an intensification, as does any wrenching effect. The extratonal sequence, though previously common enough, begins to replace the tonal sequence with the Romantics. The ease with which the melodic element gains ascendancy over the harmonic element is also evident in this fact.

The technique attained by the sequence in Wagner's music became fundamental for the entire subsequent output of the Romantic period. It is easy to outline with individual examples. . .[336]

Ex. 5.4 [K193] *Tristan*, Act 1, Scene 5 [Schirmer, 92]

The individual sequential segments are marked off here with brackets. The relationship of a tension chord and a resolution chord represents in each case the motivic formation, the first chord always as a dominant with a leading-tone intensification of the fifth, i.e., G7 with a D♭, A7 with E♭, B7 with F, etc. Consequently, the succession of these individual motivic groups, the interrelationship of the resolution chords, is no longer tonally but rather melodically determined, as a constant shift up a major second (simple transposition) of the whole cadence of these motivic groups, C major, D major, E major, [and] subsequently by a minor third (G major). The procedure of maintaining the same interval as the basis of the sequence and then *changing* the *distance of the shift*, evoking new, enhanced effects from the altered relationship of the harmonic progression, is common.

It is interesting to contrast this with the way the same motive is sequenced in the Prelude (mm. 36ff) such that the sequential motion is based, not on the resolution chords, but rather on the *tension* chords. This circumstance leads to a distinction [337] because here [in Ex. 5.4] the resolution chord is not always in the same relationship to the tension chord, so that the three resolution chords no longer form a sequence. This dual possibility in the same sequential motive shows how flexible the whole principle of sequence is. These are the measures.

Ex. 5.5 [K194] *Tristan*, Prelude to Act 1, mm. 36–40

Initially, the motive is set with the harmonies G7–C7, again with the fifth of the first harmony altered to D♭. A simple repetition at the octave ensues in the next measure, shifting from strings to woodwinds (notice how the sequential principle is always closely linked with that of simple repetition). The second time, the motive appears with the harmonies A7–D7 (the tension chord [A7] once again has its fifth altered), accordingly moved up a major second. After yet another repetition [of the chord pair] at the octave, the sequence continues such that the first chord [B7], in all its tones, is again moved up a major second higher than the second tension chord [A7]. Only this time [the tension chord] acquires a new meaning, not as a dominant to the resolution chord but rather as identical with it.[11]. . .Both are B9, [338] only at first with the leading tone f [bass] (actually e♯)

---

[11] [LR] Kurth explains what he means by one chord being "identical" with another in *Romantische Harmonik*, 206, 209–10. See Kurth's discussion of Examples 4.15 [K109] and 4.16 [K114].

to f♯. Consequently, the sequence lies only at each *beginning* (roots of the tension chords: G–A–B), not at the *endings* of the motive, as in Example 5.4. The third resolution chord no longer forms a sequence with the first two...[12]

[352] Concerning the moderating of the sequence principle regarding its more essential, *melodic* premises, the following motive illustrates the beginning of a continuous process.

Ex. 5.6 [K206] *Tristan*, Prelude to Act 3, mm. 11–15 [Schirmer, 216]

[353] The sequenced motive extends as far as the first phrase marking indicates, and is *internally* tonal (A♭: I–ii). Initially, an extratonal sequence using this motive ensues, lasting up to the onset of measure 4; the sequence is designed such that the lower voices [mm. 1–4] slide chromatically downward. From this point onward, however, the passage continues – if only for the brief ending portion – such that this melodic flow engages all voices and draws them [chromatically] downward until they meet in the final C7 chord, which again, like the initial chord, is in a simple tonal relation with the main key (F minor).[13] The melodic motive of the sequence disintegrates; consequently, the sequence simply undergoes a dis-

---

[12] [LR] Kurth chooses his musical examples carefully, for their structural properties as well as for their dramatic contents. In the case of Example 5.4, the dramatic content is especially poignant. The music follows immediately after Tristan and Isolde have drunk the love potion and, in a mixture of surprise and confusion, slowly begin to feel its effects. Kurth alludes to the dramatic element, but without explanation. Regarding the structural properties, he mentions the change in the sequence interval from whole steps to a minor third, but again without explanation.

As Kurth indicates, the passage in Example 5.4, together with the preceding music, is analogous to a passage in the Prelude to Act 1 (mm. 32–41; see Ex. 5.5). There, the sequence leads up by whole step (C–D), just as in Example 5.4, and continues with a harmonic progression that leads to a B7 chord (bass: F–B), hinting at E major. The net bass motion is thus C–D–B. Example 5.4 leads, not to E major, dominant of the Prelude's A major/minor orientation, but to a G7 harmony, which introduces C major, the closing key in Act 1, and signals the approaching end of the act (sailors' entrance). The sequence sets in just after a D-minor chord has been tonicized and leads, normatively, to the G7 harmony via the net bass motion C–D–E–G.

[13] [LR] Although Kurth does not mention the idea of controlling basic pillars in connection with Example 5.6, his remark about the C7 being "again...in a simple tonal relation with the main key" indicates that he is aware of larger harmonic processes in operation. The remark implies that the comprehensive harmonic design up to measure 15 of the Prelude to Act 3 would be f: i (m. 2) III (m. 11), V (m. 15).

solution into free-flowing voices and, accordingly, into free-flowing harmonies. Everything begins to flow and streams downward, up to the convergence on the final chord. This leads to a further principle, intimated only briefly here, that becomes very significant for the later Romantic period, and that also appears apart from direct dependence on the sequence: vis à vis the chordal organization, the lines often assume primary importance for entire passages, and produce the harmonic progression as a by-product. . .

[342] Large-scale sequences, with motives of greater dimension. . .also have a singular technique, which becomes universal in the high Romantic period. They usually embody the expression of great solemnity in their broadly extending cycles. [343] Wagner's *Nibelungen* is especially rich in examples [of this technique]. Note in this regard the harmonization of the second strophe of the *Nachtgesang* in Act 2 [Scene 2] of *Tristan*, for instance, beginning at the words "Barg im Busen sich uns die Sonne. . ." [Schirmer, 166]. A *technical feature* that typically characterizes Wagner's large sequences manifests itself here, namely a *truncation of the sequenced fragments* in the course of their unfoldment down to a brief compression of the escalating waves. All of the first six measures, starting in A♭, constitute the initial sequence motive; they are already rent in the middle by a descending mediant progression (A♭–E). The whole six measures are first repeated a half step higher, beginning in A ("Von deinem Zauber. . .").[14] A truncation to a two-bar sequence follows immediately thereafter, starting in B♭ ("Herz an Herz. . ."), then, after two measures, in C♭ ("Eines Atems. . ."), and finally, two measures later, in C ("Bricht mein Blick sich. . ."), after which the sequential organization stops.

At the *Liebestod* melody in Act 2 [Scene 2, Schirmer, 178], the same phenomenon of sequence truncation appears in the first sixteen measures in the following manner: the first motive, four measures long ("So stürben wir, um ungetrennt. . ."), begins in A♭; the next four measures ("Ewig einig, ohne End'. . .") are a sequential shift of the first four measures up a minor third, beginning in C♭ and leading enharmonically into the second cycle, as explained on [Kurth's] page 281. Wagner is especially fond of such *enharmonic linking of sequence groups*. Then a truncated sequence ensues, so that only the *two*-measure head-motive is treated, once again shifted up a minor third (augmented second), beginning in D with the two measures [at] "ohn' Erwachen." Subsequently, yet another minor third up, the two-measure group "ohn' Erbangen" enters in F, the next two measures in A♭, and then the next two in C♭. The same steady and ever impelling truncation of the segments can be observed in almost all of Wagner's broadly structured sequences. . .

---

[14] [LR] Note that while the *harmonic* design of the sequence continues past the A-major harmony, the *melodic* design changes. The association of the keys of A♭ major and A major by means of harmonic and melodic sequence here is not fortuitous (NB the Death-Motive).

[353]...Yet to be mentioned is a completely different expansion of the sequence idea, in which the melodic movements in the *large* become a guiding element for the development of the harmonic design. Often, in the midst of a broadly escalating passage, a theme (and usually the following events as well) periodically moves a step higher or, conversely, a step lower. These are no longer sequences in the strict sense because the intervening sections up to the new beginning are no longer completely alike. The guiding formal idea, however, is based on the stepwise movement up or down of the beginnings of these individual developments and thus derives from the sequence idea, which is spatially expanded here and thus internally moderates its strict imitative principle. In this manner, the harmonic design evolves in large *stratified tiers*, which, especially in Wagner's music drama, are motivated by a poetic idea or a certain scenic vividness. [354] They, too, are also only a special case of the technique of the undulating intensifications that emerge as a formal principle with the late Romantics.

The symphonic interlude preceding scene 4 of *Rheingold* can be recalled as a very clear example of this procedure [Schirmer, 156–57]. Summarized simply, the "Giant-Motive" appears in the second part [of the interlude], from *moderato* onward, initially in C major, a little further on in D major, and then in E major. Each time the subsequent motives and events are also moved one step higher, although the repetitions are not exact. Barely consciously, musical hearing and formal perception follow these tiers. Nevertheless, they conceal not only the fundamental idea of formal coherence but also the feeling of a steady musical intensification. In the case at hand, a certain scenic vividness also comes into play, which may have led Wagner (consciously or more likely in unconscious intuition) to this design. The scene on the "summit of the earth" (Giant-Motive!) arises from out of *Nibelheim*, with Wotan and Loge, who ascend to the heights, toward Valhalla.[15]

This [type of] harmonic-formal exposition occurs very clearly and beautifully in *Walküre*, Act 2 [Scene 4, Schirmer, 152–54], at the beginning of the Death-Proclamation scene: at the slow approach of the Valkyrie, the Fate-Motive [our Ex. 4.16, Kurth's Ex. 114] and Death-Proclamation-Motive (with their repetitions and sequels) move up by step (diminished third) over a broad span from F♯ minor to A♭ minor. It is a sequence of a very large dimension and of enormous, uncanny tensions.[16] Similarly, the two appeals by the Royal Herald to the heavenly court in

---

[15] [LR] The ascending stepwise sequence Kurth points out continues past the E-major harmony. Although the Giant-Motive disappears, the harmony ascends further to F minor and then to G7 (Schirmer, 158).

[16] [LR] Many analysts have discusses the harmonic events in the Death-Proclamation scene, notably Josef Schalk, in "Das Gesetz der Tonalität II," 383–87; and Anton Bruckner (see Wason, *Viennese Harmonic Theory*, 79). Werner Breig offers an interesting interpretation in "Das Schicksalskunde-Motiv im 'Ring des Nibelungen'," 223–34.

Lohengrin, for example (Act 1 [Scene 1, Schirmer, 38, 40]), appear first in D minor, then, after a brief intervening scene, in E♭ minor, spreading tension-filled anticipation over the whole event with this intensification.[17]

Such a design is found somewhat more obscurely, for example, in a section of the Prelude to Act 2 of *Tristan*. The passage from measure 33 to measure 50 appears a whole step higher at measure 50 [Schirmer, 106–7]; for the most part, [it is] repeated exactly, [355] changed slightly only in the final measures (the section from the last half of m. 46 onward). This sequential idea occurs yet further expanded in *Tristan*, even spanning two passages from the first and second scenes of the first act. The motive of the sea voyage appears initially in E♭ major [Schirmer, 6–7] and later, in the second scene, in F major [Schirmer, 19] (where Brangäne exits to the ship's deck). A [tonal] brightening and powerful momentum are also symbolized here in the broad, indistinct sequence idea (observe its frequent occurrence in expository sections!).[18] In the first movement of *Bruckner's* Seventh Symphony, the preparation for the reprise is carried out similarly: the main theme appears first in C minor [Nowak ed. (1954), m. 249], then, after a few intermediary passages, in D minor [m. 261]. [It] disappears once again and returns in E♭ major [m. 277], and finally in E major [m. 281], with which the main key and the return of the opening – the start of the reprise – is reached. The fact that here the last two of these graduated thematic entrances are placed so close together is an expression of the preparatory tension focused on this moment [in the piece]. The same idea also occurs with powerful effect in *Salome*, by Richard *Strauss*, in the symphonic interlude prior to the Prophet's ascent from the well. The motive of his prophesy appears first in E♭ major, then again in E major, complete with the subsequent surging developments.[19] The whole formal idea can be found repeatedly in the large forms of the Romantic era, as well as in symphonic poems.

---

[17] [EK] Something similar is found in Bach's *St. Matthew Passion*: the third chorale ("Erkenne mich mein Hüter") is first in E major and then, after a brief recitative, is transposed without changes to E♭ major ("Ich will hier bei dir stehen") in a solemn [tonal] darkening.

[18] [LR] The passage with the motive of the sea voyage is in Kurth's Example 37, *Romantische Harmonik*, 100–01; Schirmer, pp. 6–7. The music turns toward the key of F major before the Voyage-Motive returns in that key in Scene 2 (Schirmer, 17). The tonality at the opening of Scene 2 hovers between E♭ major and C minor, leading soon to the Death-Motive, in C minor (Schirmer, 16). The tonality then shifts gradually to F major, which begins to establish itself where Brangäne speaks of Tristan's renown ("dem Wunder aller Reiche," Schirmer, 17). At her words "des Ruhmes Hort und Bann?" there is a deceptive cadence in F. The music then oscillates around F up until Isolde sings "O, er weiss wohl, warum," where an excursion to C minor intervenes, a modally mixed dominant to F. After a cadence in C, the Voyage-Motive enters in F, on a V7. In sum, Scene 2 opens by moving toward and then establishing the key of F major, modulates to a dominant-related key, and finally back to F for the Voyage-Motive. The tonal shifts occur at dramatically significant moments: at the Death-Motive, at the reference to Tristan's fame, and at Isolde's reference to her past encounter with Tristan. A dramatic heightening thus parallels the harmonic "brightening" and "momentum" which Kurth mentions.

[19] [LR] Richard Strauss, *Salome*, piano-vocal score, ed. Otto Singer (1905), 33–34.

It embodies a certain epic breadth and lends perspective to the stratification in the harmonic development.

PATHS OF TONAL DEVELOPMENT
PATHS OF HARMONIC EXPANSION

[314] To begin, this topic involves the foundations for getting an overview of large-scale tonal development.[20] The entire technique of broad coherence, in its internal logic, derives from fundamental processes that are exemplified in short, [tonally] closed developments, and that ultimately evolve from the fundamental harmonic motion of the most straightforward cadence. However, not only does the tonal development grow to enormously expanded proportions, but also the whole range of [tonally] disintegrative forces. If we view large contexts, it is above all, and to a much more significant extent than before, the disintegrative force of endless melody that influences the tonal plan. It transforms the [tonal-harmonic] cycle, which in closed musical forms tends to return to the initial key, into a continuous stream of harmonic developments. This stream preserves the tonal unity generally only for specific passages of widely varying length, which often dissolve altogether into discrete harmonic effects in the manner described.[21] Consequently, regarding the question of large-scale tonal developments, we must always first decide whether, and to what extent in individual cases, a cyclical and overarching [tonal] design really occurs, and whether it is intended, at least roughly, i.e., with certain deviations. The influence of the music drama here, and especially the pioneering status of *Tristan* in the evolution of Romantic music, strongly encouraged [315] a compositional principle that, in contrast to Classicism and early Romanticism, extended tonal closure less and less over large cohesive passages, and yielded more to a free modulatory development.

On the other hand, *Tristan* in particular exhibits the above-described internal expansionary processes of tonality up to the outermost limits. Accordingly, given

---

[20] [LR] This section translated here is from the beginning of part 5, chapter 1 of *Romantische Harmonik*. In this first sentence Kurth refers to the ground he has covered in the two chapters of part 4, p. 229–313, sections of which are included in the present volume, pp. 127–29.

[21] [LR] Kurth is referring to the end of part 4, chapter 2 in *Romantische Harmonik*, 305–13, entitled "Constructive and destructive forces," which summarizes the findings of chapter 2 (on absolute progressions and absolute chords, in this volume pp. 119–29), but also considers the whole alteration technique. Destructive forces are those energetic melodic and harmonic forces that undermine the tertian structure of individual harmonies and distort their normative tonal connections and coherence (neighbor-note insertion, chromatic progression, extratonal sequences, absolute chords and progressions). Constructive forces are those that preserve tertian structure in chords and promote broad tonal coherence (chords beyond the seventh, which fortify tertian structure, basic pillars). Heightened to their maximum, however, constructive forces become destructive ("Alles Konstruktive übersteigert sich ins Destruktive, im Klang wie in der Tonalität," *Romantische Harmonik*, 311).

the distinction made earlier [between interior and exterior expansion], one should think here more of the phenomena of interior expansion and dissolution than of the exterior phenomena, i.e., of the expansion of tonal coherence over widely spaced framing points [*Gerüstpunkte*], since there are only a few sections [in *Tristan*] that are unified cyclically over long passages of music.[22]

The tonal unfolding [*Entfaltung*] employs all technical elements that, emanating from even the simplest cadence, enlarge the network of related harmonies. An organic growth process begins with these harmonies in every instance where paths for development are prefigured in the nature of harmony. However, while with the Classicists the [tonal] unfolding was carried out in a certain equilibrium even in cases of large [tonal] units, it is characteristic of the intense desire in the Romantic period for expansion that everywhere the urge for intensification grows powerfully and transforms the harmonic development into a restless, fitful, elementally unbanded flux. The growth of harmony proliferates wildly in all directions. Sensuous as well as energetic elements [of harmony] achieve tremendously magnified effects.

It is in the nature of the tonal maturation process, which includes ever more remote relationships and strives to embrace ever freer harmonic contexts, that it culminates in undefinable transitions and generally also unifies all individual technical elements. Consequently, specific, selected examples and references can illustrate the process only as stages in an ongoing evolution. Since the basic processes have already been discussed, a summary in broad outline can now follow and confine itself to examining a few models.

One of the few tonally closed pieces from *Tristan* is, for example, the *Prelude* to the third act; it is almost self-contained, although it does lead directly into the beginning of the first scene. It illustrates an extraordinary amount, above all a general trait typical of the high Romantic temperament: [316] even though it is not very long, it does contain a wealth of bold and far-reaching tonal digressions in its internal development. The method by which these digressions are always linked to a firm tonal framework illustrates clearly one model of harmonic expansion. This method reflects a line of tonal development which, in innumerable forms, runs through Wagner's music, as well as through that of the stylistic trend influenced by him. This line begins with a basic idea embodied in the simple cadence and projects it over larger dimensions. It, too, can lead to greater or lesser weakening of tonality. At first glance, the short prelude to the third act of *Tristan*

---

[22] [LR] Kurth discusses interior and exterior expansion of tonality in *Romantische Harmonik*, 280. Briefly, exterior expansion occurs when extratonal chromatic passing chords connect the "basic pillars," i.e., the tonal harmonies (see the discussion following our Ex. 5.2). Interior expansion occurs when the basic pillars exhibit exceptional harmonic relationships, e.g., mediant or more remote relationships. See *EKATA*, 200, 204, 207.

exhibits confusing departures from the main key of F minor. The tonal connections appear when we mark them off in larger spans instead of tracing the individual [harmonic] turns. Moreover, these connections are highlighted for the most part by pronounced fermata-like caesuras, although Wagner actually notates a fermata at only one of these places. The prelude is divided up into short sections, and even though they may lead into remote tonal areas, their initial and final harmonies are clearly and simply rooted in the main key. Since we are concerned here only with the large-scale path of tonal development, with the overall organization, it will be sufficient to highlight essentially only these structural pillars [*Eckpfeiler*].

The first motivic group lapses in measure 10; it begins on IV in the key of F minor, and closes with V (indicated by e′′′–g′′′).[23] (The individual developments contained therein have already been discussed on [Kurth's] pages 53 and 251.) The subsequent section reaches from measure 11 to measure 15, is developed internally as a sequence (see [our] p. 139), and is bounded as its beginning by f: III and at its end by f: V7⁷. Measures 16–25 are a repetition of the initial motive, altered only at the ending, and link f: IV to f: VI, concluding with a quasi-fermata. The subsequent sequential passage of measures 26–30 picks up from f: VI [m. 26], with the chord of measure 30 leading directly into the next motivic group, which reaches up to measure 37. The harmony in measure 30 is, as explained on [Kurth's] page 58, a tension chord that is identical with its resolution chord, i.e., a ninth chord, G–B–D–F–A♭, distorted by alteration; that is the applied dominant in F minor. Starting with that applied dominant, the phrase discussed earlier ([Kurth's] p. 239) [317] likewise leads to a close on the same G9 chord (m. 37).[24] Finally, in measure 38 the last section begins similarly, with a tension chord that is identical with its resolution chord (m. 39), thus once again a ninth chord distorted by alteration; C–E–G–B♭–D♭ (f: V9). This final section ends in measure 52 on the tonic, with the entrance of the shepherd's pipe on stage.

The large *tonal* continuity is thus preserved by means of the beginning and ending chords, from which the individual segments branch out to their more remote harmonic developments. Those chords represent among themselves an extremely simple, cyclical cadential progression in F minor, with a secondary dominant, the applied dominant harmony in measure 30 and 38, [and] otherwise with nothing but chords of the main key.[25] By means of these cadential chords at

---

[23] [EK] The first chord is not to be understood as f: II (G–B♭–D♭–F)! See [Kurth's] p. 53. [LR: In *EKATA*, 201, I suggest that I–V, rather than IV–V, describes the overall harmonic motion in measures 1–10. See note 24 below.]

[24] [LR] Kurth's references in this paragraph to pages 53, 58, and 239 are to his Examples 4, 9, and 139. *EKATA* comments on those examples in the discussions around Examples 6.3, 8.16, and 7.5, on pp. 139, 180, and 156, respectively. I discuss Kurth's analysis of the prelude to Act 3 on pp. 201–04.

[25] [LR] Kurth calls the harmonies in measures 30 and 38 applied dominants (*Zwischendominant, Wechseldominant*), although only the harmony in measures 30–37 is an applied dominant. The harmony starting in measure 38 is the dominant, f: V9, as Kurth explained at the end of the preceding paragraph.

the boundary points, the individual segments are strongly distinguished from one another in the structure of the prelude. If we were to assemble these boundary chords into a progression, disregarding everything lying in between, it would be extremely simple:

[mm. 1   10   11   15   16   25   26   30   37   38   52]
f: IV – V – III – V – IV – VI – VI – V/V – V/V – V – I

This [schema] expresses the principle by which the tonal development is accomplished. For these boundary chords are the framing pillars [*Gerüstpfeiler*] which support the whole prelude. It is nothing but a *growth* of the simple cadential relationships to larger dimensions, whereby the individual original chords of a cadence are transformed into the core structures around which entire *chord groups* unfold. In order to reconstruct the tonal coherence, we must examine not the successive harmonies of the prelude but rather the individual, prominent ones which, as bearers of the tonal development, produce its basic design. The intervening passages can strive variously to break out of the key. In the present case, this occurs especially by means of free sequences [discussed above], albeit in relatively brief digressions. This entire development model is very old. Works of the Classical and pre-Classical epochs conform to it, and it derives ultimately from the cadential fermatas of the Protestant chorale. Notwithstanding all other features of the [Romantic] compositional technique, the model acquires new forms in the Romantic style not only through its expansion but rather chiefly through the restlessness and wealth of the digressions. [318] The basic idea itself is thus not new. From Wagner's later style onward, however, it is significant that the clear, accentuated statement of the tonic chord is forcefully and characteristically suppressed. As in small contexts, such suppression is also evident throughout the entire third prelude of *Tristan*. The first entrance is not even an F-minor chord, and that harmony appears somewhat suppressed in the initial motive, only emerging out of the compressed tension formations at the end of the second measure. The individual segments themselves are not bounded by the tonic. Even within them it is sounded

---

It is interesting to compare Kurth's harmonic-formal partition of the prelude with that of Alfred Lorenz (*Der musikalische Aufbau*, 132-34). Lorenz disagrees with Kurth's grouping of measures 26-30. According to Lorenz, "something new starts at measure 30 without question" (p. 133n). Consequently, he ends the preceding segment at measure 29, on the dominant of a G♭ major harmony (expressed with Riemann's function symbols, the D of the S). It is true that, harmonically, texturally and orchestrationally, something new begins at measure 30. It does seem somewhat arbitrary, however, to close a formal unit at such a metrically weak moment, and on the dominant of a modified subdominant harmony. Lorenz does this in order to distinguish the *Abgesang* in the local bar form (mm. 26-29) from the ensuing global *Abgesang*, starting in measure 30. In addition to the harmonic and metric peculiarity of his reading, by cutting off measure 29 from measure 30, Lorenz neglects the phrase markings (clarinets, horns, bassoons), which extend to the downbeat of measure 30.

only a few times. Analogously, the harmonic framework of highlighted chords avoids it. Thus as the scene [1 of Act 3] opens, the conclusion on the tonic at the end of the prelude has the effect of an enormous release of harmonic tension.

With this developmental principle, too, the possibilities for expansion are contained in the technique itself. They can originate either from the harmonic framework itself, which can veer off to several applied dominants or to even more remote chords, or from the intervening passages, which can expand further and suppress and conceal the stable points, and are also capable of unbounded unfolding into remote tonalities.

Actually, the very old idea of the autonomous tonal digression in individual passages interpolated similarly into a tonal framework and branching off from tonal chords can be viewed, on the other hand, as an enormously broad expansion of the idea of applied dominants. Instead of individual chords, entire developments nest between the actual tonal harmonies.

The third of the *Tristan* preludes thus represents a [compositional] principle whose generalization follows naturally, and which embodies myriad possibilities for application.

PART III

Bruckner

6

Bruckner's form as undulatory phases

The translations in chapters 6 and 7 of this reader are from *Bruckner*, vol. I, part 2 ("The dynamics of form"), chapter 2 ("The Symphonic Wave"). Part 1 provides the cultural background for the composer's work, and includes a psychoanalytically oriented biography. For Kurth, Bruckner was a mystic, whose personal and creative tensions combined to produce a music shaped by dynamic processes. These Kurth expounds theoretically in part 2, chapter 1 ("Bruckner's formal principle"). In the ensuing chapters he then illustrates analytically various facets of the process, starting in chapter 2 with some basic traits of "wave dynamics" (*Wellendynamik*), such as wave initiation and dissipation; reverberatory waves; the illusion of symphonic "space"; dynamically determined motivic transformations; and the organicism in wave structure. Most of the musical examples are relatively brief, the longest being the openings of the first and last movements of the Sixth Symphony. Kurth discusses these longer passages in short segments, the goal being to show how Bruckner hierarchically builds the overriding continuity and dynamic logic from short segments.

Readers should keep in mind that some of Kurth's analytical commentary depends on first-edition scores that are now considered obsolete. Analytical statements that rely on unauthentic orchestration, registration, dynamics, and phrasing, for example, may not hold up in light of modern editions of the symphonies. Although certain of Kurth's analytical statements may no longer be fully supportable, his idea of dynamic form, and the musical criteria employed to illustrate it, are nevertheless significant and remain valid in principle. In order to appreciate and learn from Kurth's work in *Bruckner*, it is necessary to evaluate his analyses in the context of the unauthentic scores. My notes point out the textual discrepancies that led Kurth to interpret the music as he did.

THE SYMPHONIC WAVE

Introductory example and general characteristics

[279] Although thematic content, arrangement, construction, [and] outline cannot be ignored in Bruckner's formal principle, we cannot gain an understanding of [it] by pointing to an actual theme and [theme] groups, etc., but rather by illustrating how basic symphonic motions appear in developmental waves, as energetic events, in light of which themes and, likewise, the further expansion up through the

formal design as a whole first become understandable. The challenge lies in grasping the forms synthetically instead of analytically. However gloriously and directly the theme may shine forth in Bruckner's music, the most essential property is its efficacious verve and unfolding (*Entfaltung*). On the other hand, we very often encounter the phenomenon where Bruckner does not begin with the theme at all but rather with a preliminary development that builds up to it, as the following examples will now show.

Just as in [Bach's] monophony the *motive* appears as the unit of a dynamic phase [*Bewegungsphase*], so too *developmental waves* appear as uniform respirations [*Atemzüge*] in the overall symphonic motion.[1] And just as it would be misguided to view a melody as pieced together from motives, the examination of symphonic music can also proceed from the larger undulations, whose course more properly refers back to the smallest component waves [than vice versa]. Moreover, it will become clearer that with Bruckner so-called endless melody prevails, which even in the individual line does not permit the component motives to be separated but more often illustrates their fluidity. To a far greater extent that is the case with symphonic waves.

If it is a matter of first isolating certain typical primary motions from the formal principle, then we must not shy away from focusing [280] at times on seeming minutiae. As in all of the phenomenal world, essential elements are often concealed. Ultimately, the details coalesce quickly into continuities, and the view of the symphony is then finally able to corroborate them from other [larger] perspectives. The comparison of the beginnings of two movements, for example the beginnings of the first and last movements of the sixth symphony, illustrates various techniques. The latter movement is better suited as a point of departure.[2]

---

[1] [LR] Kurth discusses the motive as the unitary dynamic phase in *Grundlagen*, 24–25: "An indivisible [melodic] formation which represents itself to us mentally as a complete, distinctive unit, as a dynamic phase, is to be designated a motive when, in the course of the compositional process, it controls a work or a part of a work..." (*Grundlagen*, 24). Regarding dynamic phases, see our chapter 1, p. 42, and note 8. When Kurth says monophony, he has in mind the melodic style exemplified in Bach's solo violin and cello works. He expresses this opinion in *Grundlagen*, 145 (see our chapter 1, p. 49).

[2] [EK] The premise for the musical examples had to be to give the reader a simplified score, not in the strict sense of a "piano arrangement," even though it is reduced, as far as possible, to the summary view of a piano setting. Hence from the outset we have abandoned the idea of adapting certain orchestral performance indications – such as, for example, tremolo or the like – to the distinctive and modified performance mode of the piano. Individual tones were doubled, too, when their inclusion was required in two different sections of the orchestra. Whoever has been trained according to the old orthodoxy of piano instruction may be confused by this at first. That was not the intent, however, and one will very quickly become accustomed to this clearer presentation, which does prevail in all better piano scores. Often, for the sake of clarity, the range of the piano had to be exceeded without apprehension. On the other hand, simple modifications – such as omitting inner voices or occasionally even octave changes – were considered permis-

Ex. 6.1 [K1] Sixth Symphony, Finale, mm. 1–7[3]

[281] It is the first initiative of a very broadly escalating development. The illimitability of such a component wave, its formal tension directed at larger surges, is the first thing that presents itself purely intuitively. However, the purely technical phenomena cooperate in creating that effect, down to the smallest strands. In order to penetrate Bruckner's technique of formal development, we must first learn to translate the sonic image into an energetic image.

Viewed as a whole, this first small surge illustrates how, formally and dynamically, its beginning and end correspond. At the beginning there are sonic and symphonic stirrings in the first quivering of the softest tremolo, a mere whisper, more an energetic than a sonic impulse. After the release of the upper voice, there is an arpeggiation in the quickening bass line (with the fourth skip A–E), amid the

---

sible if they served clarity. Otherwise, however, in the case of individual examples, reproducing the score with varying completeness was determined by the various things that had to be clear in the example, according to the explanations, now more the internal structure, now more the overall summary, which was subject to the greatest simplification (similar to when it is necessary to take in a natural phenomenon, now in a close-up view, now in a wide-angle view). In part, it was a matter of illuminating [*beleuchten*] the exterior of symphonic motions, in part of throwing light onto the *interior* [*durch*leuchten]. Thus it would have been useless schematicism to simplify all examples according to the same model; the purpose of the discussion had to be decisive from case to case. In other words, the simplification of the score to a sketch could not always be effected in similar proportions.

[3] [LR] Kurth probably used a version of the first published edition of the score, prepared by Cyrill Hynais (Doblinger, 1899), which according to Deryck Cooke is "unauthentic" due to tamperings with dynamics, phrasing, and tempo markings, as well as to suggested cuts (Cooke, *The Bruckner Problem Simplified* [New York: Novello, 1975], 12). Nowak discusses the genesis and publication of the Sixth Symphony in the preface to his Bruckner-Society edition (1952). Example 6.1 matches the Nowak edition.

continued quivering of the tremolo's energetic impulse.[4] Following the initial linear progressions, the tremolo rings out again for an instant and allows the growth and ferment that engendered the initial lines of force and the sonic density to resound once more from the void. It is a reversion to nothingness from the initial sonic materialization. Taken as a small symphonic component wave, the whole exhibits a formal unity that could not be more dynamic: everything is vitally directed toward coming events, in this case toward the theme. For this is hardly a matter of foreshadowing the theme in the formalistic, i.e. in the motivic sense, but rather more generally [it is] the *motif of evolutionary growth [Werden]*.[5]

This motif explains the sense, will, and the beauty of the unpretentious dynamic lines that arise from the initial symphonic impulse of the two-measure tremolo. The upper voice, too, is only an individual strand, only the onset of a motion faintly drifting downward in gentle spirals [282], neither a theme nor a "melody" in the traditional sense, but rather a first emergence from silence of linear quiverings along with the inception of the *bass part*.[6] The bass, too, appears hurried and also exhibits an overall descending tendency amid weak rebounding waves. Notice that these waves do not run parallel to the upper line (except for a single spot in m. 5, where [the parallelism] has a completely coincidental effect).[7] The [bass] line, resounding in sharply plucked, soft *pizzicato* notes, is likewise just an instrumental effect that serves the formal dynamics. It is the as yet *immaterial, brittle tone production* that *Bruckner* always employs *mainly in evolving* or *dissipating developments*.[8]

---

[4] [LR] Melodically, the beginning and ending of Example 6.1 correspond with F–E–D, although the association is weakened in measure 6 by the fleeting rhythm, by the abbreviated F, and by the lack of octave reinforcement. Allowing the end of a wave to dissipate to an energetic level below that of its beginning makes an ensuing escalation appear more vivid and dramatic.

[5] [LR] Several authors, among them Max Auer (*Anton Bruckner*, 354), Karl Grunsky (*Anton Bruckner*, 40–41), and Ernst Decsey (*Bruckner*, 125, 142 [quoting Oskar Lang]), have noted the characteristic beginnings of Bruckner's symphonic movements. August Halm calls Bruckner a "Master of beginnings" ("Musikalische Bildung," *Wickersdorfer Jahrbuch 1909* [Jena: E. Diederichs, 1910], 61; reprinted in *Von Form und Sinn der Musik*, 219). He singles out the Fourth, Seventh, and Ninth symphonies as clear examples. Of such beginnings he says, "We sense it: a piece of music is not beginning here but rather music itself commences" (*Die Symphonie Anton Bruckners*, 42).

[6] [EK] This is one of the cases where, in *performance*, it would be incorrect to bring out the lines in the violins with feeling. It is an art in itself to shape them as the spasmodic primordial formations that they are. From the first measure on, the movement could be ruined if one tries here to wring out something lyrical or the like.

[7] [LR] Actually, the bass and soprano do run parallel for the most part. Significantly, the contrary motion at measure 4 occasions a dramatic peak, where the clarinet becomes melodically active and the key of A minor crystallizes momentarily. The slight crescendo further reinforces the peak. The complementary diminuendo and parallel motion in measure 5 signal a dissipation.

[8] [EK] Wherever *pizzicato* has this common formal significance of brittle tones, no matter how minimal the external dynamic, or how delicate the *diminuendi*, one should play it as a plucking with a certain inner power, not as a playful strumming, and above all mindful of its explosive sonic dynamic. (It is clear that this is not the only kind of *pizzicato* in Bruckner's music, but even elsewhere it is never used playfully in his works; it is always an instrumental expression of tension.)

Like the tremolo, the *pizzicato* appears in this small initiatory gesture as a partial instrumental expression of the gesture's tremendous formal tension.[9] Looking deeper into the inner structure, we come to sense the formal logic in small, still less pretentious embryonic phenomena. An inner voice in the clarinet is also present. If we were to examine the score purely analytically, this clarinet voice would seem to be merely a partial reinforcement of the violin part. Viewed synthetically, the tiny voice means something else within the total dynamic. The voice likewise represents energetic impulses, churned up from the internal motions, but not lasting beyond the energy of the first volitional gestures [*Willensansätze*]. The impulses are absorbed in the more turbulent motion of the upper voice (unison) after a small upward spiral barely arose independently. That is the animated dynamic content of the small "imitation" on the second quarter of the fourth measure, a content that can in no case be understood from the thematic-formalistic standpoint. [283] Small though the phenomenon may be, it reflects the whole *mode of comprehending imitative* and other formalistic *phenomena* in Bruckner's music on a large scale. Looking ahead, if we recognize in the activity of the inner voices one of the most essential interior processes in the impelling growth of formal waves, then it becomes even clearer that we have [here] more and something different than an instrumental "reinforcement" or a "variation" on the main line by the clarinet. If unfulfilled impulses linger even here in this unpretentious inner voice, then the *timbre* of the thin and "transparent" *clarinet tone* also agrees, orchestrationally, with the dynamic-formal phenomenon of a gentle undulatory intensification surging from within. This surging is always a chief trait of wave formations, even when as a whole they are in the process of deintensifying.

But we must guard against seeing all of this too much with the eye. Even the individually demonstrable lines are to be felt, not for their own sakes, but merely with regard to the totality out of which their entire structure is generated. The lines, including the upper voice, are only formal symbols that serve the idea of initial primordial shaping [i.e.,] energetic impulses, a first casting of symphonic mist. Despite all the simplicity [of the process], it is evidence that the symphonic, not monophonic, melos prevails, even where one voice may predominate. The individual strands and component phenomena, by contrast, reach [our] consciousness only afterward.[10] Tracing the total symphonic undulation seems difficult

---

[9] [LR] The low register and rhythmic steadiness of the pizzicato notes, together with the quick tempo, jointly convey a strong sense of restlessness and anticipation. The accented dissonances in measure 4, beats 3 and 4, and on the first beats of measures 5 and 6 heighten the tension. Kurth does not mention these details, but they contribute to the anticipatory character he senses.

[10] [LR] Earlier (our p. 152), Kurth compared Bach's monophonic dynamic phases to Bruckner's symphonic undulations. Now, referring to monophony again, Kurth contrasts the mono-linear dynamism of Bach's solo string works with the multi-linear dynamism of Bruckner's symphonic texture, where even a momentarily predominant line has meaning only in the context of the surrounding linear forces.

only from an erroneous viewpoint. In reality, [tracing the undulation] is simple to the point of being self-evident since it corresponds to the creative process, which should not at all be thought of as "calculative." Precisely here we can observe that amateurs often have one of the many advantages of impartiality over professional musicians.

If with Bruckner it is above all a matter of listening to the development, then we must also turn our attention to the interaction of the interior *curves* themselves. The upper voice, as the initiator of a subsequent long and powerfully expanding developmental progression, exhibits something very characteristic: although it is a hint of a large intensification, the upper voice itself drifts downward in a *de-intensifying* process and, on closer inspection, exhibits a *downward* drifting motion in all of its component motives as well. Thus a force arises even on the small scale which later, in the context of large series of waves as well, is [284] apparently contradictory, i.e., when viewed analytically, but which is highly logical with regard to the synthetic reality. Bruckner is fond of the power of large *tierings* [*Schichtungen*], whose individual component motions do in fact lead downward from the very outset, but which build up linked series of intensifications. Even here, the frequent, multifariously occurring idea of inner conflict manifests itself.[11] The undulations do not unfold directly but rather amid the urge from other, partly cooperating, partly conflicting forces, very much in the manner of natural rolling and storming. Further, the upper voice itself exhibits in all of its individual motions the outline of a play of curves permeated in its overall motion by a chaotic interior dynamic, as if it were moving resolutely, without counterforces, in a straight line. A similar feature is present in the bass, only in a different form. Hence the individual lines [in Ex. 6.1] exhibit the reverse of the subsequent development in the overall series of waves that adjoin this initial six-measure component wave. For the individual lines assert their downward urge over the opposition of rebounding motions. By contrast, the entire subsequent wave series is an intensifying force that prevails over the individual symphonic waves of primarily downward tendency. Such an undulant buildup that arises from downward hastening tiers is, on a large scale, one of the most powerful formal ideas [i.e.,] a forward urgency transcending constantly waning and newly waxing force. The constant overreaching initiatives, surmounting previous ones, achieve in this way an interior agitation completely different from the mere gradual ascent of the individual upper-voice

---

[11] [LR] The "synthetic reality" consists of the tremolo, low-register pizzicato, the small melodic rise in the clarinet, as well as the overall sense of sonic growth and attenuation over the course of Example 6.1. Timbral, registral, and articulatory criteria, as well as the comprehensive dynamic curve, override the general descending melodic tendencies. Direction alone, Kurth points out, does not always determine whether the dynamic function of a passage is progressive or recessive.

beginning. It becomes a struggle and a hastening onward amid the threatening depletion of forces.

If we trace the very extended undulatory buildup that culminates ultimately with the emergence of the main theme, the component waves appear everywhere determined by the lively activity directed at the ensuing development. In order to get an understanding of a few main features of Bruckner's wave dynamics, it will be sufficient initially to pick out some individual characteristics. At first, the same component wave is repeated, unchanged, from measures 7–11 (without the two introductory tremolo measures). Of course this repetition does not occur in the sense of a *partially completed* symmetry [285] but rather in the opposite sense of an *inaugural* tier, pointing forward. *Repetition* can mean various things, and it would be good if the consideration of Classical traits of form would also free itself from disabling bias in understanding the repetition principle. Repetition can contribute just as well to the intensification as to the lapsing process. The subsequent measures [mm. 11–13, Ex. 6.2] clarify how the repetition fits in with the developmental progression. The recurrent, descending component tier [*Teilschichtung*] flows into the following wave tier, which is also repeated and exhibits a highly characteristic reference to the very first tier.

Ex. 6.2 [K2] Sixth Symphony, Finale, mm. 11–13

It is a foreshortened and also internally abating fade-out of the beginning. Among the lines of force in the [downward] drifting wave motion – still involved in a vague, primordial stage of formation – it is the upper voice that first loses its spiraling shape and runs downward without reversal. It summarizes the entire original progression of the initial wave (Ex. 6.1) in a brief impulse. It is not the "imitation" of a section that is decisive here but rather the formal symbolism of the whole: a slackening of tension within the whole first initiative. Thus rectilinearity is by no means always an expression of increasing energetic tension. On the contrary, as a release from the undulating countertendency [*Gegenstrebung*], here it is the manifest linear symbol of the final, rapid lapsing of force. In this instance the bass is likewise rectilinear, except for its last arpeggiated fragment. Conversely, it is highly characteristic that just at this point, during the weakening of the principal motion, the barely revived inner voice (clarinets) surges upward from its first, unconsummated impulse. In a vigorous arch, it intercepts the fading [286] final tone of the upper line (violins). Intoned in the airy, transparent sound of the clarinet, the inner voice gains scope and strength, though still not impelling strength.

Hence the energetic process of this small symphonic component wave [mm. 11–13] is as follows: it does have a lapsing quality, but that is only a part of a whole, of a beginning, which heads not toward a complete dissipation but on the contrary toward the first large-scale development. It is characteristic of Bruckner that here both processes manifest themselves in the individual wave, the fading out of the component tier and, with regard to the overarching, comprehensive development, the will toward growth. Bruckner shapes such interaction – *an anticipation, derived from the momentary dynamics, of the subsequent dynamics of broad continuities* – by the most diverse means and in countless ways, of which one of relatively simple immediacy in its individual linear forces is present here. Again, it is the idea of an internal countertendency, and once again the typical picture manifests itself. Beyond the entire descending and dissipating motion, the symphonic component nevertheless surges upward from within: the wave form.[12]

When Bruckner repeats these two measures unchanged ([mm. 11–12 repeated in] mm. 13–14), the repetition occurs in the same sense as the earlier, opening measures, as a symbol of the continued influence of an initiated basic motion, in both cases [mm. 7–10 and 13–14], as part of a subsiding partial de-intensification integrated within the [overall escalating] developmental course. That course prevails over all of the attenuating stages of these initiatory waves, practically to the point of complete quiescence. This [process] occurs as follows.

Ex. 6.3 [K3] Sixth Symphony, Finale, mm. 14–19

[12] [LR] Recall that in Example 6.1 the clarinet first ascended at the local wave crest, in contrary motion to the violins (m. 4), and then descended with the strings in parallel motion. In measures 11–12, by contrast, the clarinet does not reverse directions. Instead it ascends steadily, in contrary motion to the violins and basses, and opens the way to further development.

Ex. 6.3 (cont.)

[287] The upper voice is reduced to the residual two-note motives (d′-e′). But one should consider that, as small motivic fragments, they are *initiatory gestures in the midst of the ebbing away*, not repetitions of the final fading two-note motive ([i.e., of the tones e′-d′] in the upper voice in the preceding measures). A more essential element lies concealed in the directional reversal: embryonically, a will to ascend, to evolutionary growth. Behind the reversal, there lies none other than the dynamics of countertendencies (if yet slight) in the *feeling of anticipation arising from the current* passage *directed toward imminent events, and toward the whole*. The wave lapses with the will to continuation – vitality permeating the most concealed elements. Accordingly, this sonic attenuation cannot be understood in light of individual linear strands. Dynamically, it is easy to detect what will become of the remaining voices. The inner voice (clarinets) first shifts from its rising arch into an oscillating motion, encircling stationary tones, that seek the equilibrium of complete tranquility. This repetition of the inner-voice motive also exhibits a regression, a flagging will, here within individual linear strands, just as previously in entire component waves. The same process is present in the bass, in the repetitions of the arpeggiated fourth leap, which likewise evolves out of the fundamental will of the overall wave, as a pendular motion swinging to a standstill. And what remains at the end, again in all unpretentiousness, is a trait of the pervasively animated formal dynamic: beneath the viola tremolo, once again sounding alone, remains only a motion drifting downward in the bass – in the depths, a final, diffuse *pizzicato* echo of the initial formative symphonic gesture, a rhythm just barely pulsating beneath the surface.[13]

---

[13] [LR] Kurth focuses on significant details of linear contour, which are often overlooked, for example the oscillating motion in all voices, leading to a bass descent. In addition to those linear details that Kurth cites as sustaining formal tension, notice also that the violins and clarinet stagger their peak notes (e′ in the violins, c′ a beat later in the clarinet), further contributing to the ongoing ferment. Kurth might also have mentioned that the music in Example 6.3 dwells on the dominant, a half cadence, which adds to the anticipatory character. The phrase rhythm, too, has quickened over the course of measures 2–17 (at first four-bar, then two-bar phrases, culminating in the breathless two-note motive in the clarinet at mm. 14–17). Finally, the harmonic rhythm accelerates considerably in measures 15–16, and so strengthens the feeling of intensification. Previously, the melodic bass outlined a single harmony in each bar. In measures 15–16 the bass becomes more harmonic, alternating rapidly between dominant and tonic roots, the latter subordinate to the former.

If we now scan the whole beginning of the movement up to measure 18, a larger component development emerges once again at its conclusion, analogous to the small-scale case at the end of measure 6 (see Ex. 6.1). [288] The unpretentious tremolo acquires new meaning each time. For when symphonic buildups occur over larger stretches of music and are on the verge of lapsing, instead of the complete stillness of a pause, the continued quivering of the one activating tone embodies a formative will whose influence continues throughout all of these ascendent accessory motions, and drives the formative process onward.[14]

Everything up to this point is merely the continued influence of the descending, dissipating motion that was engendered by the first wave. But that is only a fragment of the forthcoming development, of new initiatives and emerging forces. As mentioned, the first broad intensification peaks initially with the surfacing of gestures of the subsequent main theme.

Ex. 6.4 [K4] Sixth Symphony, Finale, mm. 29–31

---

[14] [EK] In *performance*, even in measures such as the last two of Example 6.3, where in the very typical manner of Bruckner's processive shaping the tremolo alone resounds for a few moments, a perceptive conductor will give the tremolo a special intensity. It would not exactly be an *external* reinforcement; that would be superfluous since the tremolo is in any case the only thing remaining. Rather, it would be an internal reinforcement by means of agitation, an acceleration of the quivering into an intense expression of a growth impulse focused into a single point. For the playing of a tremolo, there is an enormous difference, in general, whether it is part of an overall waxing or waning development. But in all such cases, as should surely be self-evident, one ought *not* to have the tremolo played *rhythmically exact* – in sixteenth notes, or thirty-second notes, or triplets or the like – but rather thoroughly blurred, and above all like the *quivering of a force*. Initiatory tremolo tones in particular, such as the ones in the examples given above, are for Bruckner something between force and tone, are impulses of the will becoming sound [see note 5 above]. Of course this by no means implies a neglect for the accompanying sonic appeal; and in cases where the tremolo spreads out over several tones, one must especially pay attention to *sonic uniformity* (thus not rhythmic uniformity!) among the individual voices. There is no more heedless a transgression against sonic uniformity than a restive tone production. Enveloping Bruckner's orchestra, with all of the interior dynamics, is a sonic enchantment, whose projection is among the basic requirements of an orchestral performance.

[LR] Several authors have commented on the importance of Bruckner's opening tremolos. Max Auer compares them poetically to the breaking of dawn (*Anton Bruckner* [1923], 354). Frank Wohlfahrt interprets them spatially, as a sign of Bruckner's unique ability to "hear retroauditively into the distance" out of which the symphonic aura gradually emerges (*Anton Bruckners Sinfonisches Werk: Stil- und Formerläuterung*, 17; cf. Oskar Lang, *Anton Bruckner*, 95). Fritz Oeser, using a Gestalt-psychological idea, interprets the sonic aura of the tremolo and the emergent thematic material as "ground" and "figure," respectively, in a figure-ground relationship.

[289] For if we look ahead in the score, this [passage], too, is only the [preliminary] apex of a huge comprehensive wave that first ebbs away, then intensifies anew, and leads to the actual delineation of the theme. It is not difficult to recognize, then, that the entire first main theme is nothing but a single symphonic surge of expansive dynamic quality, which later ends precisely at the entrance of the second, contrasting theme (m. 50, rehearsal letter D).[15] Although in retrospect it is not difficult to establish a distant motivic connection between the individual components of the main theme and the introductory measures (cf. the separate discussion of the symphony on this), what remains essential is that the thematic connection is supported primarily by the logical connection of the whole dynamic unfoldment (*Entwicklung*), from the preliminary gestures up through the emerging central idea. The preliminary development is not, conversely, a formalistic toying with "motivic fragments," etc. The essence of the thematic content of the preliminary symphonic development is that it starts from more general, relatively undifferentiated lines of force, from apparently "meaningless" primordial motives, and that the art of endless melody is also able to occasion that *internal* transition to the pronounced individual thematic structures (this passage also illustrates distinctly the influence of harmony on the formal logic: after the preliminary development in the minor, an incipient fulfillment in the major).[16]

The small, initial gestures discussed were, of course, lifted from the overall development leading up to those points. But even as very simple phenomena, they teach that the wave is the actual formal kernel, that it does not exist for itself alone, that it acquires meaning, as well as its particular momentary shape, only in light of the inner tension directed toward large-scale unfoldment. Herein lies also its vividly potent beauty. Only the undulatory play, which supports thematic construction in the first place, and gives rise to large sections, [290] leads to the formal design and permits us to see the logic of its unfolding (*Entfaltung*), at first on a small scale. But even from that stage on, besides the expanded dimensions there is also an essentially different internal organization than with the formal grouping and structural technique of the Classicists. That difference has already become a source of misunderstandings: failing to comprehend the large dimension and becoming lost in details.[17]

---

[15] [LR] In the Haas and Nowak scores, measure 50 is not rehearsal letter D. In the Doblinger score, rehearsal letter D is at measure 65. Kurth must have had some other edition, with rehearsal letters placed differently.

[16] [LR] Kurth's view of Bruckner's formal structure differs sharply from that of Werner Korte, who hears the music as an "additive" rather than a dynamic process. Note 19 in our chapter 7 discusses Korte's opinion.

[17] [EK] In *performances*, this [problem] even became a source of frequent makeshift solutions, in resorting to uneven, variable *tempi*. Further, some conductors believe they should gain control of the large continuities by means of a rushed tempo. By doing that, they only concede from the outset to being overcome by the formal control. There is a place for length, too; Bruckner's form cannot be "tossed off" but rather must be mastered by retracing the creative tensions. There is nothing hasty in Bruckner's [formal] unfolding processes (*Entfaltungen*); he himself took every opportunity to caution against fast tempi in his music

Additional characteristics in individual illustrations: parts and whole

[291] The basic idea of the wave technique will be amplified in its essential, additional features if we compare the beginning of the first movement [of the Sixth Symphony] with that of the Finale. While in the latter the initial developmental growth, with its linear forces, begins only indistinctly and leads gradually toward the theme, the first movement begins immediately with the main theme. Nevertheless, here too a process of growth and development is present, but of a different type. Even though the thematic contours are present from the very beginning, still it is just a preparation for the enhanced, full emergence of the theme at an apex. We recognize in a completely different illustration that the formal content is not the [thematic] structure itself, however brilliant, but rather a huge coherent development. [Growing] from a mysterious beginning to a towering and resplendent mass of sound, the development spans the entire primary section of the movement, which is dominated by the first theme. The initial flickering of the principal line beneath the peculiar glimmering in the high register is an instance of pure Brucknerian mysticism.

[LR: see Max Auer, *Anton Bruckner*, 354]. The basic movement in Bruckner is that of festive ceremony. The resolute expansiveness is in complete opposition to the highly strung person of the twentieth century. Only in serene tempi is there room for frenzy, of which Bruckner's music is capable; in its tranquillity it is the most buoyantly mobile, alongside that of Richard Strauss. It is generally known, though of course no longer well known to many performers, that for example the words *allegro* or *andante*, or even *adagio* can mean different things. With Bruckner, one ought always to interpret such designations fairly broadly. Only the Scherzi can tolerate a proper "modern" tempo, sometimes (as with the Ninth Symphony) pushing it all the way to the limits of performance.

Additionally, if we say that the basic pace derives from the thematic character (which incidentally is obvious for *any* music), that says the tempo designations point more toward the thematic character than toward the actual tempo. The switch to a new theme automatically produces a new tempo; but within the [individual] developments, nothing is more mistaken than constantly changing the tempo. It is particularly necessary to caution against rushing when nearing a [formal] goal or, conversely, in the moment prior to a climax, against those ritardandi with which some conductors make prominent sweeping gestures, and which are completely inappropriate for Bruckner's music. Such triteness is only proof that the person does not follow the internal tautness of the intensifying progression. If one feels that progression, the tempo barely requires controlling. All of the impatient haste, which distorts Bruckner from the outset, is often due to the customary overloading of the concert program. One often witnesses a Bruckner symphony being appended, as a filler, to all kinds of tiresome offerings. And there are localities where this is even strategically manipulated by Bruckner opponents.

[LR] August Halm talks about the length of Bruckner's symphonies in "Musikalische Bildung," 62–63 (reprinted in *Von Form und Sinn der Musik*, 220–21). According to Halm, audiences of the late nineteenth century were "spoiled" by the "short-windedness" (*Kurzatmigkeit*) of the Classicists, and so could not understand Bruckner.

Ex. 6.5 [K5] Sixth Symphony, first movement, mm. [1–8]

[292] Here, too, [as in the Finale] there is a two-measure incipient primal motion in vividly quivering rhythm prior to the entrance of the principal line. This C♯ in the violins has a meaning similar to the tremolo at the beginning of the Finale (Ex. 6.1): right from the start, a highly agitated whirring in the sonic atmosphere (moreover, it is the intense major third of the tonic chord). The glimmering, wonderfully vivid principal line of the basses beneath starts out as a closed four-bar gesture (mm. 3–6), at first leading downward, then striving upward in a more agitated gesture (quarter-note triplets), and curving back to the initial tone from the highest peak. As a line in itself, it is an urgently undulating unity beneath the steadily quivering crest of the total symphonic sound image. Despite thematic prominence, it is only one part of the internal dynamic. The registral contrast in particular enhances the internal energetic will of surging undercurrent, and the large spatial distancing of the voices also heightens this internal tension. (Looking ahead, we can recognize the fulfillment of this internal

tension in the ultimate emergence of the bass theme in the high register [Ex. 6.9]. And it will become evident how the intensification directed toward that point highlights precisely the idea of freshly surging currents flowing up from deep waves toward a magnificently vivid development.)

This expansive formal drive in the bass line continues such that, in a few unpretentious measures, it conceals a phenomenon [293] that merits extensive attention. In bars 7 and 8, before the bass line re-enters and amid the constant whirring of the high tones, a brief intervening horn motive resounds which, according to the analytical view of form, simply represents an echo-like imitation of the previous [bass] motive. Viewed that way, the force would again be concealed by the phenomenon, and precisely that which manifests itself as "simple" is always most intimately linked to the basic aspects of a total artistic-expressive will. Imitation, echo – all of that is superficially understood sound. What we must see is the active energetic gesture dissipating into the boundless distance. The last melodic gesture (the motive A–F–E [in the basses]) extends its influence and, in a moment of sonic attenuation [*Klangausschwebung*], reaches out into the *void* [*Leere*], toward *another tier of sonic perspective*, which opens up the way for elaboration until, after two measures, the [thematic] entry coalesces. The imitation is merely a reverberation of the thematic impulse (its final fading away) cast out into the *distance*.[18] Here it is unpretentious, noticeable only to one who is otherwise familiar with Bruckner. It functions merely as a foreshadowing of what other contexts will exhibit in much larger dimensions. The principal lines, or their components, are followed very often in Bruckner's music by intervening resonances that symbolize distance, directions, a type of *symphonic space*, toward which the music points.[19] They are often very brief, as here, but can be extremely vivid and spun out to considerable lengths. Only in the first case [brief sonic intervention] do they tend to be occupied with such echo-like repetitions that, in subsiding, entail a *shift to sonic attenuations* [*Klangverdünnungen*]. The intervening resonances do not always involve actual thematic fragments but rather modified, or even new continuations, as we shall often see later. In that case, they tend to be dominated by various motives that pass quickly, not just by closing motives, and in a far clearer impression of a completely altered sonic dimension.[20] Then, the void is not serene and majestically broadened, as here, but rather filled with restless

---

[18] [LR] Kurth, following the Hynais edition, places a *crescendo–decrescendo* marking in the horn part, measures 7–8. That brief swell reinforces the sense of a distant, intervening "sonic perspective." However, the Nowak edition lacks the *crescendo–decrescendo* marking and shows instead a steady crescendo across the whole motive, starting at *piano*.

[19] [LR] Consider, for example, the first theme in the first movement of Bruckner's Fifth Symphony, measures 57–59 (see Ex. 7.2).

[20] [LR] Kurth discusses an instance of this technique in connection with Example 7.2.

linear forces. In Bruckner's music such passages always reveal something of the formal will in the development to which they belong. Bruckner employs reverberant extensions of a concluding motive [294] especially often after a far-flung upward reach. In this way, the formal urge is elevated into the ethereal realm, from the palpable tones of the principal line into a delicately fading resonance, sometimes almost resembling an imaginary reverberation. Thus here, too, the intervening arch is occupied completely with the expression of great longing, an expression that the arch carries beyond the upswing of the principal line, to release. Hence also the shift from strings to the soaring tone of the horn, as a gently fading intermediate [timbral] density in the ascent toward the rarefied atmospheric tones of the high register.[21] Bruckner does not shape his sonic material into a *uniformly spread transparence*, as for example *Bach* does with his ethereal, metaphysical lines, but rather projects sonic formations of *multi-tiered depth*. Bruckner creates a sonic abundance full of *luminescence* and *ambiguity*, and its dispersal into the *void* – the world and *vast background*, purely in the *view of the mystic*.

Accordingly, when a brief attenuation, a regression, leads from the initial sonic buildup and material consolidation back into the void, formally it is in essence a matter of something like the tremolo pressing repeatedly to the fore in the Finale opening discussed above, despite the completely different expressive will that here [in Ex. 6.5] determines the shaping of the moment of void. There [in the Finale, it is] the activating force, here [in the first movement], more a dissipation, and that [difference] is closely related to the way both movements begin. In the Finale, the whole beginning is a preliminary impulse directed toward the theme; in the first movement, however, the theme starts immediately and *occasions the contrasting effect of evolved material and a void*. In both cases, such intervening passages point toward the evolving *opposition of sonic mass and sonic space*. (We must attune ourselves, beyond the sound of the piano, to the sonic space of the orchestration by means of the simplified arrangements.) This [contrast] arises in a brief, passing glimpse, by allusion, but it is often heightened to become powerful moments

---

[21] [LR] Fritz Oeser explains the sense of space in Bruckner's music similarly, as resulting primarily from dynamic contrasts and orchestrational contrasts (*Die Klangstruktur der Bruckner-Symphonie* [Leipzig: Musikwissenschaftlicher Verlag, 1939], 65–66). More recently, Leopold Nowak has written about the "expanses" (*Weiten*) in Bruckner's music, which he associates with the architectural spaciousness of St Florian, without claiming, however, that the music is a conscious representation of such architecture (Nowak, "Der Begriff der 'Weite' in Anton Bruckners Musik," *Über Anton Bruckner: Gesammelte Aufsätze, 1936–84* [Vienna: Musikwissenschaftlicher Verlag, 1985], 126–35). Kurth comes back to the notion of musical space in connection with Example 7.2.

The sense of a new sonic space in measures 7–8 results not only from dynamic, timbral, and registral shifts but also from a tonal shift. When the horn enters, the harmony is a C♯ dominant seventh chord, implying a shift from A major to F♯ minor. In addition to the wide registral gap between the melody and accompaniment, and to the registral-timbral shift from the low strings to the horn in measures 5–8, the suspensive chordal fifth that closes the motives in measures 6 and 8 (E and G♯) reinforces the feeling of vastness.

where the entire cumulative buildup, replete with sonic mass, reverberates outward into the void of psychic space. (More later on the nature of this interior vision of space.)

Notice how, in the whirring of the high region, the harmonic blurring into the dissonance, [295] c#''''/b'', corresponds to this shaping of space and boundlessness. In its sonic appeal, it is an image similar, perhaps, to refracted, blurry light. This heightened dissonance results also from the overall dynamic development. The incipient, broadly surging development, merely initiated by the theme, is held in suspension here solely by the brief intervening segment. In this momentary void, the tension attained becomes perceptible due to the sonic refraction of the high register into a dissonance. And once again this, too, is that image of internal opposition, in a new, highly ingenious version, which allows a concealed, fresh accumulation of operative forces to arise precisely in moments of marked de-intensification. It is not only a heightening of dissonance but also a harmonic agitation in the development from the A-major chord toward the F#-major chord. What [powerful] internal dynamics reside, therefore, in the unmediated shading [of the F#-major chord] into F# minor at the end of measure 8! (See the upbeat of the next example [Ex. 6.6], which follows immediately after the half measure of the previous example.) Motivic, harmonic, instrumental, and other details cooperate in Bruckner's sense of dynamic form in this highly refined manner.

Accordingly, what happens in measures 7 and 8 is a complete transformation of the "imitation," only one of the countless transformations that show how all traditional formalistic elements, in the large as well as in the small, are permeated by a new spirit, and pervaded by the overall, sustaining formal trait. The intervening motive does not sound from *out* of the distance (*piano* imitation) but rather *into* the distance (linear oscillation that fades out into boundless space, with the will to transcend palpable sonic materiality). Superficially, there is a relationship to the Classical linkage technique [*Weiterführungstechnik*] based on the smallest, primal motivic fragments, as refined especially by Beethoven. The echo-like effect as such would also permit some comparative historical references. Softer repetitions of motives, or even of somewhat longer fragments, abound especially in instrumental music from the seventeenth century onward (but fade from view in the first perceptible beginnings of more artful vocal polyphony). Repetitions in Bach's chorale preludes and cantatas in particular often show quite clearly that echo effects in the manner of the old *forte* and *piano* alternation are intended to symbolize the vastness of space and effects of endlessness. There, the [contrasting] components [296] are limited with a certain rigidity to changing dynamic shades; the mere contrast suits the clearly tranquil inner spatial design in Bach's feeling of endlessness. With the late Romantic influence on the world-view and its inner structure, that mere contrast is replaced by the fundamental experience, profoundly affecting our spatial sense, of developmental forces and growth. In Bruckner's music this experience shows that the phenomenon of contrast has been expanded into infinitely fluid interaction between motivic and sonic-environmental variations, has been transformed to the point where shared features [among contrasting elements] are barely recognizable, and is thereby thoroughly interwoven with the newly spiritualized idea of classical motivic techniques.

The subsequent measures [mm. 9–14 in Ex. 6.6] exhibit the same basic characteristics, with slight variations, which result from a keen dynamic sense.

Ex. 6.6 [K6] Sixth Symphony, first movement, mm. 8–14

[297] While the progressive stratification manifests itself through the principal line in the bass returning a third higher than the first time, the quarter-note triplet exhibits a directional reversal, which is totally different from toying with a motivic variant. The line dips downward in order to swing directly upward from the pivot point toward the expanding figure in the next measure. The ascending trend in this trailing figure [m. 11] is thus supported by an enhanced initiatory

gesture. The ascending trend determines the next change as well: this time [in mm. 11–12] the trailing figure does not curve back [as in mm. 5–6 of Ex. 6.5] but rather stretches straight upward (from A♯ up to B). And this [ascent] is followed once again by a reverberative intermediary passage (mm. 13–14) with the same timbral change as before, but with a different linear direction. Compared with the analogous passage in measures 7 and 8 (Ex. 6.5), it is an exact directional reversal. Following the previous ascending tendency, the motion now first swings downward and contains a slight descending tendency in the boundary tones g′ and f♯′ [mm. 13–14]. The influence of the preceding motion stretching upward into space is coupled with a dynamic feeling tending toward equilibrium, a feeling that holds the overall development up to this point in suspension. As a whole, that development is only a fragmentary initiative, whose culmination is delayed and induced only later, amid highest tension, by new tiers of developmental waves.[22]

The components of the subsequent development must therefore also be understood in light of the long-range dynamics of the whole. The undulatory tiers in the next four measures exhibit the following new picture, which further illuminates motivic formation in relation to basic formal questions.

Ex. 6.7 [K7] Sixth Symphony, first movement, mm. 15–18

---

[22] [LR] In addition to linear aspects in measures 8–14 that escalate beyond the dynamic level of the previous music, tonal and textural elements also come into play. Kurth mentions that the bass enters a third higher in measure 9 than it did in measure 3. Tonally the music has ascended as well, both in the local and trans-local dimensions. Locally, the music has ascended a fifth, from the implied F♯ minor tonality in measures 7–8 to C♯ minor. Trans-locally, the music is now a third higher than it was at the opening (A major). The texture has become denser through the added horns in the middle register and through the filled-in open octave in the upper register (c♯‴–g♯‴–c♯⁗). Note also that the upper-register dissonance, a″/b″ (m. 11), now enters *before* the reverberatory echo, rather than with it, as was the case with c♯‴/b″ in the earlier passage (m. 7).

[298] The principal line begins with two new upward surges from below. The two-measure motive clearly results from the dynamics of the moment within the overall development. It is a *tiering* motive of the broadest movement, and also contains in the dotted rhythm of its beginning an expression of a reinforced gathering of momentum, an uninterrupted ascending surge throughout the first bar, subsequently peaking on a suspended tone [*überhangenden Ton*].[23] The motivic connection with the principal theme is pressed more into the background; it resides in the half-notes at the conclusion (m. 16), which is similar to the leap of a fifth in the principal theme (Ex. 6.5, m. 3). We should not artificially reconstruct such connections but rather recognize that, with Bruckner, it is the *power of development* that inflects, or even creates, its *motives as lines of force* most vividly. And it is moreover highly characteristic here that the long-range relationship to the basic thematic unit first emerges at the moment of relaxation (in m. 16 of the last example [Ex. 6.7]). (In any event, [299] one can also recognize a faint connection with the half-note triplets [Ex. 6.5, m. 4] in the dotted-rhythm ascent in m. 1. Such connections become illimitable and indefinable.) Because such lines of force, as projected by the momentary dynamics, usually embody something prototypical, i.e. embody basic forms of motion of a certain universality, it is almost always possible in an inquiry to maintain a connection between those lines and all of the more pronounced motivic forms, hence also with forms deriving from the principal theme. In a most artful manner, Bruckner knows how to bring out that connection gradually and distinctly in cases where he had perhaps suppressed it for a time. It is evident that here, in simple embryonic forms, a highly significant, fundamental trait of Bruckner's thematic-formal development manifests itself in this interaction and reciprocity between individually etched *initial themes* and the more general *lines of force* in *developmental motives*.[24] Until now this fundamental trait has been thoroughly misunderstood precisely in its uniformity. It, too, is a central element of the technique of "endless melody," which Bruckner found splendidly exemplified in Wagner's music. He placed it in the service of the thematically closed symphonic forms and surely would have perfected it, since that was present in the basic intellectual conditions of contemporary sensibility, which Bruckner fulfilled in the pure musical form.

Bruckner moves a third higher with the second entry (m. 17) [Ex. 6.7] as well. As before, this may not be dictated by the fondness throughout the high Romantic

[23] [LR] As Kurth has explained, and as I mentioned in the previous note, the overall development has been a steady escalation, tonally, texturally, melodically, and registrally. Measures 15–18, arriving after an initiatory and an escalatory gesture, represent the third phase in a four-phase escalation. As such, measures 15–18 intensify beyond the previous two phases and yet remain dynamically subsidiary to the final one (Ex. 6.9). The music in Example 6.7 does this in ways Kurth explains presently.

[24] [LR] Kurth's discussion of developmental motives in Bach's music is in our chapter 2, pp. 65–74. See also *EKATA*, chapter 3.

period for the coloring effects of sequences by third. Rather, it is clear in such cases that it is a dynamic sensibility as well which leads Bruckner to employ the third, prefigured in the overtone series, as the natural *structural* interval of music.[25]

Contrasting figures enter (woodwinds) in measures 16 and 18 (mm. 2 and 4 of Ex. 6.7) amid the continued quivering of the high whirring motive. Strikingly agitated, iridescent lines in the high register always characterize the mystic's view into the dazzling distance. Technically, having easily recognized [in the woodwinds] imitative inversions of the foregoing bass ascent, we can see that their appearance in the sonic play of forces and their particular form is dynamically determined. Once again a subtly felt directional change [300] produces a certain state of poised suspension that bridges the tension between the dissipating principal motivic line and the newly entering one. However, it is a different type of imitation than previously, at the directional reversal in the intermediary passage of measures 13 and 14 (last measures of Ex. 6.6). Above all, the counterpointing figures certainly do not appear as reverberations, even superficially, but rather are thrust into the principal lines as high-register reflections of the onrushing formal will, as undulant reflexes arising from the outer layer of the sonic environment – reflexes that sustain the dynamic counterweight in moments of slowing and local deintensification of the principal curve. That is the formal meaning of the inverted "imitation."[26] Moreover, the harmonic dispositions of the main tones are everywhere dynamically determined: the peak and pivot tones of the bass line [are] *appoggiatura* effects with downward-pressing tension, thus impinging on the linear contour with full clarifying poignancy. The pivot tones of the high, contrasting imitations (in the woodwinds [F♯ in mm. 16 and 18]) also appear as dissonances, which glance off the lower voice.

The onset of the escalating development has the following additional effect:

---

[25] [EK] See chapter 5 [*Bruckner*, vol. I] on the harmony in these opening measures. [LR] In a note on pages 545–46, Kurth explains how Bruckner expands the harmonic space at the beginning of the first movement of the Sixth, working out from A major to the dominant and related harmonies of E major and C♯ minor (mm. 9–16), then to the subdominant-related harmonies of F major and D minor (mm. 18–20), and back to E major and A major (mm. 21–28). He says the beginning of the movement foreshadows this harmonic journey: the brilliance of C♯, the chordal third, in the high register at the opening suggests dominant-related ("sharp") harmonies, and the G♮, B♭, and F♮ in measures 4–5 suggests subdominant-related ("flat") harmonies.

[26] [LR] The distinction in Kurth's mind between a technical and a dynamic interpretation of musical events is especially clear here. Technically, measures 7–8, 13–14, 16, and 17 are melodic imitation. In measures 7–8 and 13–14 Kurth interprets the imitations as reverberations that convey a sense of sonic perspective (depth, distance). That reading gives the imitations a dynamic function in the musical unfolding process. Further, because dynamic functions are processive and reciprocally influential, Kurth distinguishes measures 16 and 18 from measures 7–8 and 13–14. The processive logic of the overall escalation leading to measure 25 (Ex. 6.9) occasions a shift in dynamic function in measures 16 and 18. They are no longer strictly reverberatory but rather impelling elements. Accordingly, the melodic contour (inversion) and intensified timbres (high winds) are necessary and intrinsic to the dynamic unfolding process.

Ex. 6.8 [K8] Sixth Symphony, first movement, mm. 19–24[27]

[301] It is once again a dynamically engendered figure, related only distantly to the principal idea. The figure casts the developmental progression of the principal line repeatedly upward in a brief, concise gesture. The sharper definition of the formal development is also expressed in the transfer of the principal line from the lowest strings to the timbre of the trumpet (reinforced by the clarinet), and the formal function of the orchestration becomes even clearer from measure 21 on (m. 3 in Ex. [6.8]). From there on, the last motive, tension-laden and repeated several times, ultimately in a swirling acceleration, is sustained on a high note so that, of the two instruments, only the clarinet tone – at first nearly absorbed by the trumpet tone – remains as the bearer of the airy impression of height.

---

[27] [LR] Kurth's piano reduction differs from Nowak's edition of the full score in only a few details. Kurth marks the clarinet and trumpet parts in measures 19–20 *mf*; Nowak shows *f*. Further, in measures 23–24 Kurth places individual slurs over each motive in the clarinet, continuing the phrasing of measures 21–22. In Nowak's edition one long phrase marking spans measures 23–24.

Additionally, there is the general sonic attenuation to *pianissimo*, again as an expression of the highly tense suspension, still quivering, against which the whirring violin motive resounds as almost the sole surviving content. The two final measures (mm. 23–24 of the passage) thus bear a characteristic formal significance: by no means [do they constitute] a stalling or flagging, nor a de-intensification, despite the sonic attenuation. Rather, on the contrary, [they contain] an extension of the critical tension, which evolved out of the repeated tiering in the foregoing large arch, and which prepares the emerging fulfillment. The fulfillment occurs in the next measure with a powerful effect of discharged tension, together with the most forceful eruption of the principal theme.[28] [302]

Ex. 6.9 [K9] Sixth Symphony, first movement, mm. 24–28

[28] [LR] The motivic repetition in measures 23–24 is set with E-major harmony, the dominant (A: V), which sustains harmonic tension right up to the climactic statement of the theme (m. 25). The harmonic development has steadily heightened the level of tension throughout measures 1–14. It begins with ascending thirds with A-major, C#-minor, and E-major harmonies (mm. 1–9, and 15). G-major harmony in measure 17 is the link between the cycle of thirds and a brief cycle of fifths: G major, C7, and F (mm. 17–19). The cycle of thirds then resumes with F-, A-, C-, and E-major harmonies (mm. 19–21). Measure 25 thus arrives with a powerfully satisfying effect following a dynamic, ascending harmonic arch. Kurth sometimes omits the explanation of harmonic phenomena when he feels it may be too complex for lay persons (*Bruckner*, vol. I, vii). Kurth finds enough other, more easily identifiable and readily explainable dynamic processes, allowing him to illustrate the formal development without over-complicating the analysis.

[303] It is an apex whose significance for the principal theme is similar to the curve of the Finale discussed previously; only there the actual thematic features first appear at the apex. Note also, with the forceful reassertion of the theme at the apex, how its principal line is also cast up into the high register. This, too, occurs as a result of the intensification, with its constant fresh initiatives from below. The high-register rhythm has evolved into such impulses that it now causes the entire sonic depth to quake! Fulfillment is also evident in this change of register. What was previously a hint of an initial aura of quivering now permeates fully the wildly convulsing sonic mass from its foundations. (Note also the fine elemental effect in the present [harmonic] setting of this motive with root, fifth, and octave, [and] further, the participation of the timpani.) All in all, the whole "registral exchange" between the principal line and the rhythmic countermotive is merely an expression of the energetic process. A formalistic characterization, such as that of double counterpoint or the like, would be completely superficial and meaningless.

This passage, too, contains imitations: the full-blown initial motive of measure 25 (first [full] measure in Ex. 6.9) is intoned by the horns in the next bar. It is likewise not a sonic or formalistic [*formspielerisch*] process, nor mere filler, but above all a process of energy: a continued quaking of the powerful initial thematic motion transferred into the trembling rhythms of the low regions (as previously the transfer from the low melody into the high-register imitations!).[29] The reverberation in the horn parts, measure 27, of the quarter-note triplets (woodwinds and trumpet) in the previous bar (m. 26 in Ex. 6.9), illustrates even more clearly the dynamic character. The stepwise line [in m. 26] is [in m. 27] transformed into very large chordal skips – a vivid symbol of the broadening embodied in the dissipation of this dynamic thematic impulse (which is why the impulse ultimately fades with an octave leap [horns, m. 27]).

Although these four measures arise from the preceding development as a brilliant apex, they are superseded by yet another escalation, the principal line being driven a third higher (m. 31 [304], last bar of Ex. 6.10), as in its first appearance [mm. 3 and 9]. That is accomplished after a short intervening procedure (mm. 29 and 30 in Example 6.10), which merits special attention because it offers a clear and vivid illustration of the fundamental dynamic processes on which Bruckner's symphonic shaping process is based.

These are the two measures whose position would correspond exactly to the reverberative intervening development in measures 7 and 8 (Ex. 6.5). However, they [mm. 29–31] do not contain any sort of imitative reverberation. In other ways, too, they contain a completely different picture, but are nevertheless dynamically

---

[29] [LR] Observe also the collision between A and B♭ on beat two of measure 26, impelling the phrase toward its midpoint.

Ex. 6.10 [K10] Sixth Symphony, first movement, mm. 29–31

determined, once again referring back to the dynamic meaning of that reverberation in the sonic attenuation of measures 7 and 8. With the fulfillment of the escalation, however, the energetic process of this intermediary development is completely changed. Instead of the effect of endlessness in the final reverberative motivic component observed there [mm. 7–8], [305] a powerful and sonically compact upsurge appears here, a fresh current streaming up from below.[30] As a new impulse, this current penetrates between the segments of the principal line, mediates the tension between them, and gathers the entire force of the upward tendency in an *intervening wave*. Accordingly, it is merely a supporting element within the whole bold buildup. For while the new motivic initiative in measure 31 (Ex. 6.10, last bar) is, on a large scale, only a further heightening of the line that was interrupted in measure 28 (Ex. 6.9, last bar), now the initiative appears freshly reinforced from below or rather – since the dynamic development must be grasped, and not the static image – it appears freshly impelled by the powerful forward drive of the two intervening measures. It is the *model of after-surging support waves* so essential and common in Bruckner's symphonic works.[31] It is thus a differently fashioned linkage of component waves, which are clearly much more than the simple linking of one developmental arch to the preceding one. The waves of energy *interweave*

---

[30] [LR] Note 22 above mentions how context can change the dynamic function of previously stated material.

[31] [EK] They are also always distinguished by a darkening in the overall color and, in their upward drive, are also always formed as a great fermenting, [and] not perchance as a "mediatory accompaniment."

and overlap with one another to create an kinetic symphonic image of principal and accessory waves, [i.e., of] exterior and interior undulation, like the lively undulatory play of natural forces.

(In the measures given, yet another unpretentious detail illustrates how Bruckner is profoundly affected by the force of the overall shaping dynamics. In measure 25 [Ex. 6.9] a short sixteenth-note upbeat, e, precedes the thematic entry of the principal line, also an E. At the *intensified* continuation in measure 31 [Ex. 6.10], this sixteenth-note upbeat is not identical to the entry note G♯ but rather enters from below, on F♯, with *upward-driving force*. This minute change is so full of vitality that it could never be produced by a clever contrivance [but] only by a permeation with the most subtle sense of form. The change also appears in the first thematic entrances [see mm. 3 and 9 in Exx. 6.5 and 6.6].)

Concerning the subsequent development, we can say preliminarily that here, too, (as in the Finale) the entire first thematic development up to the entrance of the new, contrasting theme [306] (m. 49, rehearsal letter B [Doblinger and modern editions]) completes a unified undulation. Accordingly, the whole section involving the principal theme is a single formal arch, a closed progression pervaded multifariously by component waves. One can easily see in an overview how the mass attained at the apex passage dissipates in individual undulations from measure 41 on (analogous to the section following m. 19), and how finally, from measure 47 on, only the figure from measures 21–24 remains in the airy sound of the flute as the last, slightest ethereal swirling away in the heights – almost like a complete void after the accumulation and discharge of tension in the whole preceding development. Only then does the second principal theme enter. We can see from the two beginnings discussed so far [first and last movements of the Sixth] how poorly we would manage using *only* concepts such as theme *groups* and the like, and how these very things are borne by an interior shaping progression, the penetration of which is the basis for understanding Bruckner's formal principle.

Furthermore, like the beginning of the Finale, the theme appears in consolidated form at the peak of the whole wave; in passages of tension, by contrast, it flickers everywhere in motivic allusions.[32] Such allusions embody the will toward the

---

[32] [EK] For those readers who lack professional training, it is noted here that motive means the smallest unified fragments; theme usually means a larger formation which yields the basic content of a section of a movement. A theme normally consists of several motives; only exceptionally is it held to the brevity of a single motive. [LR: Kurth refers the reader to a note in *Bruckner*, vol. I, 274, which speaks of linear energy and its larger manifestation in the "more expansive melos."]

[EK] When a theme consists of several longer linear progressions, however, and no one of them can clearly be designated as a principal line, then it is generally better to speak of "component thematic lines," as long as a clear orchestrational indication disallows an abbreviated reference, e.g. "horn theme" etc., amid the network of the total structure.

[LR] In explaining briefly the difference between rudimentary ideas such as "motive" and "theme," Kurth shows that he includes the non-professional reader in his potential audience.

theme. Given everything discussed so far, one can recognize a unique and new association of motive, theme, and form in general based not only on [such motivic allusions] but also on the whole motivic procedure, at least with regard to the formal arches that incorporate a theme. While all of the motives appear to serve the thematic content in some way, the themes [in turn] serving the structure of the movement, in close interaction with those procedures it will become apparent how closely motivic and often even the thematic formation itself depends on a specific formal-dynamic function.

[307] In the Finale, it could be observed in the arch concluding at measure 18 that the tremolo re-emerging at the fadeout corresponds to the introductory one, and hence that this whole arch in the undulation is framed by deep-lying tremors (see Ex. 6.3). In the first movement, the larger dimensions of the whole first thematic complex exhibit an analogous phenomenon, only in a different form: in the first measures, the initiatory quivering of the agitated high-register triplet; in the last two measures (mm. 47 and 48) only a reverberative quivering of the final vestige of the dynamic motive, which likewise fades by oscillating around one note in a thin, high [flute] tone. In this case, the beginning and ending are neither motivically nor timbrally similar. While the beginning was in the violins, the conclusion ebbs with the flute, whose tone (as often) symbolizes a final lapsing, a de-materialization, compared with the strongly generative tone of the string entry. We already can see from this that Bruckner does not set down a theme as such. Rather, he elevates the entire growth process and the unfolding of symphonic forces to the essential problem of creating musical shape, from the first incipient stirrings and first energetic impulses, to the final ebbing away. This is the way components of a movement are formed. Bruckner's creative impulse is an unleashing of expansive psychic forces.

As different as the themes and the entire developmental model are in the two openings discussed, a number of shared traits appear amid the differences. Above all, the general question concerning the relationship of part to whole arises repeatedly. This relationship is based on Bruckner's enormous *psychic power* of *constant, expansive prospective hearing*. It is a principal feature of high formal art always to create shape according to the necessities occasioned by large continuities. With Bruckner, every individual developmental wave is directed at later events, often in infinitely subtle contexts, and likewise recalls earlier ones. With him, the *function* always controls the *present moment*; a sense of destiny guides him even in the formal process.[33] The ability always to hear prospectively and retrospectively entails

---

[33] [EK] [This view is] the exact opposite of the one proverbially attributed to him due to a lack of understanding – a lack that deserves to become proverbial itself – [the view] of an alleged stringing together of individual ideas without regard for form. [LR] See Oskar Lang, *Anton Bruckner*, 2nd., edn, 60–61.

[LR] Readers familiar with the critical response to Bruckner's work, originating mainly with Eduard

the same secret that underlies his [308] incredible harmonic art. Beyond the independent luminescence of all harmonic changes, he feels and anticipates the modulatory paths leading forward and backward over long passages, and always senses the tension between individual harmonic successions and the overall harmonic development across the largest spans. Essentially it is the same large-scale tension that, much more generally, preserves the suspensive relationship between individual moods and the overall character of a work, as well as between all manifest and concealed contents of music. Bruckner gives Romantic sensibility its purest expression in absolute and closed musical form, a sensibility that in its whole outlook heightened the reciprocal tension between parts and the unified whole to extraordinary turmoil. Bruckner enhances the significance of the individual phenomena and with hitherto unknown escalation of power simultaneously forges them into unified wholes whose simplicity appears as though ordained by nature.

The illimitability of the interior processes: the symphonic melos

The illimitability of the individual waves manifests itself in a lengthwise as well as in a crosswise profile [*Längsschnitt, Querschnitt*]. The former illustrates the reciprocal flow of successive component waves, each carrying within itself the momentum that it discharges. It is possible to isolate a wave only in individual instances, e.g. in the case of initiatory waves or at apexes. Even then, however, isolating a wave would be more happenstance. For the inner tension directed toward the subsequent and overall context still remains essential – a break is still not a termination – and the growth, logic, and beauty of such a component structure would not be understood if we were to examine that structure purely on its own. The same is true if, instead of individual waves, we isolate larger

---

Hanslick and his followers, Gustav Dömpke and Max Kalbeck, need no reminder of the harsh reviews Bruckner received after performances of his symphonies in Vienna. Hanslick described Bruckner's work as formless, bloated, and unnatural. Dömpke referred to the counterpoint in the Seventh Symphony as "musty smelling." Various letters from Bruckner to Hans von Wolzogen, Moritz von Mayfeld, Siegfried Ochs, and others, make clear that Bruckner was acutely aware of Hanslick's power to "destroy" (*vernichten*) a composer (letter of May 9, 1884, to Anton Vergeiner, printed in Max Auer, comp., ed., *Anton Bruckner: Gesammelte Briefe, Neue Folge* [Regensburg: G. Bosse, 1924], 162 [letter no. 131]; see also letter no. 299, p. 280, as well as letters in Franz Gräflinger, comp., ed., *Anton Bruckner: Gesammelte Briefe* [Regensburg: G. Bosse, 1924], 143–45). Accounts of contemporary responses to Bruckner's works may be found in several sources, among them August Göllerich, *Anton Bruckner: Ein Lebens- und Schaffens-Bild*, ed. Max Auer (4 vols., Regensburg: Bosse, 1922–37), vol. IV.1, 247, 480, 642; vol. IV.2, 436–40, 449; vol. IV.3, 89, 93, 100; Erwin Doernberg, *The Life and Symphonies of Anton Bruckner* (London: Barrie and Rockliff, 1960), 72–78, 95–96; Max Dehnert, *Anton Bruckner: Versuch einer Deutung* (Leipzig: Breitkopf und Härtel, 1958), 73, 81, 89; Hans Conrad Fischer, *Anton Bruckner: Sein Leben* (Salzburg: Residenz Verlag, 1974), 107, 169, 182; Hans Hubert Schönzeler, *Bruckner* (New York: Grossman, 1970), 48, 74, 87. Kurth discusses Hanslick and the Viennese anti-Bruckner sentiment in *Bruckner*, vol. I, 122–26, 136, 204–06, 216–22.

undulatory dimensions. Whoever approaches this music with the demand for defined boundaries, besides misunderstanding the style, has also not grasped that the art of form applied to illimitable elements requires far more power, and also a stronger, subtler sense of balance, than the art of form applied to defined boundaries. In their *crosswise profile*, however, the waves exhibit their trait of internal illimitability in that their *coexistent*, tiered dissipations cannot be fully distinguished because they lapse variously [309] into sonic motions and then dissolve. From this we can see how their constant mutual overlapping in the crosswise profile aids in determining the reciprocal flow in the lengthwise profile.[34]

The following measures [Ex. 6.11] illustrate both profiles even more clearly than the previous examples, partly in a new illustration of the interior dynamics. There are also some small-scale features to be seen that will help later to clarify the large-scale outlines of Bruckner's music.[35]

Ex. 6.11 [K11] Fourth Symphony, second movement, mm. 1–12

[34] [LR] Kurth refers several times to the lengthwise (longitudinal) and crosswise (transverse) profiles without sufficiently explaining how they represent complementary views of musical texture. Lengthwise and crosswise profiles of dynamic-formal waves in music, with their variously surging and ebbing textural strands, would be analogous to waves of water, as viewed in a long, narrow glass tank, with their various component currents. We may observe the tank either from the side (lengthwise profile) or from the narrow end (crosswise profile). In the lengthwise profile we can see the collective internal swirling that impels each wave into the next, thus creating an interlocked series of undulations. In the crosswise profile, we can see the individual, overlapped currents that contribute to the collective internal swirling.

[35] [LR] Kurth's ideas on Example 6.11 are based on Franz Schalk's and Ferdinand Löwe's edition of the symphony (Vienna: Albert J. Gutmann, 1890), which Deryck Cooke calls "completely spurious." Cooke notes that by failing to sign the printer's copy of the manuscript Bruckner withheld his approval of the Schalk–Löwe score (Cooke, *The Bruckner Problem Simplified*, 11). The editors made numerous changes in the orchestration throughout the score. For example, in Bruckner's score the first violins do not divide in measure 6. Instead, the second violins take the lower of the two notes, beginning with eb' on beat three and continuing up to g' on the downbeat of measure 8. The main difference here is that the Schalk–Löwe edition doubles the cello part with second violins, as shown in Kurth's short score, necessitating the division in the first violins.

Schalk and Löwe also rearrange the voices in measures 9–10. In Bruckner's 1878/80 score (Nowak, 1953) the cellos and second violins do not drop out after the downbeat of measure 9. Instead, they continue by playing the parts scored by Schalk and Löwe for divided first violins and violas, notably with the cellos *above* the violas.

Ex. 6.11 (cont.)

[310] Illustrated here is, above all, how even seemingly independent principal thematic lines often recede into the embracing undulatory symphonic dynamics rather than exhibiting any defined boundaries. For even the magnificent curve of the cello melody does not independently determine the form of the overall contours, even though everything else appears to be merely subordinate accompaniment. In reality the accompaniment is something totally different, or at least a variety of "accompaniment" that differs fundamentally from the conventional type. Examined more closely, it becomes apparent that precisely this [accompanimental] veil, which surrounds the principal lines and initially sounds alone for two bars, subsequently becomes the chief element for the entire developmental dynamic.[36]
[311] Thus even where a principal melody is sounding, it is a remarkable characteristic of the dynamic formal principle that the melody does not constitute the chief element in the actual course of the form. And what presents itself as accompaniment to the fleeting glance are structures aiding the development, *an enveloping*

---

[36] [LR] The accompanimental voices in the original, 1874 version of the movement (Nowak, 1975) are not nearly as refined as they are in the revised, 1878 version.

formal urge.[37] To overlook that fact would be to neglect the creative process and activity in the theme itself.

As with the quivering vibrations of the high-register aura (Ex. 6.5) in the opening theme of the Sixth Symphony, and as with the initiatory impulse of the tremolo (Ex. 6.1) in the Finale opening, so also these two introductory measures are a first trace of growth, though of course of a completely different character: the most delicate awakening in a lightly swelling billow, filled with the calm of the ensuing movement. Here too, however, the theme appears enveloped in a symphonic aura as a result of the calm. Viewed by themselves, these two preliminary *pianissimo* bars represent a brief symphonic ripple: a gentle swell in the inner voices and, after a gentle surge, a fading away into the unison C in measure 2. Rather than speaking of inner voices, one would almost prefer to speak here of inner wisps of sound. For they do not sound like two distinct lines but rather drift more like veils through the interior motion of the mellow string sound, like shadowy thirds within its borders, within the floating, gentle rhythmic pulsations on C [c′–c″].[38]

This initial gesture immediately draws the broad principal melody in the cellos into an undulatory motion. If we trace the whole motion further, it also shows that the inner undulatory current (visible in the crosswise profile) is again a multi-faceted one, that the undulatory surges of the enveloping strings ebb away around the expansive, independent contours of the cello melody, at first every two measures, then subsiding irregularly. If we observe this activity, a beautiful image of dispersal and vaporization is revealed, observable from many perspectives. [It is observable] primarily with regard to the course of the enveloping string sonorities [312]. Their undulatory motion cadences twice at two-measure intervals and begins anew in measure 5, which remains open and continues in measure 6 with a new three-bar ascending tier. This tier finally peaks with the highest tone, E♭. From there, it does sink back to the two Cs in the uppermost part (first violins) as before, but if we look at the other parts, beyond such a boundary it has already

---

[37] [EK] The beginning of the Third Symphony shows what highly ingenious formal ideas this technique can lead to in Bruckner's music. There, (as will be discussed more thoroughly in the study of the whole work) at the very first principal theme the surrounding activities of the string lines are not a "shell" but rather a direct radiative outcome of the thematic energy itself in a completely new type of treatment.

[38] [LR] The rhythm, too, slowing gradually into measure 2, outlines a miniature convex arch that reflects the motion of the inner voices. Interestingly, the long, suspensive pause at the beginning of measure 2 is subsequently filled with the cello's steadily ascending apexes at analogous spots in measures 4–8. The rhythm escalates slightly when the long pause is interrupted in measure 6 by the first violins (e♭′ on beat two). It intensifies further when the whole two-bar pattern is interrupted and shifts to a constant eighth-note stream in measures 6–8. Clearly, the rhythm reflects the dynamic growth in the small and large dimensions. The melodic shape of the string accompaniment is identical when the main theme returns at rehearsal letter G. Observe, though, the subtle changes in the accompaniment at letter A, where the inner-voice arch from measures 1–2, now amplified, is freed of its former c′–c″ octave boundary.

frayed into separate strands, for these other parts do not join in the close. (Thus the second four-measure group [mm. 5–8] dissolves into lapsing component waves and interior motions – a hallmark of the internal dissolution of all symmetry even in the small, which will be examined later. Even amid its preservation, e.g. in the two-measure boundaries of the opening gesture, the symmetry is already breached and destroyed by the changing internal dynamics of the component motions, and it loses its traditional meaning and power in the process, to the benefit of the newly-emerging concept of force.)

There are two more very remarkable internal processes that must be examined more closely in this connection. Above all, the enveloping wave in the strings that begins in measure 5 has dissolved. The first violins grow to a more densely woven veil of two voices [in m. 6] – this division itself being a hallmark of hazy wisps of sound – [and] push toward the peak in measure 8, while in the inner string parts (violas) a new branching out occurs in this general internal dissipation. A medial wave forms here [in the violas, m. 7], likewise broadening out to two voices.[39] It intersects rhythmically with the wave in the upper parts (first violins) and extends beyond its peak in measure 8. In the tapering off of these different waves, the free, inner movement spawns a strand (second violins) which is swept along by the principal melody in the cello. Within the overall movement, that process [the cellos engaging the second violins] is the interior dynamic content of this unison "reinforcement," which is much more than an exterior dynamic growth of the principal melody.[40] But there is a second noteworthy internal process that affects the relationship of the principal melody to the symphonic play of forces. In various upward thrusts the principal melody ultimately arches up to its peak, c'', in measure 8 (second quarter).[41] This peak does not coincide with that of the first violins. Rather, from measure 6 on, their ascending wave appears in a new connection. Their upward reach was a presentiment of the approaching peak in the principal line, [313] and that presentiment is aided by the whole internal growth that has just been examined. The *overall wave*, not a principal melody, is on the verge of an *apex*. That apex is founded, however,

---

[39] [LR] The first violins "growing to a more tightly woven veil," in measure 6, and the violas "broadening" into two voices in measure 9 reinforce Kurth's idea about the accompaniment determining the dynamic shape of the passage. However, as pointed out in note 35 above, the first violins in measure 6 and the violas in measure 9 are not divided in Bruckner's 1878/80 score.

[40] [LR] Kurth's comments here, about the second violins being "swept along" by the cello melody, are based on the Schalk–Löwe score. In Bruckner's 1878/80 score the second violins do not double the cello in measures 7–9. See note 35 above.

[41] [LR] Modern editions of Bruckner's 1874 and 1878/80 scores, (Novak, 1975, 1953) notate the cello beginning on c''' in measure 8, but this is a notational convention: the pitches sound an octave lower, Kurth follows the Schalk–Löwe edition, which doubles the second violin and cello at the unison in measures 7–8. The modern editions of Bruckner's 1874 and 1878/80 lack the doubling.

not on a single peak tone of a particular line (which is not the highest line here either), but rather on an internal *dynamic tension* that pervades the whole wave.[42] Viewed from the perspective of the crosswise profile, the peaks are thus offset from one another, the principal melody and first violins by a quarter note. But those are not the only peaks. The inner voices (first and second violas) also carry their waves to peaks independent of the cello and first violins. Further, it should be noted that the principal melody, even before its definitive summit tone, also injected local peaks *amid* the surrounding buildup [at mm. 4, 6, 7] (never coinciding with it), and so forth. In other words, even this simple opening exhibits enormously subtle internal differentiation, which aims at making the *overall wave, not a principal melody, the bearer of the intensification process*. That fact alone puts the unpretentious string envelopment in a completely different light than that of an "accompaniment." Despite the melodic prominence of another voice, the enveloping string parts grow *formally* to become the supporting symphonic environment, on whose broad melos Bruckner's conception is based. (Thus away with the all-too-naive notion that this mind composed the melody first and then the encasing motives!) We can even see in this still very simple, externally almost "homophonic" example how the characterization of the style as homophony with independent activation of the voices remains sterile, superficial, compared with the fundamental significance of the dynamic formal sense that created his style here. That significance of the overall wave emerges even more distinctly in the ensuing music.

For if we look further, following this whole intensification, it is the enveloping sonic motion alone that takes over the continuation and retrogression. The [harmonic] darkening manifests itself and drifts downward with the emergence of a gently rocking figure in measures 9 and 10, beginning on g♭″ (in the first violins). Again, it is a developmental motive engendered by the dynamic state, namely a delicately swaying motion headed downward, which is borne by the vague inner-voice motion of the violas (note here the singularly primal meaning, psychologically, of swaying and rocking figures [314] as calming motives in Bruckner's music!). That descending progression in the inner voices becomes the sole content in measures 11 and 12, in *pizzicato* again, symbolizing dwindling force, while the dotted motive from the first violins in measure 9 reverberates languidly and calmingly in the horn.[43] Formally, however, this motive conceals something very

---

[42] [LR] In Bruckner's 1874 and 1878/80 scores, the c″ in the cello line *is* the highest instrument sounding at measure 8.

[43] [LR] Schalk and Löwe make the retrogression in measures 9–12 even more explicit by marking measure 9 with *pianissimo* and the end of measure 12 with *decrescendo*. Further, the initial horn echo, in measure 11, is marked *piano*, the second one *pianissimo*, hence reinforcing the sense of fading away. Bruckner's 1878/80 score lacks these details. It has a triple-*piano* marking for the strings in measures 9–12, with no *decrescendo*, and both horn echoes are marked *pianissimo*.

essential. For at first it is the enveloping string choir that rises in measure 9 to become the subsequent bearer of the development, even shedding the role of a mere "accompanimental figure" in its external design. On the other hand, however, this string emergence reaches back once again, in a very subtly concealed manner, to the previous principal melody: the first violins incorporate in that rocking motive an allusion to the dotted motive from the principal line in the cello – just a rhythmic allusion, of course, set within an altered directional and developmental dynamic. Thus a synthesis between a main melodic element presented up to this point and the sonic envelopment arises in an ingeniously simple manner. The rise of the [string] envelopment to a guiding rôle first attains, thereby, full power.

Remarkable motivic connections also extend over the entire twelve-measure development. The development exhibits a sonic growth and decline on either side of the principal melody, with motivic uniformity prevailing across the whole twelve-measure wave. The introductory motive [m. 1, second violins] is none other than the later descending figure [in inversion] of the principal line (as it enters for the first time on b♭ in m. 4 in the cello), but without the enhancement of the dotted rhythm [from m. 4], still as an indistinct "pre-figurational" hint of the subsequent main [thematic] shape. Thus if the aforementioned slackening process, from measure 9 on, contains motivic gestures of the main [thematic] shape (particularly in the cited dynamic transformation), then once again more and something other than mere "imitation" resides in these connections.

Within the cello melody itself, the dotted motive always appears as the first turnabout after the [melodic] curve swings upward (b♭–a♭–g in m. 4, etc.). The rhythmically more restless diversion from the surrounding [rhythmic] uniformity lends sensitive expression to the critical unrest of the apex turnabout. [315] The motive thus possesses *dynamic meaning even within the melody*; indeed, the motive is occasioned by that meaning. Note also how these apexes always protrude upward *between rhythmic* stresses. In its curving action the principal line again exhibits countertendencies unusually powerfully in between the upward-thrusting urgency and the descending stepwise series, over which the upward urgency prevails with ever-increasing momentum. Note in this connection how the descending linear fragment following the first upswing (m. 4) is shorter than subsequently. Note further how that first [downward] reaction yields merely an oscillation around the initiating tone g, which is taken up again in measure 5, while thereafter the upswings as well as the stepwise lines leading downward increase in size. Also, a downswing reaching below the initial tone of the curve no longer occurs (as in m. 4, with f) – a highly vivid illustration of how a countertendency in Bruckner's music strengthens the reactive components and does not, perchance, undermine them. The dynamic empathy thus also shows how his melodic art is never founded on a trivial display of the abundant beauty, even in cases of such serene elegiac expression, but rather on inner dynamic turmoil. That, however, leads directly back to the initial problem, to the *illimitability* that emerges here *regarding the lengthwise profile* within the individual line.

For it is precisely the dynamics of the countertendencies that show how wrong it would be to rend the melody into separate phrases such that the descending stepwise lines would always be isolated. It is not a counter*positioning* but rather a counter*tension* that constitutes the inner force of the melody, not a rending but rather *unity*. Consider, for example, measures 7 and 8. If the empathy is directed only toward the successive downward-drifting stepwise lines, the result is a feeble tiering process that misses the point: the heightened counteraction of the [foregoing] upswing, which finally discharges [its tension] over an entire octave, and which in no way requires a slur for a coherent performance. The highest tone (e.g. c″ in m. 8) must not be played as though the preceding upswing interval had no significance. In performance, the shaping energy must remain active across enormous tone and motive series, complete with local closures. Here (as everywhere), phrase markings in the score [316] are easily completely misunderstood. For one thing, it is unfortunately still impossible to determine to what extent foreign influences intruded (see p. 249n [in Kurth's text]). However, even if, for example, the phrase markings (given in Ex. 6.11 faithfully according to the score) go back to Bruckner himself, they in no way mean what the current nit-picking over phrases eagerly makes out of them (in the same way that individual slurs in Bach's manuscripts, for instance, by no means always refer to phrasing, as has been proven).[44] They could be optional suggestions for playing legato. Furthermore, Bruckner did not insert phrase markings with the strictness that was later attributed to them. More generally, he wanted continually to urge the players to a flowing connectedness by means of slur markings, and above all did not intend

---

[44] [EK] Actually, in order to clarify the real continuities, several slurs would have to be superimposed over one another in the cello part, i.e., longer ones would have to subsume the shorter ones. Or it would better suit the wave progression in the first violin part, for example, if a larger, *two-bar* slur were placed over the two small component phrases in measures 1–2, likewise over measures 3 and 4. Furthermore, a slur in the first violin part from the second eighth note in measure 6 (eb′) up through measure 8 would suit the component progression, and so forth. Of course too many directives never lead to anything good, and it is best to leave the phrase groupings to the instinct of the performer. Bruckner wanted it that way. In general, the phrasing indications of the score have been preserved in the following examples of this book, even though there was grave doubt at times. The piano arrangements of Schalk and Löwe even depart from them occasionally. The addition of larger embracing slurs that subsume the component phrases seemed warranted to me only in special cases. A special discussion on this issue in every single case would have burdened the book too much.

[LR] Neither the Haas edition (1936) nor the two Nowak editions (1953, 1975) contain the slurs of Kurth's example, which follows the corrupted Schalk–Löwe score. Bruckner's original score (1874; Nowak, 1975) does slur each dotted eighth/sixteenth-note pair (mm. 4, 6, 7, and 8). See our chapter 7, note 8.

every slur ending to be felt as a boundary. The best proof would be the obvious inconsequence of the slurs in these measures, in case one were to take them for strict phrase divisions. Measures 3–6 would then apparently no longer correspond to measures 7–8 (the interval of the upswing, for instance, is at first included under the slur, and is then split off [from it]; the upbeat phrasing also changes with the phrasing at measure endings amid identical motives, etc.). Hence in this case one may not adhere literally [to the phrase markings] and must recognize the purposeful incorporation of component motions into the unified interplay of forces.[45] The dictate of "endlessness" rules here, too. The fluency may not be removed from the continuous development. [317] The delineation of parts in such longer melodies in no way requires strict clarity (from the standpoint of the whole principle of melodic style), as is appropriate to small, individual developmental motives (which will be discussed more specifically[46]). For these [developmental motives] are simple gestures of force, which exert their influence in one impulse and thus appear alternately in various voices. In the motion of a melody, by contrast, a process of fluent broadening prevails, which links tension-laden phrase endings into subsequent music, as could be observed in the broader melos of the whole symphonic process with regard to the component waves. With Bruckner, even the single-line melody carries concealed within itself the type of flux in that wave current.[47]

---

[45] [LR] See note 47 below. Schenker also expressed frustration over printed slurs. Although the two men approach the problem from different angles, the reasons behind their frustrations are in fact similar (Schenker, "Weg mit dem Phrasierungsbogen!", *Das Meisterwerk in der Musik*, vol. I, 41–60; trans. Sylvan Kalib as "Let's Do Away with the Phrasing Slur!", in "Thirteen Essays," vol. II, 53–83).

[46] [LR] See pages 195–98 below.

[47] [EK] Accordingly, how should the practical *performance* be carried out? Here a fanaticism over clarifying misunderstood phrasing has already turned a great deal of sense into nonsense. Everything cannot be forced into the same mold. The efforts of many orchestra conductors focus on the most scrupulous adherence to all phrasings, down to minutiae throughout every instrumental part of one section. That is an achievement (widespread especially through Riemann's theory of phrasing and, in practice, since Bülow's groundbreaking influence) which is always beneficial in compositional styles based on strong [phrase] segmentation, hence especially in the Classical style (of course one can also frequently hear it exaggerated in the extreme, mottling the continuity of pieces into a patchwork, the music into hairsplitting [*Kleinspielerei*]!). In the case of other linear styles, this practice often turns into the nonsense of a totally misconceived orchestral discipline. Besides, the Classical style exhibits a strengthening of the rhythmic accentuation, unique in music history, which rather unilaterally takes control of the phrasing. That, too, is relaxed considerably in Bruckner's music. Whoever listens somewhat closely to Bruckner's music will have to admit that the magnificence of his linear unfolding (*Linienentfaltung*) lies not in fragmented pieces but rather precisely in its fluid and dynamic integration. If, for example, in the present case [Ex. 6.11] some of the performers bring out the descending motive independently, it would be wrong to prevent others from bringing out more the integrative upswinging motive; and both motives should definitely not be drilled to achieve identical bowings among the performers. It is far more artistic to allow the appealing differences in phrasing here (as in the bowing itself) to blend, and to shape the continuously flowing progression precisely by means of their intermingling, and thereby to sustain the tension and dynamic course of the long developments from the conductor's podium. The melos is internally so manifold that it will become dull through a drilled uniformity in phrase articula-

[318] If, finally, we examine the *harmonic activity* of the whole symphonic developmental wave in Example 6.11, we will also see connections with the overall dynamics. At the moment of the retrogression caused by the emergent enveloping violin parts taking the lead (m. 9), and by the simultaneous pause in the principal melody, the pale diffraction into a strong flat-key progression occurs. The languor of the final abatement of the wave is also expressed in the subdominant cadence.[48] A full, straightforward parallelism holds, therefore, between the harmony and the dynamic design. Later examples will show [319] that even parallelism sometimes undergoes subtle disturbances, since the harmony is related, not to the momentary conditions, but to far-reaching processes, and frequently has anticipatory effects, in the spirit and service of the whole anticipatory feeling of tension in Bruckner's music.

This third preliminary example also shows ever more clearly the extent to which the unity of the expansive symphonic undulatory melos dominates the creative process and all technical phenomena, even motivic ones, and [shows] how inade-

tion. Bruckner himself gives a clear sign in the scores: often *one and the same melodic part* may well be assigned to *different instruments*, but they exhibit *different phrase markings*! This is not a case of mere reinforcement but, additionally, a subtle internal enrichment of the undulating melodic course. Furthermore, it should be clear to anyone who has understood that continuity can extend even across rests and *staccato* tones that *legato* slurs do not always necessitate a separation at phrase endings, not a severing of the melodic course. Orchestral phrasing in general ought not to be abandoned altogether, but it should not degenerate into nit-picking. For, on the other hand, the comprehension of independently arising short motives, above all, of the aforementioned *developmental motives*, for example, very clearly requires phrasing in service of the developmental dynamics. Both distinctness and intentional indistinctness in phrase articulation interact in Bruckner's melos. But where they alternate, where distinctness or indistinctness predominates, cannot be schematically determined; rather, it is a question of artistic tact, of empathy. Such fluid boundaries must of course remain unwelcome to some personalities, but ultimately they characterize all things artistic.

The drilling for uniform phrasing, considered the sole salvation by many conductors of today, rightly suits the mistaken "explication" of music even in that form of scholarly research which destroys feeling instead of awakening it, which no longer sees the flowing source of creativity because it geometrizes the surface phenomena. Here the healthy instinct of practical music making usually steps in therapeutically for the better. For the orchestra performers bring with them different ways of connecting and shaping melodies from different training, something which can only benefit the symphonic style, as a richly differentiated whole of the most multi-faceted inner life possible. This lacking uniformity in the method of instrumental training is readily lamented as a misfortune by every single school, and in reality is good fortune. It guards against the dreadful mechanization in orchestral performance, which is considered by many to be progressive, academic, scholarly, or whatever else. The search for boundaries when their absence is the uppermost stylistic principle is nonsense, an element of that impotence which always intends something good and always produces something harmful.

[48] [LR] By "subdominant cadence" Kurth means that the harmony comes from regions that lie on the descending circle of fifths relative to a given starting point, for example in the key of C major a cadence in E♭ major. In Example 6.11 the allusion to G♭ major (m. 9) is "subdominantic" (*subdominantisch*) in the governing key of C minor. In addition to the local function of G♭ major as a sign of momentary retrogression, the reference to G♭ major near the beginning of the movement anticipates certain harmonic events in the movement, for example at measures 57–58, 63–65, 101–04, and, strikingly, the reference to C♭ major at measures 225–28.

quate the isolation of a single melodic strand is, or even of several strands. Attempting to construct "thematic analyses" based on [individual strands] leads only to idle superficialities. Once the feeling for dynamics has been properly awakened in our hearing, it is just as little a prime necessity for us to become aware in a first listening of all the individual component lines in the symphonic undulation than it is for a natural wind to reveal all of its swirling air currents – just as in the furor of creation the whole symphonic wave swells and discloses all of its contributory unfoldings (*Teilentfaltungen*) only to the discerning master.

7

Details of Bruckner's symphonic waves

Our chapter 7 continues the translations begun in chapter 6, from *Bruckner*, part 2, chapter 2. As explained in the introductory paragraphs to our chapter 6, part 2 of *Bruckner* contains a series of preliminary analyses that initiate the reader into Kurth's style of analysis, and provide a framework for understanding the extended discussions of each movement of the symphonies, as well as of Bruckner's other major works, in volume 2 of *Bruckner*.

In our chapter 6, the discussions of excerpts from the first and last movements of the Sixth Symphony, and from the second movement of the Fourth, gave us the basic idea of Kurth's approach to form. The analytical discussions included below probe further into the details of dynamic formal processes. Kurth addresses reverberatory waves (*Nachbebungen*, literally "after-tremors") in a short excerpt from the first movement of the Ninth Symphony (Ex. 7.1). Two passages from the first movement of the Fifth illustrate how Bruckner creates a sense of symphonic space (Exx. 7.2, 7.3), and an excerpt from the second movement of the Seventh shows how formal dynamics affect developmental motives (Ex. 7.4). Finally, the opening of the first movement of the Eighth Symphony illustrates thematic-motivic evolution and the effect of formal dynamics on harmony (Exx. 7.5–7.8). My notes refer to other, perhaps more familiar analyses of the opening of the Eighth in publications by Hugo Leichtentritt, Werner Korte, and Constantin Floros.

Wave and linear dynamics: an exploration of additional features

[319] Wherever the small scale is comprehended in Bruckner's music, it always expands promptly into the large scale. From all sides, the examination of the wave structure spontaneously widens the view to the whole drama of the highly formative undulatory play. The dependence of the image of the individual wave on the developmental stage from which it is taken shows that, beginning with the formal elements (the symphonic waves), entirely different factors must be brought to the fore than with the elements of Classical grouping structure. Certain similarities [with Classical grouping structure], which can easily cause confusion, also acquire an altered meaning, as will become apparent. Since, in aiding the large-scale structural play of forces, all the formal possibilities of individual waves remain infinitely varied and, additionally, since further contexts are always incorporated into and dynamically aid ever larger ones, it must be clear from the outset that

we cannot aim at schematizing the wave forms. Thus dwelling on the small dimensions, besides adding to the general features, will also help in grasping [320] large contexts before the examination of form shifts to those.

If we compare a *sonic ebbing* [*Abklingen*] with the beginnings [of movements examined] so far, even in smaller waves an apparent contradiction within the whole arises, a counteraction [*Widerspiel*] under the general principle of the countertendency [*Gegenstrebung*]. The vitality of form, which occasions the creative exception, embodies the logic the necessitates all contrasts and unites them into a clearer totality. As earlier in initiatory waves, here too the progress is rarely steady: undulations and the play of recurrent small *after-tremors* arching upward exhibit a natural state even in the attenuation. It is quite easy to see in the principal line itself why the following example [Ex. 7.1] is particularly suited for observing this detail. These measures are not, incidentally, the concluding wave of a full attenuation but rather the concluding wave of a large component gesture – something which always illustrates the interactive animated processes more fully. The measures are from the beginning of the Ninth Symphony, which builds up over several large arches. The first of them generates this ascending wave at its end.[1]

Ex. 7.1 [K12] Ninth Symphony, first movement, mm. 18–26

[1] [LR] Kurth's example follows Ferdinand Löwe's 1903 edition (Doblinger) of Bruckner's original score (1896). Löwe introduced many cuts and extensively modified the texture and orchestration. Bruckner's original work did not appear until Robert Haas's and Alfred Orel's edition of 1934. Leopold Nowak published his edition in 1951.

Although Löwe's edition is corrupt, Example 7.1 is relatively free of tampering. One difference is that Löwe doubles the first and second horn parts in measures 22–26 ("right-hand" part in Kurth's reduction)

[321] Initially, certain phenomena must be explained in light of the broad overriding coherence, the highly unique thematic relations being set aside once again until the discussion of the whole work. While the principal line juts abruptly upward, the strong harmonic darkening (D minor being the point of departure) is noteworthy. The darkening peaks in the apex measure with the sharply protruding C♭-major chord. As long as we look only at this wave in isolation, this harmonic turn seems to contradict the positioning of the climax. In reality, despite its initial upward surge, in the overall context [of mm. 1–26] it is the *conclusion* of a larger initiatory section, and from that perspective the whole subdominant darkening is a wonderful expression of the overall dynamic. The wave as a whole is perceived as an ebbing away. If it were to stand alone, or in another context, with its jagged outline, the tonal darkening would be unmotivated and absent.[2] Hence the harmonic course here is based on the parallelism with *large-scale* formal processes. (This parallelism also explains the somber instrumental coloring: horns on the principal line; beneath, as in the preceding sections, a string tremolo, which however is now darkened by the four horns in sustained chords.)

In the measures isolated here, the shape of the upswing to measure 21 is easy to follow, as two gestures soaring upward very suddenly. The magnificent drama of forces in the downswing is less easy to follow. It begins in a steep, unbroken line (past m. 23), and we might expect that it would continue to the end in a descending motion, either directly or in gentle curves. However, a strong *after-trembling undulatory thrust* takes hold of the downswing from below (at m. 24); it is another local upsurge which then ebbs away more slowly and leaves only the low tremolo as a remnant (the continued ferment of the developmental forces from the beginning of the symphony). The power of the entire upward thrust has not yet exhausted itself within the one sweeping principal wave; the *after-wave* is plainly elemental, natural, an expression of the force which breaks forth time and again from below.[3]

---

with the third and fourth horns. The main difference is that Löwe places the third and fourth horns on the sixth e♭′–c♭′ in measure 21, a sixth higher (for added brilliance no doubt) than Bruckner's setting of g♭–e♭′. Kurth's interpretation of Example 7.1 does not rely on the setting of the horns.

[2] [EK] The darkening has further connections, which will come out in the full discussion [of the symphony, in *Bruckner*, vol. II, 684–88, 690–92, 695–96, 701–02]. [LR] Harmonic "shading" and striking turns toward subdominant-side harmony are discussed in *Romantische Harmonik*, 159–74. Our chapter 4 includes some of Kurth's discussion (see pp. 100–09).

[LR] Regarding the dynamically recessive character of measures 18–26, recall that the Ninth Symphony begins with a soft pedal on D, which acts as an increasingly tense background for the elemental motives D–F–D and D–A–D. The suspenseful build-up leads to the passage shown in Example 7.1. Measure 21 is at once the climax of the preceding music and the moment when the accumulated tension is discharged, hence the "dark," subdominant-side C♭-major harmony and the allusion to D♭-minor harmony (C♭: ii) by means of its applied dominant in measures 25–26.

[3] [EK] Thus in *performance* absolutely no pathos, no sentimentality should be injected into an apex tone such as the one in measure 24! No "sighing figure," as one hears over and over again, only a natural feeling of force, formal power, *pure* music!

Eliminate the after-wave [322] and imagine the downswing completing its plunge directly, and from the difference we will understand Bruckner's whole formal power in miniature. Measure 24, viewed separately, has a dynamic disposition within the framework of the five-bar retrogression (mm. 21–26) precisely analogous to that of the entire eight measures within the whole preceding opening. We see that it is crucial to view parts only as components that are dynamically determined. Therefore, if we can speak once again of a countertendency that pervades the principal course, it is of a completely different type than in previously observed concurrent counteractions. It is a countertendency in the lengthwise profile. Contradictions are thus transformed into overpowering accord...[4]

[338]...The sense of space is always a reflection of the sense of form. For the sense of space, being evoked by formal processes in the first place, is also contingent upon the particular, stylistically variable type of formal processes for the nature of its aural experience.[5]

If this phenomenon [of space], whose diversity can come to light only in the course of the investigation, is already taken up here in general, it is because with Bruckner it is most closely linked to the *developmental motives*. [339] Very vivid, distinctive linear progressions are formed, which are connected dynamically with the sonic tierings in particular, even giving shifts in tone coloring and other means of [creating] formal perspective with a clear sense of spatiality.[6] Elongated motivic gestures that imply endlessness aid in the shift toward remote spaces [while] arched, broadly curving formations aid [in simulating] the hollow interior spaces. An example from the Fifth Symphony can serve as an illustration. It is once again merely a brief reverberative intervening passage, still not one of the pronounced

---

[4] [LR] Kurth continues by explaining and illustrating after-waves (*Nachwellen*, pp. 322–27), the dynamic meaning of unison passages (pp. 328–32), and of linear and motivic procedures (pp. 332–37). He then takes up the idea of spatiality, which is the subject of the next paragraphs. The translation continues with the last sentence of the second paragraph on p. 338, at the words "Das Raumgefühl ist stets ein Gegenbild des Formgefühls..."

[5] [LR] Recall Kurth's characterization of form as "control of force through space and time" (*Bruckner*, vol. I, 239: "*Bezwingung der Kraft durch Raum und Zeit.*"). August Halm stresses the element of time in musical form: "Understanding musical form means understanding the art of time. If we are able to do that, if we recognize that time is not just the playground for music but rather a chief factor, indeed to a certain extent its content, then apparently superficial determinations suddenly become for us essential and full of life" (*Die Symphonie Anton Bruckners*, 19). In saying this, Halm is trying to distinguish between form as simple thematic succession ("*Sich-folgen der Themen,*" ibid.) and form as a dynamic temporal process. Kurth adds to that temporal shaping a spatial shaping, a metaphorical nearness or remoteness (sonic perspective) created, for instance, by means of register or instrumental timbre. Motives and themes may press to the fore or recede into the distance, as explained in connection with Examples 6.5 and 7.2.

[6] [LR] Kurth discusses developmental motives in *Grundlagen*, 417–38, and more fully in the essay "Zur Motivbildung Bachs," 89–96. Chapter 2 of the present volume includes translations from the relevant passages in *Grundlagen*. Chapter 3 of *EKATA* (pp. 55–77) is devoted to developmental motives.

and lengthier spatial contrasts like those yet to be amply investigated later. It is also one of the instructive cases where the appropriate developmental motive does not appear suddenly, as a new, independent formation. Rather, its emergence from a thematic motion is clearly recognizable.

In the first principal theme (similar to the Sixth Symphony; see Ex. 6.5), after the bass enters, an intermediary structure appears which, coupled with the sonic attenuation, contains a high-register motive in the airy sound of the flute. It is in the fourth of the following measures.[7]

Ex. 7.2 [K18] Fifth Symphony, first movement, mm. 55–60

---

[7] [LR] The reduction in Example 7.2 is based on Franz Schalk's edition of the Fifth Symphony (Doblinger, 1896), which Bruckner never saw. Schalk prepared the edition in 1893 and used it for a performance in 1894 which Bruckner was unable to attend owing to poor health. In addition to making large cuts, Schalk essentially reorchestrated the entire work, fundamentally altering the sound and texture, so that Bruckner's original conception is completely obliterated. Of such drastic cuts, Halm says wryly "Bruckner's symphonies are too long only when they are cut!" (quoted in Oskar Lang, *Anton Bruckner*, 116; see also Karl Grunsky, *Anton Bruckner*, 48). A recent study by Thomas Leibnitz on the relationship between the Schalk brothers and Bruckner puts their editorial work into perspective (*Die Brüder Schalk und Anton Bruckner* [Tutzing: Schneider, 1988]). Leibnitz discusses Joseph Schalk's version of the Fifth Symphony as an example of extensive editorialization (ibid., 280–300). According to Leibnitz, three basic things motivated the Schalk brothers to instigate and implement changes: (1) to combat claims of orchestrational "brutality" (Hanslick), and to bring the work of the supposed "Wagnerian symphonist" closer to a Wagnerian ideal through reorchestration; (2) to transform any static traits into dynamic ones; and (3) to parry attacks about formlessness and criticisms of exaggerated length by abbreviating the symphonies (ibid., 286–88).

Kurth comments only on the flute reverberation in Example 7.2, which Schalk did not change. Kurth's reduction does, however, reflect several of Schalk's editorial changes. For example, Schalk added the horn in measures 58–59, presumably to fill in the space between the abrupt end of the melody in the low string parts and the flute reverberation. Further, Schalk added a clarinet to the melody in the viola and cello. Neither the horn nor the clarinet appear in Nowak's edition (1951) of Bruckner's 1876 score. (Fritz Oeser discusses editorial changes affecting Bruckner's orchestration in *Die Klangstruktur der Bruckner-Symphonie*, 51, 53, 55.) Despite Schalk's alterations in Example 7.2, Kurth's interpretation is reasonable, although the horn in measures 58–59 may have helped to create the sense of space that the flute fills in.

The whole sonic impression of that measure seems to be captured in the one flute motive. For it is a motive that reaches out into the heights [340], that juts up into the vaulting space (of the intervening void within the principal line). Further, it is not difficult to see how this is a linear reflex of the last fragment from the principal line, especially in the first upward hurling of the angular fourth motion into the heights (hence an imitation, or better, an imitative transformation aiding the developmental dynamic). Observe how this shaping force, which reaches far into the metaphysical domain, modifies a subsequent, parallel passage, constructed from the same theme, but now set with a fuller texture.[8]

Ex. 7.3 [K19] Fifth Symphony, first movement, mm. 367–73

[8] [EK] It can also be seen (in accordance with the note on page 317 [our p. 185, note 47]) how Bruckner gives the theme in the low strings completely different phrasing slurs than in Example 7.2 [K18] and, moreover, how the woodwinds lying above are phrased collectively under one large slur. It could not be proven any more compellingly that Bruckner was thinking of an intermingling of different phrasings in spun-out melodies. It is not necessary here, either, that every individual instrumental part get the same phrasing by all players.

[341] Once again Bruckner contrasts the wonder of spatiality, of the empty interior infiniteness, with the wonder of mass and processive formation. This time the intermediary passage is also accorded a larger extension, in reaction to the denser sonic fullness. It appears as a *diminuendo* of the remaining high string tremolo, and extends over three measures [mm. 370–72]. This time the high motive does not appear until the second measure, but those are not the only changes. The previous, ideal continuation of the ascending final thematic fragment [Ex. 7.2, mm. 58–59] into boundless space appears here (again in the flute) transformed into a broader symbol of *vaulting* (successive fourth and fifth leaps stretching over a total of one and a half octaves). With the more extended sonic attenuation, it is like an emblem of a broad horizon, suggested by ingeniously short motivic flashes. (Thus we comprehend the meaning of this particular entrance only at its second measure [of the reverberatory passage, Ex. 7.3, m. 371], the rests surrounding the motive concurring fully with its dynamic of a wide swing out into the void.) There is still more: in the low strings [Ex. 7.3, mm. 371–72], there are also faint remnants of the final, much more fully orchestrated thematic motion [from mm. 369–70] added in.[9] This thin, low-register sound [in mm. 371–72] enhances the vaulting sensation – it is the contrary motion against the flute part – and joins with the flute in a broad *spatial rounding out*. (It is thus much more than a mere after-effect of the thematic material from the preceding measures, also rounded out. The thematic material itself, [342] including the counterparts appearing there, is already an expression of expansiveness.)

The comparison of these last two passages [Exx. 7.2 and 7.3] already shows Bruckner's formal power in the shaping of space, together with its motivic refinement to the smallest detail.

[LR] Schalk's editorial changes go further in Example 7.3 than in Example 7.2. Note 7 above points out some of the changes in Example 7.2. In Example 7.3, besides adding the bassoon, horn, trumpet, and various octave doublings, Schalk has changed Bruckner's slur markings so that Kurth's comments on the phrasing are not entirely correct. In the original score, the phrasing for the string parts in Examples 7.2 and 7.3 is identical, not different, as Schalk has it. The woodwind parts are, however, embraced by a single slur, so that it is not unreasonable to speak of intermingled phrasings in Example 7.3. In the string parts, Schalk seems to have extended what Bruckner meant as bow markings into long-breathed melodic phrase markings. Fritz Oeser points out the discrepancies between Kurth's account of the phrasing, based on Schalk's edition, and Bruckner's notated phrasing in *Die Klangstruktur der Bruckner-Symphonie*, 29–31.

Besides the editorial changes, there are a few errors in Kurth's reduction. Like Schalk, Kurth failed to put in flat signs for the As in the melody at measure 368. Further, Kurth's reduction shows C♯s rather than C♭s in the bass instruments (lowest staff) in measure 373. These errors are corrected in our example.

[9] [LR] Measures 369 and 370 of Example 7.3, the ones Kurth says are scored "much more fully," are in fact not scored quite so fully in Bruckner's version as they are in Schalk's edition. Schalk added the bassoon to the lower line (cellos and violas), divided the oboes in octaves, and set the first and second clarinets in octaves. He also added trumpets and horns in measures 368–69. Nevertheless, despite Bruckner's sparser scoring in measures 369–70, measures 371–72 are thinner by comparison, and thus could be heard as being "remote," especially in light of the ensuing *fortissimo* entrance.

The relationship between developmental dynamics and thematic content

If we now explore further the technique of developmental motives, that is, the influence of formal dynamics on the linear content as such, the dynamics show the way in all cases. For the phenomenon of developmentally determined structures penetrates to the small and even to the smallest dimensions, to the formal atom, and likewise expands into the large dimension, into the developmental course. An individual example like the following [Ex. 7.4] can illustrate concisely and relatively simply the aforementioned connections among dynamics, thematic content and development, symphonic accompaniment, motivic content, and the undulatory course. Proceeding inconspicuously in its overall effect, on closer examination the example illustrates how the dynamic action shapes every linear strand in all details, thus facilitating its course. Precisely therein lies the unobtrusiveness, the "naturalness" of the overall symphonic impression.[10]

[344] The measures shown are only an excerpt from a larger undulatory escalation, in the vicinity of the apex section, hence neither at the beginning nor at the end of the wave boundary. The principal melody is spun out in the cello. However, one senses in a first hearing that the cello cannot be designated as the actual bearer of the development, that the development resides in the overall

Ex. 7.4 [K20] Seventh Symphony, second movement, mm. 67–74

---

[10] [LR] Kurth probably used the edition of the score published in 1885 by Albert Gutmann. Bruckner, with the help of Joseph Schalk and Ferdinand Löwe, made changes in the orchestration in 1883, the year he completed the work. The Gutmann edition contains further changes made by Schalk and Löwe *after* their collaboration with Bruckner. Except for a tie missing in the double-bass part between measures 70 and 71 – the same tie is missing in Kurth's example – there are no major differences between Example 7.4 and the passage as it appears in Nowak's edition (1954).

Ex. 7.4 (cont.)

surrounding motivic content, despite the cello's melodic prominence. The upper voice [first violins] aids that content in a highly characteristic manner. Purely motivically, it is related to the sixteenth-note figure in the cello melody. But this "imitation" is once again not the fundamental aspect but more a unifying, overarching individual progression.[11] The upper voice takes up the sixteenth-note figure only in order to place its supple mobility in service of the leading idea of the whole developmental dynamic. These motivic transformations could just as easily be derived from a fragment of any other melody and, with a different motive, would conform to the same developmental motions, which are decisive. The actual [compositional] difficulty and art is not at all a matter of such motivic association

---

[11] [LR] The sixteenth-note motive actually goes back to the theme that enters at measure 37 (rehearsal letter D). Various ascending and descending sixteenth-note figures appear – at measures 38, 43, and 50, to mention a few – so that the violin and cello motives in Example 7.4 are heard in relation to those earlier events, and not just in relation to each other. It seems curious that Kurth would say the violins imitate the cellos, when in fact the violins play the sixteenth-note figure first. Kurth may be hearing the violin figure as an imitation of the cellos in the two measures preceding Example 7.4.

itself, in the way formalistic investigation generally stresses it as the be-all and end-all. Motivic unity is surely masterful and noteworthy, but the actual art resides in the way the *fluid transformation into developmental motives* is *derivable from every* motive or melodic fragment.

Since the first two measures are still a part of the escalation, this sixteenth-note figure, taken into the uppermost voice purely as a development motive, [345] *stretches* directly upward. Precisely at the apex point, beginning at measure 69, it curls into a *wavering* figure that maintains the buoyancy of the apex. At the descent (from m. 73 on) [there is] a transformation into a highly vivid *downward-climbing* formation, at once loosening the original motivic relationship (all the more unobjectionable since here the principal melody in the cellos has ceased). The inner voices (second violins and violas) contain in their "accompanimental figures" a thoroughly essential element of the whole measured, fluid dynamic. They are not "rhythmic arpeggiations of chords" but rather, apart from their effect of filling out the harmony, they are developmental motives of a fluent type of *expanding motion*. And this motivic dynamic escalates artfully in the sustained contrary motion between the second violins and violas. The aura of widening and narrowing unites the two voices (just as, in general, it is a feature of the symphonic style that individual voices unite illimitably into separate sonic motions).[12] Even with the principal cello melody it can be observed how, at its peak (from m. 69 on), its sixteenth-note motive twists into a *curling wave* form. With greatest sensitivity, Bruckner thus gives it an inverted wave motion in relation to that of the first violins, since the motives alternate in the two voices, and thus the undulant swaying between them reflects their balanced opposition (inversion), down to the most minute linear formation. The staggering of apexes in the individual lines is thus also manifest, something which likewise affects the inner voices. Not a single one of the measures exhibits simultaneous peaks in any two lines, and in this respect the developmental progression illustrates still more. In measures 71 and 72, where the upper voice and the cello melody have already reached their highest points, internally an intensification of the inner motions continues, which maintains the tension.[13] Even here the peaks of those two inner voices do not coincide. In the descent from measure 73 on, it is further characteristic that the soaring, upward-striving expanding motives in the viola immediately reverse into a downward motion, and further that the second violin part is simplified into a plain descending developmental motive – its chain of syncopations resisting the overall

---

[12] [LR] As the music approaches the local apex (mm. 69–72), it is noteworthy that the second violins restrain their rocking motion slightly by introducing a neighbor-note gesture in measures 61–66, and then restore the uninterrupted rocking motion at measure 67, just before the apex.

[13] [LR] Note also that as the wave reaches its highest point (m. 71), the low G♯ in the bass drops out, effectively exposing the high register. At measure 73, when the descent begins, the low G♯ returns.

motion sinking gently downward, [346] more a downward swaying motion within the overall dynamic. The entire symphonic aura is thus woven with dynamics down to the finest strands. (We will return to the noteworthy *external* dynamics, the *p* at the peak in m. 69, in connection with the forms of energy in wave summits.)

The perspective on larger contexts: the art of motivic unity

The beginning of the Eighth Symphony below throws some light on how little the *motivic uniformity* is impaired amid this whole art of dynamic continuities, refined down to the smallest linear strands, how it [the motivic uniformity] in no way degenerates, perchance, into free "coincidental forms." For here even the second principal theme appears as a developmental structure derived from the first theme such that there is at once the greatest logic and vividness of the energetic motions, as well as the most rigorous motivic economy [*Konzentration*]. Looking ahead, the course is that the first principal theme, which enters as a highly differentiated, jagged and by no means simple structure, is soon drawn toward simpler, typical energetic motions at its continuation and is dissolved until, finally, a new version of those motions gives rise to the second theme. Other characteristic hallmarks of the wave technique can also be considered at the same time.

The principal theme appears at the beginning in magnificent spasmodic gestures, once again mysteriously from the depths.[14]

Ex. 7.5 [K21] Eighth Symphony, beginning of the first movement [mm. 1-6]

[14] [LR] Kurth probably used Joseph Schalk's 1892 edition of the Eighth, which is a corrupted version of the revised score that Bruckner made, with Schalk, between 1887 and 1890. Nowak published the 1890 Bruckner-Schalk version (without Schalk's pre-publication alterations) in 1955, as well as Bruckner's original 1887 score in 1973. Haas published yet a different version (1939), which mixes Bruckner's 1887 original with the Bruckner-Schalk 1890 revision. Deryck Cooke explains the circumstances in *The Bruckner Problem Simplified*, 13-14.

There are no substantial differences, in orchestration or otherwise, between Kurth's reductions in Examples 7.5, 7.6, and 7.8, and the Bruckner-Schalk 1890 score. According to Manfred Wagner, the differences between the 1887 original and the 1890 revision are, in general, less extensive than in the cases

[347] The bass line lurches sharply upward and sinks back to the fifth, C, as a formation whose tremendously powerful *initiatory* character needs no special mention. Here, too, a primal impulse of a mere tremolo leads off once again.[15] (An initiatory harmonic duskiness is contained in the subdominant darkening of the principal tonality, C minor.)

No sooner have we looked beyond the first entrance than, in addition to all of the vividness (dynamic flexibility) of the actual main waves, we are confronted from all sides with the way Bruckner allows the most varied constituent waves and effects of sonic perspective to appear. [He does this] in order to relate the small-scale [formal] arch, already full of inner tendencies, to the large arch, and to reconcile both into a cooperative accord of their energies.

With the initial lapsing of the bass line at the beginning of measure 5, the sound again opens outward into the void. It allows the primal impulse of the tremolo

of the Third and Fourth Symphonies (*Der Wandel des Konzepts: Zu den verschiedenen Fassungen von Bruckners Dritter, Vierter und Achter Sinfonie* [Vienna: Musikwissenschaftlicher Verlag, 1980], 39, 52). Wagner points out that the orchestration in the 1887 score is more distinctively Brucknerian than in the 1890 revision, which he says is more Wagnerian (ibid., 39). Ultimately, he considers the two versions equally valid in their own right (ibid., 52).

[15] [EK] The energetic impulse of the tremolo is here, as very often, masked and tempered by a brass part (horn) on the same tone, so that more of a flickering from out of a serene interior comes about.

[LR] Kurth's analysis of the opening of the Eighth as having a "powerful initiatory character" and, a little further on, as being full of "inner tendencies" differs from Werner Korte's description of the initial thematic gestures of the Eighth as being self-contained, i.e., "'complete' structures, which discontinue their melodic thrust at the last tone." According to Korte, Bruckner's thematic genius lay in understanding how to set forth pithy, self-sufficient melodic formations, then to "unlock" their potential and evolve logically additional melodic material (*Bruckner und Brahms* [Tutzing: H. Schneider, 1963], 25). Korte's comments apply to Bruckner's thematic structures in general, but they derive specifically from the opening of the Eighth Symphony.

Constantin Floros explains the opening theme of Bruckner's Eighth in a very different way. Based on a combination of biographical and musical evidence, Floros shows that the theme derives from an aria sung by the Dutchman in Wagner's opera *Der fliegende Holländer* (1841). As biographical evidence, he cites a letter Bruckner wrote to the conductor Felix Weingartner in 1891, giving a programmatic outline of the symphony. Since the date of the letter may imply that the program was conceived several years after the original score was finished (1887), Floros offers additional evidence to substantiate Bruckner's programmatic intentions. He cites a memoir of Bruckner's friend August Stradal, who reports a conversation he had with Bruckner in 1886, in which the composer, then working intensively on the score, interpreted the Eighth Symphony programmatically (Floros, *Brahms und Bruckner: Studien zur musikalischen Exegetik* [Wiesbaden: Breitkopf und Härtel, 1980], 183, 185; see also Floros, "Zur Antithese Brahms–Bruckner," *Brahms-Studien*, ed. C. Floros [Hamburg: Karl Dieter Wagner, 1974–], vol. I, 82). The conversation and letter speak of a Death-Resignation-Motive (*Todesverkündigung, Totenglocke, Ergebung*). Floros points out the similarity between this dramatic motive and that of the Dutchman's aria and shows, furthermore, how Bruckner's theme resembles the aria melodically and rhythmically (Floros, *Brahms und Bruckner*, 211; see the Schirmer piano–vocal score of *Der fliegende Holländer*, pp. 38–40, at the words "Nur eine Hoffnung soll mir bleiben," and at "Wann alle Toten aufersteh'n"). Floros's programmatic explanation of the Eighth contrasts sharply with the customary "absolutist" view of Bruckner's music. Kurth rejects the interpretation implied in the 1891 letter as merely a suggestion, not be taken literally, to help Weingartner prepare a performance of the Eighth (*Bruckner*, vol. II, 1048n).

to push once again to the fore (raised one step and also reinforced by octave doubling). Additionally, a soft and airy intermediary motive resounds in the clarinet. The motive expands upward in an open fifth (simultaneously expanding the chord to its fifth!). Everywhere the same phenomenon in a new portrayal: at the moment of a merely transitory loosening of the accumulated sonic mass – just a brief relaxation in the formative main progression – sparse structures appear, as though in exterior sonic spheres. Here, briefly and inconspicuously, it is an intervening reverberation of the type already encountered at the opening of the Sixth Symphony (see [our] page 164), a type of reverberation that soon achieves significance in larger contexts, but undergoes internal modifications in the process.[16] In the continuation this process takes shape in the following way.

Ex. 7.6 [K22] Eighth Symphony, first movement, mm. 6–10

[348] Now the bass presses onward once again. The ending of the [bass] line shows most vividly that this segment, too, is not a closure of the preceding initiative but rather another initiative that fades out similarly with an open arch. It ends by stretching upward. *Ascending developments that stretch upward at the conclusion are open arches directed aggressively at subsequent fulfillment.* Closure, or even partial closure after such a lively buildup, would produce a downturn. And it is an extraordinarily subtle stroke here that in the last measure of this [bass] line (eighth measure from the beginning) a delicate viola part surfaces which contains such a slight inversion. It introduces a delicately implied partial closure into the yet open and forward-pointing initiatory development. Bruckner's unlimited dynamic sense shapes the *overall* tension and the *momentary tension at the same time.* What follows is once again the sonically attenuating effect of a reverberation, but this time in the heightened tension owing to the now fuller tremolo [at m. 9], together

---

[16] [LR] Unlike the "spatial" reverberations encountered in Examples 6.5 and 6.6, which momentarily suspend forward motion, the reverberation in Example 7.5 presses forward by leaping upward a fifth, thus forcing an ascending fifth progression from an implied chord on C (beginning of m. 5) to one on G. That ascending fifth progression is the second of two such progressions, the first one being from an implied F chord in measures 1–4, to the C chord in measure 5, and finally to the G chord in measure 6 (anticipated in m. 5).

with the intensive shading effect of a strong subdominant progression to the Ab-minor chord.[17] However, the intervening woodwind motive (mm. 9–10) is no longer the open fifth [as in m. 5] but rather is essentially differentiated to become a chromatic figure, transformed now more clearly into a reverberation of the recent fragment of the principal line, and extended in the process to correspond very vividly to the distant remove of the newly opening sonic tier. The sharper sound of the oboe also adds substance to the ethereal tone of the clarinet. The whole intervening reverberation [349] is thus a significant [textural] consolidation compared with the void of the preceding reverberation in measures 5–6 – within the overall intensifying progression, [it is] an illustration of how such intermittent flashing into the distance plays a part in consolidating the whole atmosphere. Retrospectively, we also recognize that the initial motive of a fifth in the clarinet (mm. 5–6) is not to be understood directly as an "imitation" derived from the bass line (as is superficially always more or less easily possible to reconstruct), but rather as a *pre*-figuration of the woodwind motive in measure 9. For these woodwind fragments stand in a separate *reciprocal* relationship, above and beyond the principal line, whereby the woodwind line, initially a simple symbol of rounding out and expanding, first attains its aforementioned motivic relationship to the principal line at the second appearance (m. 9). Hence once again the prodigious master builder shapes two developmental tiers simultaneously.[18]

This procedure occurs in the course of the movement in a yet larger dimension; the ensuing measures steer toward still other phenomena. Lasting up through the retrogression of the [local] wave, the first de-intensification of the opening theme is shaped as follows.

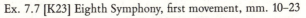

Ex. 7.7 [K23] Eighth Symphony, first movement, mm. 10–23

---

[17] [LR] See note 2 above regarding "shading" and subdominant progressions. Kurth means that, instead of an Ab-major chord, we get an Ab-minor chord, which is in a remote subdominant relationship with the C-minor tonality of the piece. Ab-major harmony is "shaded" into Ab minor by lowering C to Cb, which is highlighted as the lowest voice. Additionally, the texture thickens at measure 9, when the second violins divide and a third horn enters, changing the horn texture from open fifths (mm. 1–8) to a tightly voiced triad.

[18] [LR] Earlier in this paragraph, Kurth spoke of how Bruckner shapes two dynamic tiers at once, the ascending tier that presses forward (ascending bass line into m. 9), and the hint of an imminent, temporary lapsing (descending viola counterpoint to the last fragment of the bass line). It is interesting that the descending oboe–clarinet motive derives from that viola part. In other words, not only has Bruckner shaped both tiers at once, he has in fact dovetailed them.

Ex. 7.7 (cont.)

[350] At first, the powerful ascent of the principal line continues, swooping downward in more moderate arches (also more relaxed rhythmically) before it dissolves into concluding fragments. These also stretch upward at the end both times, and are similarly interrupted by the intermediary woodwinds, with the intervention of *harmonic dynamics* coming very nicely to the fore: after the A♭-minor chord [in m. 10], an immediate turn toward the sharp-key region as an expression of surging, and doubly intense owing to the previous wide swing toward the dark flat-key region (one of the typical forms of initiatory harmonic dynamics with Bruckner). The harshness of this harmonic current is caused by the acute tension of the imminent apex. Again there is also a highly effective refinement in the woodwind motive in measures 13 and 14. Registrally, Bruckner moves it no higher than in measure 9; rather, he reinforces the tension through repetition, by adopting the same pitch level yet letting the internal intensity swell slightly by means of the enharmonic transformation [from G♭ to F♯]. The intervening woodwind motive moves further up only at the next entrance (m. 17), where a striking harmonic phenomenon occurs.[19]

---

[19] [LR] Notice also the four-two position of the chords in measures 13 and 17, as well as the poignant dissonance of the syncopated f♯″ and a♭″ in the woodwinds, all of which adds to the "critical tension" leading to the dissipation. The bass line, too, intensifies, converting c♭ (m. 9) into b♮ (mm. 10–11), which in turn induces the continued ascent to c′ and c♯′ (mm. 14–15). Notice also that the first ascending bass gesture dips down a diminished fifth at measure 12, while at the analogous spot (m. 16) the second bass gesture dips down only a half step. The second bass gesture thus reaches a full fourth above the peak of the first one and so effectively

[351] Although the intensification reaches its apex at this point, a harmonic *darkening* occurs. The wave reaches its summit with the seventh chord G7, which leads toward C minor and, beyond that, into the harmonic darkening of the retrogression. The *apex* itself [at mm. 17-18] exhibits a harmonic retrogression in contrast to the dazzling previous escalatory sections, and so *already embodies harmonically* the tension directed toward *the dissipation*. That dissipation occurs here relatively simply by means of a straightforward dominant chord.[20] Frequently, and in multifarious ways, *harmonic darkenings* enter into Bruckner's *apex sections* (often together with *instrumental* darkenings). The apparent formal contradiction stems from the anticipatory motion of its dynamics. Bruckner thus does not endow the apex with a pure, unrefracted beam but rather imbues it with the presentiment of a forthcoming retrogression. It is an extremely characteristic correlate to the phenomenon where, in apparently dissipating *depths*, *harmonic brightenings* suddenly *fore*shadow the coming renewal, a process that will be observed frequently. An understanding of [dynamic] heights and depths in the imaginative formal activity shows how Bruckner, as the tragic poet of Eulenspiegel's merry wit, does not linger in the moment, in order to give it meaning in light of forthcoming events. In particular, the [harmonic] darkenings at the moment of achieved apexes, often transformed beyond all harmonic color to become a profoundly impressionistic presentiment of depression, are again a partial expression of Bruckner's whole temperament, of the burgeoning anxiety precisely while embracing all exuberance (see [*Bruckner*, vol. I], 176-77).

---

escalates the drive toward the apex in measure 18. Korte, rather than stressing the dynamic unfolding of the theme to measure 18, points out the "chaining structure" (*Kettenstruktur*) of the thematic events, and describes them as "additive." He goes on to liken the additive character of the opening thematic material of the Eighth with that of the First, Fifth, Sixth, and Seventh Symphonies (*Bruckner und Brahms*, 28-32, 36 ["*Additionsthema*"], 65-69 [summary]). Korte's commentary addresses only the external characteristics of the openings of these symphonies. In the Sixth and Eighth Symphonies (Exx. 6.5 through 6.9 and 7.5 through 7.7) Kurth points out internal dynamic qualities that impel the music onward and so counteract a segmented, additive process. Instead we hear a fluid, dynamic process based not only on hypermetric organization, as Korte explains (ibid., 39-43) but also on textural, timbral, registral, and harmonic criteria. Kurth explains that the principle of endless melody predominates in Bruckner's music and overrides the additive features Korte points out (see our chapter 6, pp. 152, 161). In differentiating Bruckner from Schumann and Wagner, Korte, however, denies the "art of transition," in Bruckner and hears instead a joining of "cell to cell, group to group" (*Bruckner und Brahms*, 39).

[20] [LR] It is not the G7 *per se*, an energetic dominant, that signals the dissipation. As Kurth says, it is the contrast of G7 with the previous harmonic development that conveys the sense of attenuation. Specifically, the B7 and D♯ diminished-seventh harmonies in measures 11-14, followed by the F♯7 in measures 15-16 carry the harmony upward by fifths, momentarily suggesting the keys of E major and B major. The arrival of G7 in measure 17, with the bass significantly on f′, abruptly breaks the upward spiral toward remote dominant regions and instantaneously forces the harmony "downward," skipping over several mediating fifths. Notably, the G7 does not resolve. When the recapitulation of the opening events starts in measure 23, the implied F-minor harmony there represents yet a further step by fifth toward the subdominant region.

The instantaneous transformation of the motives as a result of the dynamic impulse is characteristic for the retrogression. The motives acquire a descending form (m. 18) and the intervening segments cease at once. Likewise, at the moment of retrogression, the tremolo [ceases], which was the symbol of the growth impulse. Furthermore, the way that the first rapid retrogression stalls is very beautifully constructed in all component motions. First the descending motive appears in all string parts (except for the contrabass); then the inner voices cease and the motive remains only in the violins, while the basses re-enter (m. 20) beneath with the slow stepwise ascent, F–G. It [the F–G ascent] is at once a concealed *fresh initiative* [352] – in the weakened dynamic of the retrogression, a hint of the very first, short head motive of the principal theme in the bass (see Ex. 7.5).[21] This does not indicate a formalistic symmetry between the subsiding development and the opening one but rather refers covertly to what is forthcoming, to the powerful new initiative of the whole theme, to resolute will. In preceding as well as in forthcoming sections, the transformation of the motives and their whole dependence on the developmental current must be explored in a much broader dimension.[22]

Following the last measure quoted [Ex. 7.7, m. 23], the whole development appears suffused with a powerful new initiative. We can quickly survey it here. The new initiative, which cannot be described here in detail and is easy to recognize in the piece itself, introduces a renewed, much stronger and fuller unfolding of the first theme. Viewed in the large perspective, the partial retrogression in the previously cited measures [Ex. 7.7] is thus merely a gathering of force prior to a fresh, reinforced forward drive. After the second soaring ascent of the principal theme, where the much longer attenuative retrogression nears its end, the descending motive finally enters once again in the following manner.

---

[21] [LR] This "hint" becomes explicit when the basses and cellos, reinforced by horns and tuba, continue in measures 24–25 with F–G♭.

[22] [LR] It is precisely Kurth's dynamic interpretation of motivic transformations – motivic processes as reflections of the momentary stage of dynamic-formal evolution – which distinguishes his motivic analyses from those of Korte (see note 19 above) and Hugo Leichtentritt. In *Musikalische Formenlehre*, 3rd edn, rev., enl. (Leipzig: Breitkopf und Härtel, 1927), 384–436, translated as *Musical Form* (Cambridge, Mass.: Harvard University Press, 1951), 381–85, Leichtentritt discusses the motivic relationships among the themes in the exposition and development of Bruckner's Eighth. He refers to Kurth's analyses as "philosophical and aesthetic." By addressing the "technical, structural features of the symphony," he promises to deal with "important questions" which Kurth left unanswered. Leichtentritt implies, unjustifiably, that Kurth's analysis of the Eighth lacks technical content. While it is true that in the course of analysis Kurth does touch on philosophical and aesthetic issues, it is untrue that his work lacks technical content or rigor. He discusses at length specific aspects of orchestration, harmony, and motivic relationships as they affect form (*Bruckner*, vol. II, 1035–1099), and his discussion leaves no more questions unanswered than does Leichtentritt's essay. In correlating motivic transformations with formal dynamics in the opening of Bruckner's Eighth, Kurth's analysis in fact surpasses Leichtentritt's essentially topographical observations (see Kurth's commentary at the end of this chapter, pp. 206–07).

Ex. 7.8 [K24] Eighth Symphony, first movement, mm. 47–54

[353] The first four of these measures are still within the end of the attenuation; the subsequent measures (from m. 51 on) [are] the beginning of the second principal theme. Overall, the first principal theme runs its course as an enormous double wave, the first constituent wave (up to m. 22) being an antecedent, the second a consequent superseding the first. The control of the forms by the wave technique thus reveals itself in that this technique shapes and guides the outlines of the whole first part of the symphony [occupied] with the principal theme. It is then also the same developmental principle that *leads* into the second principal theme and permits it to arise from the trough of the wave as a new, gentler, fresh undulation – the *thematic shape itself* being merely *engendered* by that whole *developmental process*. In order to get an overview, we must first consider the final subsiding measures of the previous section, i.e. the first four measures of the last example [Ex. 7.8, mm. 47–50].

In those measures, just as in measure 18, the recessive descending motive from the apex fades, [and] something of an element of urgency permeates the whole symphonic fabric owing to the harmonic shift [in mm. 49–50] and, above all, to the highly unusual rhythmic dovetailing of the motive (quarter-note syncopations [alternating between the low strings and oboe on the last half of each beat] dovetailed with a half-bar triplet).[23] It is an expression of the turmoil and blurring in the whole harmonic refraction, the tension of the moment, where the lapsing harmonic structure transforms into a new, faint consolidation. For the second *principal theme* is in fact merely a *transformation of the descending developmental motive*, which recently decelerated in the bass [Ex. 7.8, mm. 49–50]! In a delicate, fresh impulse it [the second theme] arises, as a simple [melodic] inversion, out of the clear dominant harmony, which brightens the harmonic duskiness of the wave trough and engenders new growth.[24] Even the rhythmic connection [between m. 51 and] the descending motive from the reversal at the apex (duplets–triplets, Ex. 7.7, m. 18) is clearly preserved, freed only from its recent dovetailing (prior to m. 50).

Thus even a principal theme appears to be engendered by the dynamic development, almost as if determined by it in natural clarity – here as a simple, tranquil symbol of ascent. On the other hand, however, a review will show that it developed as far back as *the first theme* before it grows melodically into a new wave, even prior to the aforementioned reversal motive, which first appeared in measure 18 (Ex. 7.7). For that motive, too, is just an inversion of a preceding gesture. [354] The triplet rhythms had already crept into the linear development from measure 12 onward (Ex. 7.7), there as a reinforcement of the accelerating intensification, just as here (with the second principal theme [Ex. 7.8, m. 51]) they function as an invigorating renewal.[25] And from measure 12 on the ascending diatonic progression of that triplet figure likewise first arose from the energetic development, from the dynamics of the individual sustaining initiatives throughout the intensification. Consequently, the triplet figure first appearing in measure 12 can be traced back even further, as merely a somewhat more expanded transformation of the ascent in measures 8–9 (Ex. 7.6), which reaches upward in the principal line (there, in a dotted rhythm). Thus *the motivic germ has been traced back directly to the first principal*

---

[23] [LR] Kurth refers to but one of several harmonic shifts that occur prior to the beginning of the second theme in measure 51. A sequential progression in measures 40–44, analogous to measures 18–22, closes on an A♭7 chord (mm. 43–44), which implies a cadence to D♭-major harmony. Instead of leading to D♭ major, the A♭7 resolves deceptively to a B♭♭ chord in measure 45. That deceptive resolution is one of three harmonic shifts on the way to the G-major tonality of the second theme. A second one occurs when the B♭♭ chord moves to a first-inversion E♭7 by chromatic-melodic motion in the first violins and violas (f♭′–e♭′, mm. 46–47). Kurth points out the last and most striking harmonic shift (mm. 49–50), where an A♭7 chord, resolution of the E♭7, becomes an augmented-sixth chord, which in turn resolves to G major (see the immediately following note).

[24] [LR] The enharmonic reinterpretation of g♭″ (oboe, m. 49) to F♯ (low strings, m. 50) effects a vivid harmonic "brightening" as the music passes over the B♭♭, E♭7, and A♭7 harmonies (mm. 45–49) on the way to G major. By means of the G♭/F♯ transformation, the A♭7 harmony becomes an augmented-sixth chord, a substitute dominant in the cadence to G major.

[25] [LR] In connection with the ascending melodic progression in measures 10–17, recall the ascending harmonic progression (B7–F♯7) discussed in note 20 above.

theme, the aforementioned upward reach [in mm. 8–9] being merely an inversion of the end fragment of the very first upward spasm of the theme (Ex. 7.5, mm. 4–5). The energetic motions, previously full of urgency, are discharged tranquilly by the second theme. If once again we compare just the second theme itself (Ex. 7.8, m. 51) with the first theme (Ex. 7.5), we do not immediately recognize any connection whatsoever. On the contrary, [we see] the greatest contrast imaginable, even in the linear form (ignoring the fundamentally different character overall). However, the connection leaps immediately to our attention when, as a mediating link, we single out measure 12 (Ex. 7.7), which reveals at once its connection with measure 4 [Ex. 7.5] in the aforementioned manner (as a broadening dissolution of its angular rhythms and intervals) and, on the other hand (even more clearly), the connection with the second principal theme. The *predominance of the new formal principle, the suffusion of the developmental technique by the grouping technique* could not be expressed any more clearly and radically. For where the new "phrase group," the second principal theme, appears, it is not only engendered by the sustaining undulatory development but rather is dynamically formed, down to its motivic content, from the initial primal impulse. This similarity manifests itself without detracting from the contrasting function [of the second theme], which it acquires as a newly entering principal group.

Even if this [phenomenon] does not always occur in such a pronounced manner, it is by no means the only example of its kind, as the discussion of the symphonies will show, and it characterizes anew how the dynamics of the linear shaping process extend far beyond the "developmental motives." [355] From all sides, we see how close and boundless is the cooperation between developmental motives and distinct themes and melodies, and within the [melodic] lines even that is only a partial expression of the comprehensive dynamic principle of form.

Appendix*

Table of contents for
Grundlagen des linearen Kontrapunkts

Preface .... page ix

Part 1 Foundations of melody

1 *Melodic energy*
    Introduction; the activity of the melodic process 1
    Primal process and manifestation in melody 4
    Relationship of tensions to sonic phenomena in music 6
    The "kinetic energy" of melodic tones 9
    Differentiation of the kinetic and rhythmic impulse 12
    The genetic process in melody. The unity of the linear progression as a primary
        phenomenon in relation to individual tones 14
    The relationship of harmonic organization to linear motion 17
    Destruction of the linear concept by the harmonic-genetic explanation 19
    The "dynamic phase" as a concept of melodic unity 21
    The motive as dynamic phase 24
    General remarks on interval progression 25
    The more conspicuous manifestations of motion 27
    The totality of phenomena as an expression of interior dynamics 32
2 *Space and matter in musical sounds*
    The origin of the mental image of space in music 34
    Objectification of tones 35
    Sensations of mass in tones and harmonies 37
3 *The evolution of tension in the formation of melody*
    The basic scale 39
    Leading-tone tension 40
    The dynamics of the scale 42
    General remarks on the effects of melodic tension in polyphony 44
    Melodic dissonance 46
    The tension of the linear unit. Chromaticism 49

* Asterisks next to chapter headings or subheadings indicate that translated text from those
  sections appears in this volume.

Appendix

4 *Kinetic energy and rhythm*
   Kinesthesia as the origin of rhythm 51
   The relationship of kinetic and rhythmic energy in melody 53
   The character of rhythmic accents 55
5 *Approach to compositional technique*
   *The fundamental trait of contrapuntal design 58
   *The effect of harmonic cohesion 62
   *The interplay of contrasting elements 66
6 *The energetic relationships in harmony. Chordal tension*
   The concept of "potential energy" 68
   Fusion of tensions 70
   Some illustrative details 71
   Chords as bearers of energy 72
   The tension of the dominant 75
   The subdominant tendency of major tonality 77
   The energy of the third 80
   The problem of the major–minor contrast 81
   Major and minor as *tension* contrasts 83
   The tension of chordal dissonances 88
   The dissonance of the fourth. The "root" sensation 91

Part 2 The problem of counterpoint

1 *Features of linear design*
   Summary of basic characteristics 97
   "Contrapuntal" and "paralinear" 99
2 *The system of Fux in its approach to the problem*
   The methodological design 103
   Vertical and linear elements 106
   Destruction of latent linear tendencies in carrying out the method 109
3 *Historical evolution of the problem*
   The beginnings of polyphony. Origin of the contradiction in the concept
     of "counterpoint" 117
   The Netherlanders and the preliminary development of the harmonic mode
     of composition 121
   The thoroughbass. The differentiation of harmony and counterpoint 124
   The reflection of the historical transition in the systemic foundations of Fux 128
   The system as an instructional foundation 131
4 *The evolution since Fux*
   Internal transition from contrapuntal to harmonic theory within the old system ... 133
   The method of the purely harmonic establishment of counterpoint 138
   The failure of the method with regard to the problem 140
   *Conclusion. Fundamental approach to the theory of counterpoint 142

Part 3 Bach's melodic style

Section 1 *General foundations of the style*

1. *Contrasting traits of polyphonic and Classical melodic style* 147
   The nature of rhythmic-symmetric melodic structure 149
   Unfettered dynamic unfoldment as a principle of melodic form in polyphony 152
   Contrasts in melodic style founded on varying intensity of rhythmic sensation 155
   The march and dance as roots of the principle of rhythmic-symmetric melody 158
   Historical precursors of the contrasts in melodic style 159
2. *The connection between melodic style and compositional technique*
   Contrasts with regard to the intensity of harmony 166
   Difference in harmonic rhythm 169
   The influence of melodic structure on homophonic and polyphonic structure 170
3. *The contrasting melodic styles in relation to the most general foundations of art*
   Polyphony and Classicism 174
   The technical characteristics of polyphonic design as an expression of opposing
       traits in overall artistic sensibility 176
   The technical characteristics of melody as an expression of the identical
       contrasting tendencies 179
   The difference in the artistic expression of melody 183
4. *On rhythm in Bach's line*
   Apexes; on the linear unfoldment in relation to rhythm 187
   The character of linear emphases 192
   The dynamics of rests 194
   Transitional phenomena in Bach 198

Section 2 *Technical characteristics*

5. *Traits of formal development*
   Group formation and fluid transition as contrasting principles 203
   The thematic motion as formal energy 208
   Formal-technical phenomena in the theme in the polyphonic style 222
6. *The technique of melodic Fortspinnung in the polyphonic style*
   The effect of thematic energy in the ensuing spinning-out process.
       Kinesthesia and the feeling of form in the linear unfoldment 225
   The appearance of sequences in the course of the *Fortspinnung* 231
   The thematic-motivic technique in the melodic *Fortspinnung* 234
   Beethoven's technique of motivic fragmentation as a consequence of the
       principle of Classical melody 237
   The technique of thematic transition in the *Fortspinnung* and its connection
       with the linear style of polyphony 242
7. *The development toward linear intensifications*
   The external formal design of the polyphonic style as based on the principle
       of intensifications 249
   Melodic intensification; design of the curvilinear development 251
   Manifestations of rhythmic, dynamic, and chromatic intensification 253
   Growth of the curves and intervallic motions as a manifestation of intensification .. 255
   Manifestations of formal equilibrium in the *Fortspinnung* 256

Appendix

8 *The polyphony of a single line*
   *Effects of fullness and technical means for heightening melodic tension in a
      single line 262
   *Implications of polyphony in the single line 272
   *Further characteristics of the technique of apparent polyphony; implications
      of polyphony in sequences 283
   Rounding out of apparent voices over chordal contours 286
   The implication of harmonic bass voices in the single line 289
   Independent motivic and melodic formations in apparent voices 292
   The implication of pedal points in the single line 294
   *Richness of apparent polyphony in Bach's melodic lines 302
   *The monophonic episodes from the C-major Fugue for violin 313
   Apparent voices in connection with the overall tonal design 322
   *The evolution and dissipation of apparent voices 328
   *The interaction of apparent voices and the actual voice 333

Part 4 The polyphonic design

1 *The dynamic relationships in polyphony* 349
   The complementary rhythmic design 351
   Differentiating linear motion 357
   *Staggering of apexes and intensifications 361
2 *The influence of dynamics on harmonic relationships*
   *Enhancement of apexes 374
   The interaction of linear tensions and dissonant harmonic formations 382
3 *Manifestations of intensification in polyphonic motion*
   Increase in sonorousness and dynamic consolidation 395
   On the technique of escalating animation 397
   Linear intensification within the polyphonic design 404
4 *Consolidation and dissolution of thematic motion*
   *The unfoldment of thematic presentations and transitional passages ... 408
   *The process of thematic dissolution in the melodic content of
      transitional passages 417
   *The generalization of dynamic progressions 429

Part 5 The technique of linear coupling

1 *The contrapuntal technique as the negative of the harmonic technique*
   The compositional developments as opposites 439
   Approach to the tonal development and to harmonic phenomena in counterpoint .. 442
   Harmonic irregularities between the linear progressions; parallel dissonances
      and voice entry in open intervals 446
   The most general intervallic relationships in bi-linear coupling 453
2 *On two-voice technique*
   The overcoming of irregularities through certain harmonic relationships
      between intervals 459
   The overcoming of irregularities through leading-tone tension and chromaticism .. 470

The overcoming of irregularities through motivic energy of the lines 478
The overcoming of irregularities through the simulation of oblique motion 490
The influence of apparent voices on the technique of intervals 496
The overcoming of irregularities through the rounding out of lines over
    chordal contours 498
Summary of the viewpoints 501
The question of the dissonances and of the fourth 509
3 *The transition to polyphony* 517
    On the technique of distributing the motion 518
    The evolution of harmonic technique 526
    On the special technique of contrapuntal refinements 528

Table of contents for
Romantische Harmonik und ihre Krise in Wagners "Tristan"

Preface   *page* ix

Part 1 Foundations

1 *Approach to theory*
    Harmony as externalization of force. Music as interior dynamics. Energy and sound. Theory as a representation of energetic development. The phenomenon of the line and the nature of the sonic phenomenon. The fluctuating relationship between energetic and sensuous phenomena as a foundation for style. Intensified play of harmonic colors as a reflex of intensified dynamics 1
2 *The psychological foundations of Romantic harmony*
    Conscious and unconscious forces in the formation of stylistic expression. The confrontation of conscious and unconscious forces in the Classical and Romantic world. The manifestations of the Romantic expressive will. Personality schism. The turn toward the unconscious. The interior process of extrication from Classicism. The interior transformation in the foundations of music. The turn toward the unconscious fundamental contents of harmony; escalation of the energetic and sensuous elements; their polar development as an outgrowth of the Romantic character. The musical and the general artistic sensibility. The evolution toward the crisis with Wagner's *Tristan* 14

Part 2 The first chord

1 *The tension of alteration*
    The foundations of alteration. The uniqueness of dissonant resolution chords. Tension and resolution harmonies. The concept of dissonance. Other tension formations and their characteristics 44
2 *Transformations of the internal harmonic dynamics*
    The modifications of the chord. Their symbolism at the climax of the *Tristan* prelude. Enharmonic redefinition as an interior dynamic flux of harmonies. Evaluation of enharmonic redefinition as an expression of Romantic sensibility. Special technical possibilities of the chord. Antecedents and characteristics in *Tristan* 62

3   *Resolutions of tension*
    Tonal interpretations and their fluctuations. Modified interpretations of alteration ... 77
4   *Harmony as a symbol*
    The motivic aspect of harmony. Individual examples. Projection of the
      fluctuating internal dynamics into the symbolism. Harmonic weight and
      flexibility. The rise to independence of individual harmonic effects.
      The symbolism of initial chords 81

Part 3 From the cadence to the alteration style of *Tristan*

1   *The first cadence*
    The renewal of harmony through fundamental phenomena. Introductory example
      and its typical characteristics. Harmonic tendencies as the first aspect of
      expansion. Dominant and applied dominant. The first cadence of music and
      its dynamic origin. Tension and harmonic intensity 97
2   *Harmonic veiling*
    Transformation of stationary voices. The tinting effect of non-chordal dissonances.
      Darkening of harmony through chordal dissonances. The suppression of tonic ... 113
3   *Enhanced Tinting**
    Expansion of tonal digressions. Dynamics of harmonic progressions and color
      intensifications. Potentiated cadential motions. Precursors and exceptions:
      liberation of applied dominants; applied dominants before six-four chords;
      release from the original voicing; minor subdominant; mixtures of major and
      minor; Neapolitan chord. Dynamic vividness in the harmonic progressions.
      *Effects of color contrasts. Natural evolutionary tensions in the contrasts.
      Application in cadential effects and formal influences 130
4   *Harmonic shading**
    *The nature of harmonic shading. *Effects of light through dynamic tensions.
      *Typical shading effects and special forms. Major–minor shifts. The Romantic
      sense for the dynamic vividness of major–minor shifts. The sense for all types
      of tertian effects. The energetic dualism of harmony 159
5   *The intensive alteration style**
    Basic characteristics and individual components* 183
    On the technique of neighbor-note insertion. *Difference from alteration of chord
      tones. *Mode of application. *Escalation of the neighbor-note technique.
      Connection with alteration of chord tones. *Additional characteristics of the
      intensive alteration style. *Coincidence of tension and resolution tones.
      Enhancements of tension 186
    Distortion of harmonies and harmonic progressions. *Harmonic image and tension
      image. Melodic focal points as tension tones. *Distortion of basic harmonic
      relationships and their consequences 205
    The connection with enharmonic redefinition. Typical idioms. Modulatory paths and
      their expansion by the Romantics. Multiplicity of harmonic interpretation 211
    Chromatic connections of harmonies. *The wrenching principle.
      *Reciprocal flow among harmonies. *Influence on the play of harmonic
      colors. *General dissolution of tonality through the dynamic tensions 219

Part 4 Paths of harmonic development

1. *Harmonic structure*
   Growth beyond the triad. Dissolution and harmonic countereffect.
   Consolidation into harmonic units. The transformation of the meaning of
   harmonic dissonance 229
   The dynamics of the structure. Sensations of construction. Tiering in thirds.
   Effects of thirds in harmonies. New effects of six-four chords.
   Influence on Neapolitan chords 237
   Influence on harmonic connections and their typical forms. Underthirds. Dynamics of
   the deceptive cadence. The deceptive cadence after applied dominants.
   Influence on modulatory passages. The connection of the deceptive cadence
   with alteration and harmonic shading. The sensation of mass 249
2. *The interior dissolution of color in Romantic harmony**
   The effect of the absolute progression. *Contexts of the harmonic effect.
   *Concept of the absolute progression effect 262
   The destruction [of harmonic syntax] and its countereffect in tonality.
   *Isolation of harmonic reflexes. *The countercurrent in the sensation of
   tonality. *Evolution of wrenching effects. *Mediant and chromatic effects.
   Intensified wrenching effects. Interior and exterior expansions of tonality.
   Dissolution into flowing colors. Individual and overall effect. Interior tonal
   tension. The relationship to endless melody 265
   Precursors. Restlessness of harmonic rhythm. Autonomy in the simplest tonal
   progressions. Effects in the external dynamics. Wrenching effects in
   earlier times 289
   The absolute harmonic effect. *Dependency on the fusion type and tonal character.
   *Chords as autonomous effects and independent color symbols.
   *Atomization in individual harmonic impressions 297
   Constructive and destructive forces. Construction and destruction in tonality.
   Construction and destruction in harmony. The fundamental processes in the
   development of Romantic harmony 305

Part 5 Paths of tonal development

1. *Paths of harmonic expansion**
   *Developmental paths of tonal expansion. (Model in the Prelude to Act 3 of *Tristan*).
   Additional interior dissolutions of coherence. (Model in the beginning and end
   of the Prelude to Act 1 of *Tristan*). Tonal developments in large proportions.
   (Model in the further development of the Prelude to Act 1 of *Tristan*). The
   tonality of the *Tristan* Prelude. The dynamic perception of tonality. Turn toward
   modulatory motion. The principle of harmonic form in Romanticism 314
2. *Paths of melodic disruption**
   The sequential technique of the Romantics. *Fundamental trait of the sequence.
   *Sequential type with tension and resolution chords. Sequence and repetition.
   Mediant sequences. *Progressive abbreviation of the sequential unit 333
   Loosening of the sequential principle. Loosening into harmonic series. Loosening
   into harmonic color effects. Aborted implied sequences. Melodic sequence as

the bearer of tonally freer passages. *Release into flowing voices. *Tiering effects across large proportions. Status of tonal breaches in the Romantic period 344

Additional manifestations of melodic innovation. Emergent predominance of the perception of melodic energy. Melodic deviations from tonality. Stronger melodic breaches of tonality. Unresolved dissonant tones. Rise of the linear element. Extension of linear energy to entire harmonies and harmonic progressions. Transcendence of the principle of tonal syntax. Re-emergence [of the melodic element] to primary significance. Compositional foundations. Contrast with pre-Classical polyphony. Fundamental trait thematic combination. Energy and resistance 356

Part 6 Impressionistic traits

1 *Nature and concept of musical Impressionism*
    Relationship to the evolutionary currents of the Romantic period. The concepts of impression and expression. The most general characteristics. The immaterial. Relationship to other arts. The sonic character of Impressionism. Transcendence of the structural harmonic principle and the change in meaning of the triad. The transformation of the internal harmonic dynamics, alteration and perception of dissonance. The individual tone, tonality 384

2 *Traits and technical antecedents*
    Effects of combining harmonies. Fusion of dissonances; neighbor-note formations. Interleaving of foreign harmonic elements. Blurred harmonic formations. Seventh and ninth chords. Dissolution into individual effects. Harmonic appeal of individual intervals. Melodic and motivic elements. Rhythmic and instrumental effects. Impressionistic accompanimental figures. Their connection with tonal reflexes. Effects of impressionistic pauses 399

Part 7 Endless melody

1 *Technical characteristics*
    Concept and fundamental manifestations. Kinetic and rhythmic energy.
    Release from the Classical principle of Melody. Contrast to pre-Classical linear art. Fluid transitions as the chief trait of "endlessness". Additional technical characteristics. The technique of "endless" transitions in motives 444

2 *On interior endlessness*
    Fundamental motivic motions. Primordial motives and their symbolism in the music drama. Projection into the psychic and representational sphere. Wave motions and their basic form. The three characteristics of interior transition 465
    The expression of linear motion. The fundamental dynamic contents of melody. Manifestations of dynamic expression and their symbolism. Significance of the fundamental process 479
    The dual emanation of the expression of motion. The absolute, subjective and objective dynamic process. Fluctuation and illimitability of the projections. Impressionistic and expressionistic traits in melody. On the psychology of pre-Classical, Classical, and Romantic perception of melody 488

3   *On the psychology of motivic formation*
    The sense of absolute motion in leitmotives. An individual example:
       the Fate-Motive. Dynamics as the origin of the meaning of a motive.
       Typical characteristics of rudimentary motions. An individual example:
       the Query-Motive. Associations of meaning in the linear symbolism of
       endless melody. Typical characteristics of motivic formation. Projections of
       the contents of the absolute motion 501
    The technical traits of subjective melodic formation of the Romantics. Chromaticism
       and affective dynamics. Traits in the intervals. The uniqueness of Romantic
       tone repetitions 515
    The objectified expression of motion. Representations of movements. Variance in
       expression of typical fundamental movements. Contrast with the principle of
       programmatic composition 527
4   *The interior dynamics of endless melody in its technical and formal consequences*
    The developmental motives. The motives of absolute music as pure symbols of
       energy. The concept of developmental motives. Developmental motives in
       the polyphonic style. Transformation of developmental motives in the
       Classical style. The new interpretation of accompanimental parts in Beethoven.
       The new developmental in the Romantic period. The character of Romantic
       developmental motives. The Overall motion and developmental motives.
       The change from primary into developmental motives 535
    The large-scale development. Endless melody in the musical flux. The motivic
       content and the overall motion. The endless melody of the harmony.
       The endless melody of form. The relationship to the foundations of
       musical art 563

Index of names 572

Table of contents for *Bruckner*, vol. I

Preface   *page* vii

Part 1 Personage and environment 1

1   *Historical environment* 3
    Bruckner as mystic 3
    Bruckner's alienation 11
    Romanticism at the time of Bruckner's youth 17
    Bruckner and high Romanticism 47
    Ensnarement in the historical setting 70
2   *Bruckner's life* 80
    Awakening 80
    Initial rise 93
    Turning point 101
    Maturation and final journey 116

3 *Character and reflection* 147
   Bruckner's appearance 147
   Bruckner's relationship to the world 152
   Behavior patterns 158
   Bruckner's thought patterns 168
   Fundamental forms of psychic activity 176
   Bruckner and the opposition 185
   Effects on the creative output of the subsequent generation 206
   Basic facts on misunderstandings and interpretation 216

Part 2 The dynamics of form 231

1 *Bruckner's formal principle* 233
   The concept of musical form 233
   The dynamic trait in Bruckner's music 240
   The play of forces as a formal trait 251
   On the nature of absolute music with Bruckner 256
   The relationship of formal and aesthetic foundations with Bruckner 265
   The symphonic style as an expression of formal will 271
2 *The symphonic wave* * 279
   *Introductory example and general characteristics 279
   *Additional characteristics in individual illustrations. Parts and whole ... 291
   *The illimitability of the interior processes. The symphonic melos 308
   *Wave and linear dynamics. An exploration of additional features 319
   *Motivic vividness and interior view 332
   *The relationship between developmental dynamics and thematic content 342
   *The perspective on larger contexts. The art of motivic unity 346
   The unity of wave activity 355
3 *The formative undulatory play* 363
   Symmetries and open wave series in the large dimension 363
   Initiations and interruptions 375
   Apparent contradictions in the intensifications and cooperation of their resources .. 384
   Bruckner's typical wind-section consolidations and additional motivic formations
      of the orchestrational concentration 391
   Repetition and intensification 398
   An examination of the paths of intensification in a larger context 406
   Energetic forms of the apex and the surmounting thereof 410
   Apparent contradictions in the apexes 421
   Discharged apexes 427
   Forms and long-range effects in the ebbing of the apex 431
   The episodes of a void and turmoil 443
   On the technique of deintensification 452
   Typical forms of large-scale tension. Tendency toward tripartition 454
4 *Interior dynamics and overall outlines* 462
   Discussion of the Classical grouping principle and the thematic triplicate . 462
   The bi- and tripartite principle in the history of the sonata 467

Appendix

Solidification of the Classical framework and the course of Romantic form
before Bruckner...476
The dynamics of Bruckner's compositional design 482
A paradigm of opening movements 486
The slow movements 496
The Scherzo..500
The Finale..511
Retroactive effect of the overall form on the theme 517
The dynamics of thematic manipulation..................................521
The formal significance of the chorale theme.............................528
The "Bruckner-rhythm" as a fundamental motivic and formal motion............529

5 *Sound and processive dynamics*...538
Harmony as structure...538
Harmony as color 571
Instrumental color..583

Select bibliography

Books

Albisetti, James. *Secondary School Reform in Imperial Germany*. Princeton: Princeton University Press, 1983.
Alexander, Thomas and Beryl Parker. *The New Education in the German Republic*. New York: John Day Co., 1929.
Apfel, Ernst. *Grundlagen einer Geschichte der Satztechnik*, 3 vols. Saarbrücken: Selbstverlag, 1974, 1976.
Diskant und Kontrapunkt in der Musiktheorie des 12. bis 15. Jahrhunderts. Taschenbücher zur Musiktheorie, vol. 82. Wilhelmshaven: Heinrichshofen, 1982.
Auer, Max. *Anton Bruckner*. Zurich–Leipzig–Vienna: Amalthea Verlag, 1923.
Auer, Max. comp., ed. *Anton Bruckner: Gesammelte Briefe, Neue Folge*. Regensburg: G. Bosse, 1924.
Beldemandis, Proscodimus de. *Contrapunctus*, trans. Jan Herlinger. Lincoln, Nebraska: University of Nebraska Press, 1984.
Bellerman, Heinrich. *Der Contrapunctus*. Berlin: Springer, 1862.
Bent, Ian. *Analysis*. New York: Norton, 1987.
Berry, Wallace. *Structural Functions of Music*. Englewood Cliffs: Prentice Hall, 1976.
Boyd, William and Wyatt Rawson. *The Story of the New Education*. London: Heinemann, 1965.
Brenn, Franz. *Form in der Musik*. Freiburg, Switzerland: Universitätsverlag, 1953.
Bujić, Bojan. *Music in European Thought, 1851–1912*. Cambridge: Cambridge University Press, 1988.
Cherubini, Luigi. *Course of Counterpoint and Fugue*, trans. J. A. Hamilton. 2nd edn., 2 vols. London: R. Cocks and Co., 1841; orig. 1835.
Clifton, Thomas. *Music as Heard: A Study in Applied Phenomenology*. New Haven: Yale University Press, 1983.
Cooke, Deryck. *The Bruckner Problem Simplified*. New York: Novello, 1975.
Dahlhaus, Carl. *Untersuchungen über die Entstehung der harmonischen Tonalität*. Saarbrückener Studien zur Musikwissenschaft, vol. II. Kassel: Bärenreiter, 1968.
Dahlhaus, Carl, and Lars U. Abraham. *Melodielehre*. Cologne: Hans Gerig, 1972.
Decsey, Ernst. *Bruckner: Versuch eines Lebens*. Berlin-Leipzig: Schuster and Loeffler, 1919, 1922.
Dehn, Siegfried. *A Course of Instruction on Canon and Fugue*, trans. G. Wolff. Leipzig: Breitkopf und Härtel, 1887; orig. 1884.
Dehnert, Max. *Anton Bruckner: Versuch einer Deutung*. Leipzig: Breitkopf und Härtel, 1958.

Doernberg, Erwin. *The Life and Symphonies of Anton Bruckner*. London: Barrie and Rockliff, 1960.
Eggebrecht, Hans Heinrich, et al. *Die mittelalterliche Lehre von der Mehrstimmigkeit*. Geschichte der Musiktheorie, ed. Frieder Zaminer, vol. V. Darmstadt: Wissenschaftliche Buchgesellschaft, 1984.
Federhofer, Hellmut. *Akkord und Stimmführung in den musiktheoretischen Systemen von Hugo Riemann, Ernst Kurth und Heinrich Schenker*. Veröffentlichungen der Kommission für Musikforschung, vol. XXI. Vienna: Verlag der österreichischen Akademie der Wissenschaften, 1981.
Fischer, Hans Conrad. *Anton Bruckner: Sein Leben*. Salzburg: Residenz Verlag, 1974.
Flitner, Wilhelm and Gerhard Kudritzke. *Die deutsche Reformpädagogik*. 2 vols. Düsseldorf–Munich: Helmut Küpper, 1961–62.
Floros, Constantin. *Brahms und Bruckner: Studien zur musikalischen Exegetik*. Wiesbaden: Breitkopf und Härtel, 1980.
Funtek, Leo. *Bruckneriana*. Leipzig: Verlag für Literatur, Kunst und Musik, 1910.
Gatz, Felix. *Musik-Ästhetik in ihren Hauptrichtungen*. Stuttgart: Ferdinand Enke, 1929.
Gédalge, André. *Treatise on Fugue*, trans. A. Levin, ed. S. B. Potter. Mattapan, Mass.: Gamut Music Co., 1964; orig. 1900.
Goering, Hugo. *Die neue Deutsche Schule: ein Weg zur Verwirklichung vaterländischer Erziehung*, 2nd edn. Leipzig: R. Voigtländer, 1890.
Göllerich, August. *Anton Bruckner: Ein Lebens- und Schaffens-Bild*, ed. Max Auer. 4 vols. Regensburg: Bosse 1922–37.
Gräflinger, Franz, comp., ed. *Anton Bruckner: Gesammelte Briefe*. Regensburg: G. Bosse, 1924.
Grunsky, Karl. *Musikästhetik*. Berlin–Leipzig: Göschen'sche Verlagsbuchhandlung, 1907, 1919.
  Anton Bruckner. Stuttgart: J. Engelhorns Nachfolger, 1922.
Halm, August. *Harmonielehre*, Leipzig: Göschen, 1905 (orig. 1902).
  Die Symphonie Anton Bruckners. Munich: G. Müller, 1913.
  Von Zwei Kulturen der Musik. Munich: G. Müller; 1913; 3rd edn. Stuttgart: Klett, 1947.
  Von Grenzen und Ländern der Musik. Gesammelte Aufsätze. Munich: G. Müller, 1916.
  Beethoven. Berlin: Hesse, 1927; rep. Darmstadt: Wissenschaftliche Buchgemeinschaft, 1970.
  Von Form und Sinn der Musik, ed. Siegfried Schmaltzriedt. Wiesbaden: Breitkopf und Härtel, 1978.
Hanslick, Eduard. *Vom Musikalisch-Schönen: Ein Beitrag zur Revision der Aesthetik der Tonkunst*. Leipzig: J. A. Barth, 1854; 6th edn. rev., enl., 1881.
Hasse, Karl. *Johann Sebastian Bach*. Bielefeld and Leipzig: Velhagen und Klasing, 1925.
Hegel, Georg Wilhelm Friedrich. *Aesthetics: Lectures on Fine Art*, trans. T. M. Knox. 2 vols. Oxford: Clarendon Press, 1988.
Herbart, Johann Friedrich. *Psychologie als Wissenschaft neu gegründet auf Erfahrung, Metaphysik und Mathematik*. J. F. Herbarts sämtliche Werke, ed. K. Kehrbach, vols. V (part 1), 177–434, and VI (part 2), 1–340. Langensalza: H. Beyer & Söhne, 1892; orig. 1824.
Herder, Johann Gottfried. *Kalligone*, ed. Heinz Begenau. Weimar: Hermann Böhlhaus Nachfolger, 1955.
Hilker, Franz. *Deutsche Schulversuche*. Berlin: C. A. Schwetschke & Sohn, 1924.

Höckner, Hilmar. *Die Musik in der deutschen Jugendbewegung*. Wolfenbüttel: Kallmeyer, 1927.
Hughes, Henry Stuart. *Consciousness and Society: The Reorientation of European Social Thought, 1890–1930*. New York: Octagon Books, 1976.
Huray, Peter le and James Day, eds. *Music and Aesthetics in the Eighteenth and Early-Nineteenth Centuries*. Cambridge–New York: Cambridge University Press, 1981.
Ihde, Don. *Experimental Phenomenology*. New York: Capricorn Books, 1977.
Keller, Hermann. *Die musikalische Artikulation, insbesondere bei Johann Sebastian Bach*. Augsburg: Bärenreiter, 1925.
Korte, Werner. *Bruckner und Brahms*. Tutzing: H. Schneider, 1963.
Kretzschmar, Hermann. *Führer durch den Konzertsaal*, 2nd edn. Leipzig: A. G. Libeskind, 1891; orig. 1886.
Musikalische Zeitfragen. Leipzig: Peters, 1903.
Gesammelte Aufsätze. 2 vols. Leipzig: Breitkopf und Härtel, 1911.
Kurth, Ernst. *Die Voraussetzungen der theoretischen Harmonik und der tonalen Darstellungssysteme*. Berne: Drechsel, 1913; rep. Schriften zur Musik, vol. XIV. Munich: Katzbichler, 1973.
Grundlagen des linearen Kontrapunkts: Bachs melodische Polyphonie. Berne: Drechsel, 1917; 2nd and 3rd edns. Berlin: Hesse, 1922, 1927: rep. Berne: Krompholz, 1946, 1956: Hildesheim: Olms, 1977.
"Zur Motivbildung Bachs: ein Beitrag zur Stilpsychologie," *Bach-Jahrbuch* (1917), 80–136.
Romantische Harmonik und ihre Krise in Wagners "Tristan". Berne: Haupt, 1920; 2nd and 3rd edns. Berlin: Hesse, 1922, 1923, rep. Hildesheim: Olms, 1968, 1975.
Bruckner. 2 vols. Berlin: Hesse, 1925; rep. Hildesheim: Olms, 1971.
Musikpsychologie. Berlin: Hesse, 1931; rep. Berne: Krompholz, 1947; Hildesheim: Olms, 1969.
Lang, Oskar. *Anton Bruckner: Wesen und Bedeutung*, 2nd edn. Munich: C. H. Beck, 1943.
Langbehn, Julius. *Rembrandt als Erzieher*, ed. Dr. Gerhard Krüger, according to the 1st edn., with supplements from the 17th edn. Berlin: Theodor Fritsch Verlag, 1944.
Lange, Konrad. *Das Wesen der Kunst*. Berlin: G. Grote, 1901.
Lauer, Quentin. *The Triumph of Subjectivity: An Introduction of Transcendental Phenomenology*. New York: Fordham University Press, 1978.
Leibnitz, Thomas. *Die Brüder Schalk und Anton Bruckner*. Tutzing: Schneider, 1988.
Leibniz, Gottfried W. *Principes de la nature et de la Grace fondés en raison*. 1714?
Leichtentritt, Hugo. *Musikalische Formenlehre*, 3rd edn, rev., enl. Leipzig: Breitkopf und Härtel, 1927; trans. *Musical Form*. Cambridge, Mass.: Harvard University Press, 1951.
Lieberman, Ira. "Some Representative Works from Beethoven's Early Period Analyzed in Light of the Theories of Ernst Kurth and Kurt von Fischer," Ph.D. diss., Columbia University, 1968.
Lietz, Hermann. "Zur Einführung in die Bestrebungen der deutschen Land-Erziehungsheime," *Leben und Arbeit* 1 (1913), 1–13.
Lipps, Theodor. *Ästhetik*. 2 vols. Hamburg: Voss, 1903, 1906.
Lorenz, Alfred. *Das Geheimnis der Form bei Richard Wagner*. 4 vols. Berlin: Hesse, 1924–33; 2nd edn. Tutzing: Schneider, 1966. vol. I: *Der musikalische Aufbau des Bühnenfestspiels "Der Ring des Nibelungen"*. vol. II: *Der musikalische Aufbau von Richard Wagners "Tristan und Isolde"*.

Louis, Rudolf and Ludwig Thuille. *Harmonielehre*. Stuttgart: Carl Grüninger, 1907.
Mach, Ernst. *Beiträge zur Analyse der Empfindungen*. Jena: Gustav Fischer, 1886.
Marpurg, Friedrich Wilhelm. *Abhandlung von der Fuge*. 2 vols. Berlin: Haude und Spencer, 1753–54; rep. Hildesheim: Olms, 1970.
Meyer, Leonard. *Emotion and Meaning in Music*. Chicago: University of Chicago Press, 1956.
Mickelsen, William C. *Hugo Riemann's Theory of Harmony and History of Music Theory, Book III by Hugo Riemann*. Lincoln–London: University of Nebraska Press, 1977.
Moos, Paul. *Die deutsche Ästhetik der Gegenwart*. Berlin–Leipzig: Schuster & Loeffler, 1914.
Mosse, Georg L. *The Crisis of German Ideology: Intellectual Origins of the Third Reich*. New York: Schocken Books, 1981.
Murray, David J. *A History of Western Psychology*. 2nd edn. Englewood Cliffs: Prentice Hall, 1988.
Natanson, Maurice. *Edmund Husserl: Philosopher of Infinite Tasks*. Evanston: Northwestern University Press, 1973.
Nohl, Hermann. *Die pädagogische Bewegung in Deutschland und ihre Theorie*. 2nd edn. Frankfurt: G. Schulte-Bulmke, 1935.
Oeser, Fritz. *Die Klangstruktur der Bruckner-Symphonie*. Leipzig: Musikwissenschaftlicher Verlag, 1939.
Pastille, William A. "*Ursatz*: The Musical Philosophy of Heinrich Schenker," Ph.D. diss., Cornell University, 1985.
Paulsen, Friedrich. *German Education Past and Present*, trans. T. Lorenz. London: T. Fisher Unwin, 1908.
Prince, John T. *Methods of Instruction and Organization of the Schools of Germany*. Boston: Lee and Shepard, 1892.
Reddie, Cecil. *Abbotsholme*. London: George Allen, 1890.
Riemann, Hugo. *Katechismus der Fugen-Komposition*. 2 vols. Leipzig: Hesse, 1890–91.
Rietsch, Heinrich. *Die Tonkunst in der zweiten Hälfte des Neunzehnten Jahrhunderts*. 2nd edn., rev. enl. Leipzig: Breitkopf und Härtel, 1906; orig. 1899.
Ringer, Fritz. *The Decline of the German Mandarins: The German Academic Community, 1890–1933*. Cambridge, Mass.: Harvard University Press, 1969.
Roman, Frederick. *The New Education in Europe*. London: Routledge, 1924.
Rothfarb, Lee. "Ernst Kurth's *The Requirements for a Theory of Harmony*: An Annotated Translation with an Introductory Essay," Master's Thesis, West Hartford, Connecticut, Hartt School of Music, University of Hartford, 1971.
 Ernst Kurth as Theorist and Analyst. Philadelphia: University of Pennsylvania Press, 1988.
Rummenhöller, Peter. *Musiktheoretisches Denken im 19. Jahrhundert: Versuch einer Interpretation erkenntnistheoretischer Zeugnisse in der Musiktheorie*. Studien zur Musikgeschichte des 19. Jahrhunderts, vol. XII. Regensburg: Bosse Verlag, 1967.
Sachs, Klaus-Jürgen. *Der Contrapunctus im 14. und 15. Jahrhundert*. Wiesbaden: Franz Steiner, 1974.
Schäfke, Rudolf. *Geschichte der Musikästhetik in Umrissen*. Berlin: Hesse, 1934.
Scheibe, Wolfgang. *Die Reformpädagogische Bewegung, 1900–32: Eine einführende Darstellung*. Berlin–Basel: Julius Beltz, 1969.
Schenker, Heinrich. *Kontrapunkt*. Neue musikalische Theorien und Phantasien. 2 vols. Vienna: Universal, 1910, 1922; trans. John Rothgeb and Jürgen Thym, ed. John Rothgeb. New York: Schirmer Books, 1987.

Harmony, trans. Elisabeth Mann Borgese, ed. Oswald Jonas. Cambridge, Mass.: MIT Press, 1973.

Schering, Arnold. *Musikalische Bildung und Erziehung zum musikalischen Hören.* Leipzig: Quelle & Meyer, 1911.

Schlegel, August Wilhelm. *Vorlesungen über schöne Literatur und Kunst* (1801), in *Die Kunstlehre*, ed. Edgar Kohner. Stuttgart, 1963.

Schoenberg, Arnold. *Stil und Gedanke, Aufsätze zur Musik*, trans. Gudrun Budde, ed. Ivan Vojtech. Gesammelte Schriften, vol. I. n.p.: Fischer Verlag, 1976; *Style and Idea*, trans. Leo Black, ed. Leonard Stein. New York: St. Martins Press, 1975.

Harmonielehre. Vienna: Universal, 1911; *Theory of Harmony*, trans. Roy E. Carter, Berkeley–Los Angeles: University of California Press, 1978.

Schönzeler, Hans Hubert. *Bruckner.* New York: Grossman, 1970.

Sechter, Simon. *Grundsätze der musikalischen Composition.* 3 vols. Leipzig: Breitkopf und Härtel, 1853–54. vol. I: *Die richtige Folge der Grundharmonien.*

Shirley, Dennis. "Paul Geheeb's Leadership of the Odenwaldschule, 1910–1930," Qualifying Paper, Harvard Graduate School of Education, 1987.

Spengler, Oswald. *The Decline of the West*, trans. Charles F. Atkinson. 2 vols. New York: Alfred A. Knopf, 1926–28; orig. Munich: C. H. Beck, 1918.

Spiegelberg, Herbert. *The Phenomenological Movement: A Historical Introduction.* 2 vols., 2nd edn. The Hague: Martinus Nijhoff, 1965.

Doing Phenomenology: Essays on and in Phenomenology. The Hague: Martinus Nijhoff, 1975.

Stern, Fritz. *The Politics of Cultural Despair: A Study in the Rise of the Germanic Ideology.* Berkeley–Los Angeles: University of California Press, 1961.

Stumpf, Carl. *Tonpsychologie.* 2 vols. Leipzig: Hirzel, 1883, 1890.

Wagner, Manfred. *Der Wandel des Konzepts: Zu den verschiedenen Fassungen von Bruckners Dritter, Vierter und Achter Sinfonie.* Vienna: Musikwissenschaftlicher Verlag, 1980.

Wason, Robert. *Viennese Harmonic Theory from Albrechtsberger to Schenker and Schoenberg.* Ann Arbor: UMI Research Press, 1985.

Weber, Evelyn. *Ideas Influencing Early Childhood Education: A Theoretical Analysis.* New York: Teachers College Press, 1984.

Wertheimer, Max. *Productive Thinking* [1945], enl., ed. Michael Wertheimer. New York: Harper, 1959.

Westphal, Kurt. *Der Begriff der musikalischen Form.* Leipzig: Kister & Siegel, 1935; rep. Schriften zur Musik, ed. Walter Kolneder, vol. XI. Giebing: Katzbichler, 1971.

Winch, William H. *Notes on German Schools, With Special Relation to Curriculum and Methods of Teaching.* London: Longman's Green and Co., 1904.

Wohlfahrt, Frank. *Anton Bruckners Sinfonisches Werk: Stil- und Formerläuterung.* Leipzig: Musikwissenschaftlicher Verlag, 1943.

Wundt, Wilhelm. *Grundriss der Psychologie*, Leipzig: W. Engelmann, 1896.

Wyneken, Gustav. *Der Gedankenkreis der Freien Schulgemeinde.* Leipzig: Erich Matthes, 1913.

Wickersdorf. Lauenburg/Elbe: Adolf Saal, 1922.

Zuckerkandl, Viktor. *Sound and Symbol: Music and the External World*, trans. W. R. Trask. Bollingen Series, vol. XLIV. Princeton: Princeton University Press, 1956.

Articles

Bekker, Paul. "Kontrapunkt und Neuzeit," *Frankfurter Zeitung*, vol. 62. March 27, 1918, 1.
Bose, Madelon. "The Sound and the Theory: A Novel Look at Work and Music," *International Review of Aesthetics and Sociology of Music* 10.1 (1979), 52–72.
Braun, Werner. "Kretzschmars Hermeneutik," *Beiträge zur musikalischen Hermeneutik*, ed. Carl Dahlhaus. Studien zur Musikgeschichte des 19. Jahrhunderts, vol. 43. Regensburg: Bosse, 1975, 33–39.
Breig, Werner. "Das Schicksalskunde-Motiv im *Ring des Nibelungen*: Versuch einer harmonischen Analyse," *Das Drama Richard Wagners als musikalisches Kunstwerk*, ed. Carl Dahlhaus. Regensburg: Bosse, 1970, 223–34.
Bücken, Ernst. "Ernst Kurth als Musiktheoretiker," *Melos* 4 (1924–25), 358–64.
Capellen, Georg. "Harmonik und Melodik bei Richard Wagner," *Bayreuther Blätter* 25 (1902), 3–23.
Cohn, Arthur W. "Das Erwachen der Ästhetik," *Zeitschrift für Musikwissenschaft* 1 (1918–19), 669–79.
Cohn, Arthur Wolfgang. "Das musikalische Verständnis: Neue Ziele," *Zeitschrift für Musikwissenschaft* 4.3 (1921), 129–30.
Dahlhaus, Carl. "Bach und der 'lineare' Kontrapunkt," *Bach-Jahrbuch* 49 (1962), 55–79.
  "Ernst Kurth: *Romantische Harmonik und ihre Krise in Wagners 'Tristan'*," *Die Musikforschung* 25 (1972), 225.
  "Absolute Melodik. Ernst Kurths *Voraussetzungen der theoretischen harmonik und der tonalen Darstellungssysteme*," *Schweizer Jahrbuch für Musikwissenschaft* 6–7 (1986–87), 61–70.
Ehrenfels, Christian von. "Über Gestaltqualitäten," *Vierteljahresschrift für wissenschaftliche Philosophie* 14 (1890), 249–92.
Eimert, Herbert. "Zur Phänomenologie der Musik," *Melos* 5.7 (1926), 238–45.
Fischer, Kurt von. "'In Memoriam Ernst Kurth," *Der Musik-Almanach*, ed. Viktor Schwarz. Munich: K. Desch, 1948, 228–52.
  "Ernst Kurth (1886–1946): Persönlichkeit, Lehrer und Musikdenker," *Schweizer Jahrbuch für Musikwissenschaft* 6–7 (1986–87), 11–19.
  "Ernst Kurth-Bibliographie," *Schweizer Jahrbuch für Musikwissenschaft* 6–7 (1986–87), 20–21.
Floros, Constantin. "Zur Antithese Brahms–Bruckner," *Brahms-Studien*, vol. I, ed. C. Floros. Hamburg: Karl Dieter Wagner, 1947, 59–90.
Frecot, Janos. "Die Lebensreformbewegung," *Das wilhelminische Bildungsbürgertum: Zur Sozialgeschichte seiner Ideen*, ed. Klaus Vondung. Göttingen: Vandenhoeck & Ruprecht, 1976, 138–52.
Göhler, Georg. "Ernst Kurths *Bruckner*," *Neue Zeitschrift für Musik* 93.12 (1926), 682–83.
Halm, August, "Musikalische Bildung," *Wickersdorfer Jahrbuch 1909*. Jena: E. Diederichs, 1910, 48–73.
  "Heinrich Schenker," *Die Freie Schulgemeinde* 8 (1917), 11–15.
  "Gegenwart und Zukunft der Musik," *Das hohe Ufer* 2 (1920).
  "Heinrich Schenkers *Neue musikalische Theorien und Phantasien*," *Der Merker* 11 (1920), 414–17.
Handschin, Jacques. "De différentes conceptions de Bach," *Schweizerisches Jahrbuch für Musikwissenschaft* 4 (1929), 7–35.

Helson, Harry. "The Psychology of Gestalt," *American Journal of Psychology* 36 (1925), 342–70, 494–526; 37 (1926), 25–62, 189–223
"The Fundamental Propositions of Gestalt Psychology," *Psychological Review* 40 (1933), 13–32.
Hsu, Dolores. "Ernst Kurth and His Concept of Music as Motion," *Journal of Music Theory* 10 (1966), 2–17.
Jöde, Fritz. "*Von zwei Kulturen der Musik*," *Der Wanderer* 7 (1916); rep. *Die deutsche Jugendmusikbewegung in Dokumenten ihrer Zeit*, comp. Wilhelm Scholz and Waltraut Jonas-Corrier, et al. Wolfenbüttel-Zürich: Möseler, 1980, 70.
Kretzschmar, Hermann. "Anregungen zur Förderung musikalischer Hermeneutik," *Jahrbuch der Musikbibliothek Peters* 2 (1902), 45–66; and "Neue Anregungen zur Förderung musikalischer Hermeneutik: Satzästhetik," *Jahrbuch der Musikbibliothek Peters* 12 (1905), 75–86.
Kupffer, Heinrich. "Gustav Wyneken: Leben und Werk," *Jahrbuch des Archivs der deutschen Jugendbewegung* 2 (1970), 23–32.
Kurth, Ernst. "Die Jugendopern Glucks bis zum 'Orfeo'," *Studien zur Musikwissenschaft* 1 (1913), 193–227; orig. "Der Stil der opera seria von Gluck bis zum 'Orfeo'," (Ph.D. diss., University of Vienna, 1908).
"Zur Stilistik und Theorie des Kontrapunkts," *Zeitschrift für Musikwissenschaft* 1 (1918), 176–82.
"Die Schulmusik und ihre Reform," *Schweizerische Musikzeitung* 70.9 (1930), 341–51; orig. *Schulpraxis* 19 (1930).
Lange, Klaus-Peter. "Zum Begriff der Einfühlung (Theodor Lipps und Johannes Volkelt)," *Beiträge zur Theorie der Künste im 19. Jahrhundert*. Regensburg: G. Bosse, 1971, 113–28.
Lorenz, Alfred. "Ernst Kurth: *Romantische Harmonik und ihre Krise in Wagners 'Tristan'*," *Die Musik* 16.4 (1924), 255–62.
"Die formale Gestalt des Vorspiels zu Tristan und Isolde," *Zeitschrift für Musikwissenschaft* 5 (1922–23), 546–57; rep. *Zur musikalischen Analyse*, ed. Gerhard Schuhmacher. Darmstadt: Wissenschaftliche Buchgesellschaft, 1974, 455–73.
McCreless, Patrick. "Ernst Kurth and the Analysis of the Chromatic Music of the Late Nineteenth Century," *Music Theory Spectrum* 5 (1983), 56–75.
Mersmann, Hans. "Versuch einer Phänomenologie der Musik," *Zeitschrift für Musikwissenschaft* 5 (1922–23), 226–69.
"Zur Phänomenologie der Musik," *Zeitschrift für Ästhetik und allgemeine Kunstwissenschaft* 19 (1925), 372–97.
Mitchell, William. "The *Tristan* Prelude: Techniques and Structure," *The Music Forum*, vol. I. New York: Columbia University Press, 1967.
Nowak, Leopold. "Urfassung und Endfassung bei Anton Bruckner," *Bericht über den Internationalen Musikwissenschaftlichen Kongreß, Wien, Mozartjahr 1956*. Vienna, 1958, 449–51.
"Der Begriff der 'Weite' in Anton Bruckners Musik," *Über Anton Bruckner: Gesammelte Aufsätze, 1936–84*. Vienna: Musikwissenschaftlicher Verlag, 1985, 126–35.
Palisca, Claude V. "The Artusi-Monteverdi Controversy," *The Monteverdi Companion*, ed. D. Arnold and N. Fortune. New York: Norton, 1968, 133–66.
Parkany, Stephen. "Kurth's *Bruckner* and the Adagio of the Seventh Symphony," *19th Century Music* 11.3 (1988), 262–81.

Pike, Alfred. "The Phenomenological Approach to Musical Perception," *Philosophy and Phenomenological Research* 27 (1966–67), 247–54.

Reinach, Adolph. "What is Phenomenology?" trans. Derek Kelly, *The Philosophical Forum* 1.2 (1968), 231–56.

Riemann, Hugo. "Ideen zu einer 'Lehre von den Tonvorstellungen'," *Jahrbuch der Musikbibliothek Peters* 21–22 (1914–15), 1–26; and "Neue Beiträge zu einer Lehre von den Tonvorstellungen," *Jahrbuch der Musikbibliothek Peters* 23 (1916), 1–22.

"Die Phrasierung im Lichte einer Lehre von den Tonvorstellungen," *Zeitschrift für Musikwissenschaft* 1.1 (1918), 26–39.

Rivera, Benito. "Harmonic Theory in Musical Treatises of the Late Fifteenth and Early Sixteenth Centuries," *Music Theory Spectrum* 1 (1979), 80–95.

Rothfarb, Lee. "Ernst Kurth in Historical Perspective: His Intellectual Inheritance and Music-Theoretical Legacy," *Schweizer Jahrbuch für Musikwissenschaft* 6–7 (1986–87), 23–42.

"Ernst Kurth's *Die Voraussetzungen der theoretischen Harmonik* and the Beginnings of Music Psychology," *Theoria* 4 (1989), 10–33.

"The 'New Education' and Music Theory, 1900–1925," *Festschrift for Patricia Carpenter*. Forthcoming.

Rummenhöller, Peter. "Die philosophischen Grundlagen in der Musiktheorie des 19. Jahrhunderts," *Beiträge zur Theorie der Künste im 19. Jahrhundert*. Regensburg: Bosse, 1971, 44–57.

Sachs, Klaus-Jürgen. "Zur Tradition der Klangschritt-Lehre," *Archiv für Musikwissenschaft* 28 (1971), 233–70.

Schalk, Josef. "Das Gesetz der Tonalität II," *Bayreuther Blätter* 11 (1888), 192–97, 381–87; 12 (1889), 191–98; 13 (1890), 65–70.

Schenker, Heinrich. "Resumption of *Urlinie* Considerations," *Das Meisterwerk in der Musik*, vol. I. 3 vols. Munich: Drei Masken Verlag, 1925, 1926, 1930; trans. Sylvan Kalib, "Thirteen Essays from the Three Yearbooks *Das Meisterwerk in der Musik* by Heinrich Schenker: An Annotated Translation," vol. II. Ph.D. diss., University of Chicago, 1973.

"Weg mit dem Phrasierungsbogen!," *Das Meisterwerk in der Musik*. 3 vols. Munich: Drei Masken Verlag, 1925, 1926, 1930; vol. I, 41–60; trans. Sylvan Kalib, "Let's Do Away with the Phrasing Slur!", "Thirteen Essays from the Three Yearbooks *Das Meisterwerk in der Musik* by Heinrich Schenker: An Annotated Translation," vol. II. Ph.D. diss., University of Chicago, 1973, 53–83.

Stumpf, Carl. "Konsonanz und Konkordanz," *Beiträge zur Akustik und Musikwissenschaft* 6 (1911), 116–50.

Wagner, Manfred. "Zur Diskrepanz zwischen Urfassung und späteren Fassungen bei Anton Bruckner," *Österreichische Musikzeitschrift* 33 (1978), 348–57.

Wagner, Richard. "On the Application of Music to the Drama," trans. William Ashton Ellis in *Richard Wagner's Prose Works*, vol. VI. London: Routledge and Kegan Paul Ltd., 1887; rep. New York: Broude Brothers, 1966, 173–91; orig. "Über die Anwendung der Musik auf das Drama," *Bayreuther Blätter* 2 (Nov., 1879), 313–25.

Wellek, Albert. "Musikpsychologie," *Acta Musicologica* 5.2 (1933–34), 72–80.

"The Present State of Music Psychology and its Significance for Historical Musicology," *Report of the Eighth Congress of the International Musicological Society*, vol. I. Kassel: Bärenreiter, 1961, 121–32.

Wertheimer, Max. "Experimentelle Studien" (*Zeitschrift für Psychologie*) 60–61 (1911–12); rep. in *Drei Abhandlungen zur Gestalttheorie*. Erlangen: Verlag der philosophischen Akademie, 1925, 1–105.

Wetzel, Hermann. "Ernst Kurth: *Grundlagen des linearen Kontrapunkts*," *Bach-Jahrbuch* (1917), 173–74.

"Zur Stilforschung in der Musik: Bemerkungen und Betrachtungen zu Ernst Kurths *Romantische Harmonik*," *Die Musik* 16.4 (1924), 262–69.

Wohlfahrt, Frank. "Ernst Kurth: *Bruckner*," *Die Musik* 18.3 (1925), 200–08.

Index of musical examples

Johann Sebastian Bach
  Inventios
    No. 3 (D major): 1.14, 1.15
  Sinfonias
    No. 3 (D major): 2.11, 2.12
  Violin Sonatas
    No. 1 (G minor), Presto: 3.22
    No. 2 (A minor), Allegro: 3.24
    No. 3 (C major), Allegro: 3.5, 3.27, 3.28; Fugue: 3.8–3.21
  Violin Partitas
    No. 1 (B minor), Double 2: 3.23
    No. 2 (D minor), Allemande: 3.26
  Cello Suites
    No. 1 (G major), Allemande: 3.3
    No. 2 (D minor), Prelude: 3.4; Allemande: 3.2, 3.30
    No. 3 (C major), Gigue: 3.31
    No. 4 (E♭ major), Prelude: 3.1
    No. 5 (C minor), Allemande: 3.7
  Well-Tempered Clavier, Book 1
    Fugue in C♯ minor: 2.2
    Fugue in F♯ minor: 2.4
    Fugue in B minor: 2.5
  Well-Tempered Clavier, Book 2
    Fugue in E major: 2.3
    Fugue in F♯ minor: 2.1
    Prelude in G major: 1.5, 1.6
    Fugue in B major: 1.12
  Miscellaneous
    The Art of Fugue, Fugue 3: 1.11
    Chromatic Fantasy and Fugue (BWV 903), Fugue: 1.9, 1.10
    Clavier Duet in E minor (BWV 802): 1.3, 1.4
    Clavier Duet in G major (BWV 804): 1.2
    Fugue for Clavier (BWV 950, A major): 2.9
    Toccata and Fugue (BWV 911, C minor), Fugue: 1.13
    Toccata and Fugue (BWV 910, F♯ minor), Fugue: 2.6, 2.7, 2.8, 2.10

Anton Bruckner
  Fourth Symphony, 2nd movement: 6.11
  Fifth Symphony, 1st movement: 7.2, 7.3
  Sixth Symphony
    1st movement: 6.5–6.10
    4th movement: 6.1–6.4

Seventh Symphony, 2nd movement: 7.4
Eighth Symphony, 1st movement: 7.5–7.8
Ninth Symphony, 1st movement: 7.1

Franz Schubert
"Am Meer," *Schwanengesang*, part 2, no. 12: 4.10

Robert Schumann
"Abendmusik," *Bunte Blätter*, op. 99, no. 12: 4.11

Richard Strauss
Elektra: 4.23
Salome: 4.21, 4.22

Richard Wagner (scene in parentheses)
Götterdämmerung
    Act I: 4.13 (2)
Lohengrin
    Act I: 4.8 (3)
Die Meistersinger
    Act II: 4.12 (5)
Parsifal
    Act I: 4.18 (2)
    Act III: 4.19 (2)
Das Rheingold
    Scene 4: 4.5
Siegfried
    Act III: 4.1 (1), 4.2 (1)
Tannhäuser
    Act I: 4.9 (4)
Tristan und Isolde
    Prelude to Act I: 4.6, 4.7, 5.5
    Act I: 4.3 (1), 5.2 (3), 4.17 (4), 5.4 (5)
    Act II: 4.20 (1), 4.4 (2), 5.1 (2), 4.15 (3)
    Prelude to Act III: 5.6
Die Walküre
    Act II: 4.16 (4)
    Act III: 5.3 (3)

Hugo Wolf
"An den Schlaf," *Mörike-Lieder*, no. 3: 4.14

General index

Aaron, Pietro, 41n6
Abraham, Lars U., 49n20
absolute chords, 125–29, 135n9, 143n21
absolute progression, 119–24, 125, 126, 135n9, 136
accompaniment, 179, 179n36, 180n38, 181n39, 182, 183, 197
actual voice, 51n25, 80, 81n5, 89–92, 95n17. *See also* apparent voice and chapter 3
aesthetics, 8 (formalist *vs.* expressionist), 11 (hermeneutical), 17, 20 (psychological)
after-wave, 190, 191n4. *See also* waves
Albisetti, James, 12n35
Alexander, Thomas, 12n34
alteration, 104–09, 128, 130, 135, 143n21, 145; intensive, 110–18, 134; style, 130n1 (components)
amateurs, musical, 15, 15n42, 156
analysis, 11 (hermeneutic), 17 (schematic reconstructions), 27–28 (psychoauditive), 155 (formalistic), 187 (thematic)
Angerer, Manfred, 4n9
anti-Positivism, 7, 32
apexes, 49–57, 79, 79n3, 161, 173, 175, 195, 197n12, 202; curvilinear, 53, 53n27; extension of, 56; and harmony, 203 (darkenings), 206; placement of, 62–63; staggered, 49–52, 197; in transitional passages, 68, 83; and turnabout, 55–57, 183
Apfel, Ernst, 40n6
apparent voice, *see* chapters 2–3. *See also* actual voice
apperception, 43, 43n11
applied dominant, 121
arrangement (piano), 152n2
Artusi–Monteverdi controversy, 135n8
Asaf'yef, Boris V., 1n1
atomization, 129
attenuation, sonic, 164, 172, 174, 192 (thematic), 192–94 (motivic)
Auer, Max, 30, 154n5, 160n14, 162n17
Ausbildung (training), 7. *See also* education, reform pedagogy

Bach, Johann Sebastian, 1, 18, 22, 49, 68, 72, 72n13, 73, 73n16, 75, 76, 80, 111, 142n17, 165, 166, 169n24, 184

basic pillars, 132, 139n13, 144 (framing points)
Beethoven, Ludwig van, 166
Bekker, Paul, 3, 3n6, 24
Beldemandis, Prosdocimus de, 47n17
Bellerman, Heinrich, 39n4, 46n15
Bent, Ian, 5n12, 24 (on Kurth's notion of "linear"), 24n73 (on potential energy)
Berlioz, Hector, 123n16
Berne, University of, 12, 15, 16 (*collegium musicum*), 23n69
Berry, Wallace, 14n41, 33
Bewegungsphase (dynamic phase), 21, 42n8. *See also* dynamics, dynamism; phase
Bewegungszug (dynamic progression), 20, 21
Bildung (cultivation), 7. *See also* education, reform pedagogy
Bismarck, Otto von, 12
Bose, Madelon, 4n9
Boyd, William, 12n34
Brahms, Johannes, 72
Braun, Werner, 11n30
Breig, Werner, 118n14, 141n16
Brenn, Franz, 33
brightening effects, 104, 142. *See also* darkening, shading
Bruckner, Anton, 1, 109, 117n12. *See* chapters 6–7
Bücken, Ernst, 3, 3n7
Bujić, Bojan, 11n30
Bülow, Hans von, 185n47

cadence, 54, 135n9 (deceptive)
Capellen, Georg, 107n6, 118n14, 122n15
chaining, motivic, 203n19
Cherubini, Luigi, 61n4
Chopin, Frederic, 131n2
chorale (Protestant), 146
chord (sonority), 38n1, 40n6, 48
chordal contours, 76, 79, 82n6
chromaticism: extratonal, 131, 131n2, 137, 139, 143n21, 140; in melody, 133; in neighbor and passing formations, 104; in voice leading, 134. *See also* progression, chromatic, and chapters 4–5

230

General Index

Classical, Classicism, 54, 137 (*vs.* Romanticism), 143–44, 146, 157, 161, 162n17, 166, 167, 185n47, 188 (phrasing)
cohesion, harmonic, 41, 42n7, 43
Cohn, Arthur Wolfgang, 8, 17, 18
collegium musicum, 16
collision, harmonic, 57, 119–21
coloring, harmonic, 100 (contrasts) 105, 106, 108 (tinting), 121 (collisions), 127
consolidation, thematic, 60, 61n4, 62n5, 73, 73nn15–16. *See also* dissolution, thematic and chapter 2
consonance, 4
Cooke, Deryck, 153n3, 178n35, 198n14
Cornelius, Peter, 131n2
counterforces, 156
counterpoint, 38n1, 48; double, 89, 173; linear, 3n6, 24–25, 32, 40n6, 43, 44n12, 45n13, 47n17; melodic-genetic view of, 26–27; species, 45n15, 47n17
countertendency, 156, 158, 159, 166, 183, 184
crosswise profile, 177, 178, 178n34. *See also* lengthwise profile
curling wave, 197. *See also* waves
curvilinear development, 53n27, 79n4

Dahlhaus, Carl, 4n8, 24n73, 27n84, 40n6, 49n20
Danuser, Herman, 4n9
darkening, harmonic, 100, 101, 103, 104–05, 109, 126, 142n17, 174n31, 182, 190, 190n2, 199, 203
Death Motive, 122n15, 140n14, 142n18
Death-Proclamation Motive, 118n14, 141, 141n16
Death-Resignation Motive, 199n15
Decsey, Ernst, 31n101, 154n5
Dehn, Siegfried, 61n4, 62n4
Dehnert, Max, 177n33
de-intensification, 73, 155, 156, 158, 166, 170, 172, 201
Descartes, René, 43n11
developmental motives, 73nn15–16, 169, 169n24, 182, 185, 186n47, 191n6; ascending, 69–70; descending, 69–70; and formal dynamics, 197; and intensifications, 73, 74; and linear shaping, 207; and motivic unity, 197; and musical space, 191; oscillating, 68n10, 69–70, 166; swaying and rocking figures, 182; technique of (in Bruckner), 195; and thematic motion, 192; transformation of, 206. *See* chapter 2
Diederichs, Eugen, 8n20
Dilthey, Wilhelm, 8
disalteration, 113n8
dissolution: harmonic, 119, 125, 129, 135; thematic, 60, 61n4, 62n5, 65, 73, 73n15, 74; tonal, 144
dissonance, 42, 54, 105, 113, 135, 166, 202n19; and apex, 55, 56; and imitations, 170; implied, 77; melodic, 42n8; suspension, 54
Doernberg, Erwin, 177n33
dominant region, 121

Dömpke, Gustav, 29, 177n33
dovetailing (apex), 206
dynamics, dynamism, 14, 17, 23, 29, 31, 43, 104, 106, 108; contrasts, 100; linear, 51n24, 53, 154; long-range, 168; phase (motive), 152; tectonic structure, 19

echo effects, 166. *See also* imitation
Eckstein, Friedrich, 118n14
editions (Bruckner symphonies), 153n3, 198n14
education: adult, 11; art, 10; developmental, 13; experimental schools, 12, 13; music, 10, 16. *See also* reform pedagogy
Eggebrecht, Hans Heinrich, 41n6
Ehrenfels, Christian von, 43n10
Eimert, Herbert, 17
elementism (psychology), 17
empathy (*Einfühlen*), 18, 19, 19n54
endless melody, 28, 143, 152, 161, 169, 203n19
energy, 38, 42, 44, 70; harmonic, 111, 134, 144, 155, 176; kinetic, 22, 24, 43, 110, 135; linear-melodic, 39, 41, 42, 48, 54, 57, 73, 78; potential, 24, 106, 110, 135; psychic, 111; and shading, 103
enharmonic technique, 111, 132, 132n4, 140 (sequences)
episode, 60n2, 61, 61n4. *See also* transitional passage
equilibrium, harmonic, 37, 40, 42, 42n7, 43, 76n1, 144, 159, 168
Esslingen, 14
expansion, exterior/interior, 143–44, 144n22
exposition, 58, 59, 60

Fate Motive, 117, 141
Fechner, Gustav T., 6
Federhofer, Hellmut, 4n9
figure–ground relationship, 160n14
Fischer, Hans Conrad, 177n33
Fischer, Kurt von, 2n2, 4n9
Floros, Constantin, 199n15
force: constructive, 120, 143n21; destructive, 120, 121, 143n21; linear, 158, 165; psychic, 176. *See also* equilibrium
form, 30, 33, 58–61, 165, 166, 179, 180
formalism, 17
Forte, Allen, 24n73
Fortspinnung, see spinning forth
framing points (*Gerüstpunkte*), 144. *See also* basic pillars
Frecot, Janos, 5n11
Freud, Sigmund, 8n20
Friedell, Egon, 6n15
fugue, fugal, 58, 59, 60, 60n2, 61n4, 62, 62n5, 65, 65n6, 73
Funtek, Leo, 31, 31n104
fusion, 42n7, 43, 125, 129, 132
Fux, Johann Joseph, 22, 39n4, 45n15, 46, 46nn15, 17, 47n17

231

General Index

Gédalge, André, 61n4
Geheeb, Paul, 13
Geist (spirit), objective, 8
Geisteswissenschaften (human studies), 5
Gemütsleben (emotional life), 8
Gerüstpunkte (framing points), 144
Gesamtentwicklung (overall development), 40n5
Giant Motive, 141, 141n15
Goering, Hugo, 14n39
Göhler, Georg, 31
Göllerich, August, 177n33
Gräflinger, Franz, 177n33
Grail Motive, 123–24
Groos, Karl, 20
grouping technique, 188, 207
Grunsky, Karl, 8, 31n102, 154n5, 192n7
Gutmann, Albert, 195n10

Haas, Robert, 161n15, 184n44, 189n1, 198n14
Halm, August, 1n2, 3n6, 5n12, 12, 13, 14, 14n40, 15, 15n42, 16, 16n46, 19, 20n58, 23, 26, 27, 29, 31, 44n12, 48n19, 131n2, 154n5, 162n17, 191n5, 192n7
Handschin, Jacques, 25n76
Hanslick, Eduard, 29, 177n33, 192n7
harmony, 26–27, 38n1, 39n4, 40, 47, 121, 159n13, 177, 186, 206 (dominant); in alteration style, 110–18; contextual influence of, 119, 161, dynamic forces in, 42, 45, 202; equilibrium in, 37, 40, 42, 42n7, 43, 76n1, 144, 159, 168; shifts (second theme), 205, 206n23. *See also* absolute progression, alteration, brightening effects, collision, coloring, darkening, force, progression, shading
Hasse, Karl, 25n76
hearing, musical, 38, 39, 4, (melodic), 41 (harmonic), 176
Hegel, Georg Wilhelm Friedrich, 20, 20n59
Helmholtz, Hermann von, 6
Helson, Harry, 21n61
Herbart, Johann Friedrich, 43n11
Herder, Johann Gottfried, 20, 20n59
hermeneutics, 11
Hilker, Franz, 12n34, 12n36
Hindemith, Paul, 24n73
Höckner, Hilmar, 14n40
Hsu, Dolores M., 4n9
Hughes, Henry Stuart, 5n11, 9n23
Humboldt, Wilhelm von, 7
Husserl, Edmund, 5, 18, 19n54
Hynais, Cyril, 117n12, 118n14, 153n3, 164n18

Ich-Beziehungen (self-references), 19
identical chords, 117n13, 138n11
Ihde, Don, 18n52
illimitability (of symphonic waves), 177–78
illusion theory, 20
imitation: and bass line, 201; echo, 155, 157, 164, 166, 170, 170n26, 173, 183, 193; inner, 20; and motive, 196
intensification, 54, 55, 56, 60, 64, 65, 70, 71, 73, 141 (undulating), 142, 144, 155, 156, 157, 159n13, 162n17, 182, 197; and apex, 79, 203; curvilinear, 79; linear, 49, 50, 51, 54; and register, 173; in sequences, 137; and thematic presentations in fugues, 62, 63; and theme, 206; and tonality, 126; in transitional passages, 61

Jadasohn, Salamon, 44n12, 61n4
Jöde, Fritz, 15n42
Jung, Carl Gustav, 8n20

Kalbeck, Max, 29, 177n33
Kalib, Sylvan, 79n4, 185n45
Keller, Hermann, 25n76
Kenntnis (knowledge), 7
key, 118, 125, 126n18
kinetic energy, *see* energy, kinetic
Kirnberger, Johann Philipp, 22
Klangfarbensymbole (harmonic color symbolism), 127
Klangschrittlehre (theory of interval progression), 40n6
Koffka, Kurt, 20–21, 21n61, 22. *See also* psychology, Gestalt
Köhler, Wolfgang, 20, 21n61. *See also* psychology, Gestalt
Können (technical skill), 7
Korte, Werner, 161n16, 199n15, 203n19, 204n22
Kretzschmar, Hermann, 11

Lang, Oskar, 30, 30n99, 154n5, 160n14, 176n33, 192n7
Langbehn, Julius, 8, 9n23, 10, 12n35, 29
Lange, Konrad, 5, 20
layman, musical, 15, 15n42, 156
leading tone, 131 (tendency), 137 (intensification)
Leibniz, Gottfried W., 43n11
Leibnitz, Thomas, 192n7
Leichtentritt, Hugo, 204n22
leitmotifs: Death, 122n15, 140n14, 142n18; Death-Proclamation, 118n14, 141, 141n16; Death-Resignation, 199n15; Fate, 117, 141; Giant, 141, 141n15; Grail, 123–24; Love, 122n15, 132n3; Magic-Fire, 118, 124; Sea, 103n5; Sleep, 100, 133; *Tantris*, 131, 132n3; *Tarnhelm*, 124; Voyage, 142, 142n18
lengthwise profile, 177, 178, 178n34, 184, 190. *See also* crosswise profile
Lichtwark, Alfred, 10
Lieberman, Ira, 4n9
Liebscher, Arthur, 31n104
Lietz, Hermann, 13, 13n37, 13n39
line, linear, 44n12, 46, 47n18, 24, 159n13; and form, 59; and tensions, 133
Linienphase (linear phase), 42n8. *See also* phase

General Index

Linienzug (linear progression), 40, 40n5. *See also Bewegungsphase*; dynamics, dynamism; phase, progression, linear
linking passage, 56. *See also* transitional passage
Lipps, Theodor, 5, 19n54, 19n55, 20, 20n59, 42n7
Löwe, Ferdinand, 178n35, 182n43, 184n44, 189n1, 195n10; and Josef Schalk, 178n35, 181n40, 181n41
Lorenz, Alfred, 5n12, 28, 146n25
Louis, Rudolf, 5n12, 27, 131n2
Love Motive, 122n15, 132n3
Luserke, Martin, 12n36

Mach, Ernst, 43n10
Magic-Fire Motive, 118, 124
Marpurg, Friedrich W., 61n4
mass, sonic, 166. *See also* space, spatiality
Mayfeld, Moritz von, 177n33
Mayrberger, Karl, 117n12
McCreless, Patrick, 4n9, 5n12
mediant progressions, 123, 134, 135n9
Meinecke, Friedrich, 7n17
melody, 38–40, 42, 46, 152, 154, 179, 180, 181, 184; chromatic, 133; polyphonic, 51n25, 53n27, 76; in sequences, 135–36, 139
melos, symphonic, 155, 177, 182, 185–86, 185–86n47
Mendelssohn, Felix, 72
Mersmann, Hans, 17, 18, 19
Merz, Elsbeth, 16n46
Meyer, Leonard, 8
Mitchell, William, 117n13
modulation, 106
monophony, 49, 80, 82, 93, 95, 152, 155n10
Monteverdi, Claudio, 135n8
Moos, Paul, 19n55
Mosse, George L., 5n11, 9n23
motions, balancing of, 61, 63–65, 106 (kinetic), 74 (oscillating), 156 (rebounding), 163 (primal)
motive, 152, 159, 164, 169, 170, 175n32, 176, 183, 185n47, 186, 191n4, 191n5, 198, 201, 202, 204–05, 207; component, 156, 174; dovetailed, 205; fragmented, 161, 166–67; primordial, 161; transformed, 196, 204; transitional, 66–67, 70, 73; unity of, 161, 169, 175, 183, 197–98, 204n22, 206
Motte-Haber, Helga de la, 4n9
Müller, Johannes, 6
Murray, David T., 21n61

Neapolitan, 102
neighbor-note insertion, 111–18, 130n1, 131
New Education, 12. *See also* reform pedagogy
Nohl, Hermann, 12n34
notation (orthography), 38, 39, 116, 132
Nowak, Leopold, 153n3, 161n15, 164n18, 165n21, 171n27, 184n44, 192n7, 195n10, 198n14

Ochs, Siegfried, 177n33
Oeser, Fritz, 160n14, 165n21, 192n7, 194n8

orchestration, 155, 171, 190, 195n10, 198n14, 203, 204n22
Orel, Alfred, 189n1
orthography, 38, 39, 116, 132
overriding line, 22, 53n27, 79n4, 80. *See* chapter 3

Palisca, Claude V., 135n8
parallelism, intervallic, 51
Parkany, Stephen, 4n9
Parker, Beryl, 12n34
part–whole relationship, 176
Pastille, William A. 5n12
Paulsen, Friedrich, 12n34
perception, musical, 43
performance practice, 63, 70, 80, 85, 152n2, 154n6, 160n14, 161n17, 184, 185–86n47, 190n3. *See also* phrase, pizzicato, slur, tempo, tremolo
Pestalozzi, Heinrich, 7
phase, 44, 79, 80, 155n10
phenomenal objectivity and subjectivity, 19, 19n55
phenomenology, 5, 17, 18
phrase, phrasing, 171n27, 173n29, 184–85, 184n44, 185–86n47, 194n8, 204 (phrase group)
Pike, Alfred, 18n53, 19n55
pillars, harmonic, 145, 146
pizzicato, 154, 154n8, 155n9, 156n11, 159, 182
polyphony, 38n1, 51, 53, 93; apparent, 78, 80, 81, 84, 86, 90; and chordal devices, 82; contrapuntal structure and technique, 43, 49, 53; and harmony, 39, 39n4, 40n6, 76; linear, 39, 40, 41, 45, 46, 48, 51, 54, 55, 58, 61; and linear progressions, 76; origins, 40
Positivism, 4, 5, 8, 9, 7n17
potential energy, *see* energy, potential
Prince, John T., 12n34
profile, *see* lengthwise profile, crosswise profile
progression: chromatic, 111, 122, 123, 130–35, 143n21; dynamic, 44; progression effect, 120, 122, 125; intensifying, 201; linear, 40, 40n5, 47, 76, 93, 103. *See also* absolute progression
projected points, 78, 79, 80. *See also* apparent voice; polyphony, apparent
psychologism, 17, 19n54
psychology: experimental, 6; Gestalt, 5, 17, 20–21, 22, 43n10, 160n14
punctum contra punctum, 46, 47n17

Randstimme, see rim voice
Rawson, Ryatt, 12n34
reconstructions, analytical, 17
rectilinearity, 157
Reddie, Cecil, 13n37
reform pedagogy, 5, 12, 13, 23
register, 155n9, 170n25, 172, 173, 180
regression, retrogression, 159, 165, 186, 186n48, 201, 203–04
Reinach, Adolph, 18n52

Rembrandt van Rijn, 10
repetition, motivic, 157–59, 164, 166, 172n28, 202
reverberation, 165, 168, 170, 173, 192n7, 200–01
reversal, directional, 55–56, 78, 159, 168, 170
Richter, Ernst Friedrich, 44n12
Riemann, Hugo, 1, 3, 3n5, 3n7, 4, 5, 23n70, 25, 28, 44n12, 53n28, 62n5, 146n25, 185n47
Rietsch, Heinrich, 107n6
rim voice (*Randstimme*), 85–86, 88, 91–93
Ringer, Fritz, 5n11
Rivera, Benito, 41n6
Rösler, Hans-Peter, 4n9
Roman, Frederick, 12n34
Romanticism,.124, 136–37 (*vs.* Classicism)
Rümmenhöller, Peter, 5n12, 6n14

Sachs, Klaus-Jürgen, 40n6, 41n6, 47n17
Saint Florian, 165n21
Schäfke, Rudolf, 16n46, 17
Schalk, Franz, 178n35, 192n7
Schalk, Josef, 118n14, 141n16, 182n43, 184n44, 192n7, 194n8, 194n9, 195n10, 198n14
Scheibe, Wolfgang, 10n28, 12n34
Schenker, Heinrich, 1, 3, 3n5, 4, 5, 5n12, 14, 15n42, 16, 22, 23n70, 46n15, 79n4, 122n15, 185n45
Schering, Arnold, 1n2, 25n75, 25n77, 48n19
Schlegel, August Wilhelm von, 20, 20n59
Schmalzriedt, Siegfried, 5n12
Schoenberg, Arnold, 15n42, 27, 122n15
Schönzeler, Hans Hubert, 177n33
Schumann, Robert, 72, 203n19
Schütz, Heinrich, 111
Sea Motive, 103n5
Sechter, Simon, 27n85, 116–17n12
self-deception, conscious, 20, 20n60
self-projection, 20
sequence, 134–36, 140n14; disintegration, 135, 139–40; enharmonic linkage, 140; extratonal, 136–37, 139, 143n21; large-scale, 140–41; truncation of, 140
shading, harmonic (shadowing), 103–06; 108–09, 190n2, 201
shifts, harmonic, 101
Shirley, Dennis, 12n35, 13n38
Simmel, Georg, 8
Sleep Motive, 100, 133
slur, slurring, 171n27, 184, 184n44, 185, 185n45, 186n47, 193–94n8. *See also* phrase, phrasing
socio-cultural revival, 5, 11, 13, 16–18, 23
species counterpoint, 45n15, 47n17
Spengler, Oswald, 7n16
spinning forth (*Fortspinnung*), 51, 60–63, 66, 70, 76, 79, 82
space, spatiality, 164–65, 165n21, 166 (psychic), 191, 191n4, 191n5, 192n7, 194. *See also* mass, sonic
Stern, Fritz, 5n11, 9n23, 9n24, 10n27
Stradal, August, 199n15
Strauss, Richard, 131n2, 162n17

Stumpf, Carl, 42n7, 43
subdominant, 102 (minor), 107n6, 108; cadence, 186, 186n48; excursions into, 102n3, 108; progression (shading), 201; region, 101, 170n25, 190n2, 203n20; shifts, 100–01. *See also* darkening, harmonic
super-summative wholes, 21
suspensions, 54, 78
synergies, specific, 42n7

Tantris Motive, 131, 132n3
Tarnhelm Motive, 124
tempo, 161n17. *See also* performance practice
tension, 45, 54, 104–06, 110, 116, 155, 163, 175, 182; in chords, 45, 113, 115–16, 118, 135, 145, 147; kinetic, 54, 79; in sequences, 137–38
thematic presentation (fugue entry-group), 58–61, 61n4, 62, 62n5, 63, 65, 65n6
theme, 151–52, 154, 161–62, 162n17, 164–66, 169, 175n32 (definition), 173, 176, 180, 183, 191n5, 192 (developmental motives), 194, 199n15; and developmental process, 161, 176, 195, 205; principal, 169, 172, 175, 180n37, 192, 198, 204; second principal, 206
theory, theorizing, 38–39, 39n4, 41–42, 42n12, 44, 45–49, 45n13, 61, 62, 76, 110, 121, 127
Thuille, Ludwig, 5n12, 27, 131n2
tiering (of waves), 141, 156–58, 169, 172, 184, 191
tonality, 38n1, 48; large-scale, 143, 145
transitional motive, 70, 73
transitional passage, 58–60, 60n2, 62–63, 65n6, 72n13, 83, 86, 89; formal function, 61, 62n4, 62n5; oscillating motive in, 68, 70. *See* chapter 2
tremolo, 153–54, 156n11, 159–60, 160n14, 163, 165, 176, 180, 190, 194, 199, 200, 204
triad, 41
Tristan and Isolde, 27, 28, 111, 116, 117n13, 121, 123, 125, 126
turnabout, 55, 57, 183

underthird, 108, 115n10. *See also* cadence
undertones, 91n13
unfoldment, ascending and descending, 40, 40n5, 61, 67, 95, 161 (large-scale)
unison passages, 51

vaulting sensation, 193, 194
Vergeiner, Anton, 177n33
Versuchsschulen, *see* education, experimental schools; reform pedagogy
voice leading, chromatic, 134
void, 154, 164–5, 166, 194, 199
volkish ideology, 5, 5n11, 13
Volksbildungsbewegung, *see* education, adult
Voyage Motive, 142, 142n18

Wagner, Manfred, 198n14

Wagner, Richard, 1, 100n1, 103, 104, 105, 107n6, 109, 111, 113, 114, 116, 119, 124, 125, 127, 131, 134, 135, 137, 140, 141, 144, 145, 146, 169, 199n15, 203n19
Wandervögel, 13
Wason, Robert, 2n3, 3n7, 5n12, 27n85, 116n12, 141n16
waves, symphonic, 30, 151–52, 155–57, 161–62; component, 152–54, 156–59, 174–75, 177, 181; countertendency in, 189, 191; de-intensifying, 155, 189; developmental, 151–52, 168; initiatory, 157–58, 160, 177, 189; medial, 174, 181; rebounding, 154, 174, 189, 190; summits, 79n3, 190, 197, 198. See also tiering, reverberation; chapters 6–7
Weber, Ernst H., 6
Weingartner, Felix, 199n15
Wellek, Albert, 2n4

Wertheimer, Max, 5, 20, 21n64, 43n10
Westphal, Kurt, 33
Wetzel, Hermann, 1n2, 25, 28, 48n19
Wickersdorf, 12, 12n36, 13, 14, 14n40, 15, 16, 16n46, 23, 23n69
Wilhelm II, Emperor, 11
will, 104, 106, 111, 163, 166; expressive, 164–65; in polyphony, 45–46; in symphonic waves, 158–60, 165, 170; thematic, 175–76, 204
Winch, William H., 12n34
Wissen (wisdom), 7
Wohlfahrt, Frank, 31, 31n103, 160n14
Wolf, Hugo, 116, 131n2
Wolzogen, Hans von, 177n33
Wundt, Wilhelm, 6, 42n7, 43n11
Wyneken, Gustav, 12, 13, 13n37, 14n40, 23

Zuckerkandl, Viktor, 21n64